What the World's Most Renowned Entrepreneurs and Brands are Saying about *Elevate* and the Authors

"Elevate is the entrepreneur's playbook. If you're a business owner who wants to grow faster, work less, and live more of your life, this is your blueprint."

—**FRED SCHEBESTA**, Co-Founder of Finder.com, a $650 million company

"Jack and Tim know firsthand that business is tough, especially going from business operator to business owner. Elevate is a practical guide on how to take that step."

—**JANINE ALLIS**, founder of Boost Juice and Boost Investment Group

"Jack Delosa is a leading entrepreneur of this generation. He builds world-class companies at scale that operate without him. From scaling multiple eight-figure companies to investing in unicorns and even buying his own island…as far as entrepreneurs go, Jack is a leader of the new school. In Elevate, he is passing down his roadmap so that other business owners can walk the same path."

—**GERARD ADAMS**, Co-Founder of Elite Daily,
achieved a $50 million exit to Daily Mail

"If you're a business owner, this book will change your life. This is an absolute must-read for any entrepreneur, manager, or employee who is looking to achieve rapid growth and build a world-class company."

—**JUSTIN DRY**, Co-Founder of VinoMofo, a $100 million company

"Jack and Tim have a perspective that few people in the global business community ever get to see. They haven't just succeeded in scaling their own business; they've helped thousands of others do it too. Accelerating growth and scale in a sustainable way is not something that can be done with luck—it's by design and Jack and Tim have generously given you the blueprint for it."

—**DANIEL AND JUSTINE FLYNN**, co-founders of Thankyou,
the social enterprise that has raised over $17m to end extreme poverty

"If I could use one phrase to encapsulate everything Tim Morris does in business it's 'walk the talk.' I've experienced this first hand over three decades of friendship and two decades of us both running high-growth businesses, one of which we did together. Over the past eight years, I've watched him create and deliver incredibly relevant content for business owners while simultaneously using these same frameworks to sustainably scale

The Entourage year on year. If you're a high-growth business owner looking to unlock the next level of scale, then Elevate is absolutely the book for you."

—**DAVID ANDREW**, Founder of Naked Life Spirits,
Fast100 Fastest Growing Business 2022

"As they grow, all business owners find themselves working harder, doing more, and earning less. Elevate is the answer to this universal problem, giving you the blueprint to growing faster, doing more of what you love and less of what you don't."

—**SARAH DAVIDSON**, Founder of Matcha Maiden, host of
the Seize the Yay podcast, television presenter

"Elevate is a must-read for every business owner and their management team. This book is the complete methodology for building a self-managing company that can scale."

—**STUART COOK**, former CEO of Zambrero and Founder of TWIYO

"Delosa is one of the most influential men in the Australian entrepreneurial landscape."

—*GQ*

"This book is like having a smart, experienced business advisor in your pocket. A seriously impressive business bible packed with decades of experience, effectual insights, cautionary tales, and every last strategy you need to go from startup to scale-up."

—**TIM DUGGAN**, new media entrepreneur, author of Cult Status and Killer Thinking

"Working on your business and not in it is a universal goal of every business owner. The problem is, there is no how-to manual to make that transition. Until now. Through The Entourage, Jack and Tim have consistently helped business owners from over 100 different industries to build self-managing companies and transition from business operator to business owner."

—**MATT VITALE**, Co-Founder of Birchal, an equity crowd-funding
platform that has helped businesses raise over $70 million

"Jack Delosa, author, investor, and founder of The Entourage, is also known as Richard Branson's curriculum development go-to, BRW's rich list staple, and all-round nice guy. That is, Delosa gives back, in the form of purpose and prose, with an aim to assist others in achieving their ideal life, bank account balance and dream career."

—**FORBES**

REAL-WORLD RESULTS FROM ELEVATE

*"We felt like we had taken Verge Girl to the furthest point we could by ourselves. The business was doing well, but we were always stuck in technician mode. We had no idea where to take the business next. **Within just six months of joining Elevate, we had grown from a seven- to an eight-figure business, and within twelve months we had grown 100 percent compared to the previous twelve months.** We always knew our business had potential to grow, but we didn't know how we'd do it, and we didn't have the confidence to make the decisions ourselves. We now feel really excited about the future. If there's an area of your business that you want to master but you don't know where to go, Elevate has so much to offer. There's nothing that The Entourage can't help you with."*

—**DANIELLA DIONYSSIOU AND NATALIA SUESSKOW**, Co-Founders of Verge Girl

*"As with any business, we had a very challenging time in the beginning. I didn't have all the answers, and there was no one I could turn to. The concepts contained in Elevate gave me clarity. They gave me a very clear plan and roadmap for how to grow my business and myself. Within a few years, **we had grown from $1 million in revenue all the way to $16 million, and I grew my team from fifteen people to 100.** We have also since been named Australia's fastest-growing real estate company. I now feel like more of a leader. Elevate gave me the answers, and I can now provide the right opportunities to my team. Jack and the team at The Entourage transformed my business and changed my life."*

—**SUNIL KUMAR**, Founder of Reliance Real Estate

*"In the first three years of our business, there would have been ten, maybe even fifteen times when we thought it was going to collapse. Working with Jack Delosa and The Entourage gave us the focus we needed to get through the startup phase, get back our time, leverage our team, and get more out of the business. **By the time we exited the business, it had grown from a three-person operation to over 140 staff members. We'd achieved industry-wide recognition with numerous accolades and awards, including Smart Company's Top Digital Innovator and Top 5 Fastest-Growing Companies and a feature on the BRW Fast Starters List.** From the start of our entrepreneurial journey right up until the exit day, the effects of The Entourage have compounded."*

—**DAVID AND ROSS FASTUCA**, Co-Founders of Locomote

*"**We increased our profit from $100,000 to $600,000 in 6 months, and I doubled my team from 11 to 22 people to free up my time.** The Entourage gave me the tools I needed to reinvent myself and be the person I needed to be to elevate the company to new levels. We're now playing a bigger game, and the business is bigger than ever. I'm happier, I feel more free, and I have less stress."*

—**KATE PRIOR**, Managing Director of Face2Face Recruitment

*"My business looked shiny on the outside, but it was chaotic on the inside. I was working crazy hours, we had no plan for the future, and it just wasn't sustainable for long-term growth. Until we had The Entourage, we didn't have the systems in place to grow. Since then, **we've profitably scaled our revenue from $1.5 million to $20 million. We had 10 people working in the business, we now have over 100 people employed and it's allowed us to elevate out of the day to day.**"*

—**JYE BOHM**, Co-Founder of ProFinish Coatings

*"It had been chaotic taking the reins of my sixty-year-old family-owned business. The business was mature in terms of the years it had been operating, but it was still stuck in startup mode. I was always so busy 'doing' that I never had time to think about where we were heading, how we could modernize the business, and what we actually needed to make that happen. I needed support and coaching to develop as a leader. There was just so much I didn't know that I even considered going to university and getting a business degree. Looking back, I'm so glad I joined the Elevate coaching program. **We've profitably increased our revenues by 400 percent and the team by 30 percent, and we've put structures and systems in place to reduce key person dependency on me.** I've elevated out of the day-to-day of my business. I can see the future and I also now have my life back. After some particularly turbulent years, I attribute the survival of my business to Elevate and the concepts in this book."*

—**BELINDA DONAGHEY**, General Manager of American Doughnut Kitchen

*"We had been having a terrible time in business before we came across Elevate. We had no idea what we were doing, and we were terrified of growing the business. We were scared of taking the risk of growing to the next level because the business was totally key-person dependent on us, and we didn't know how to grow in a way that was supported by strategy and structure. As husband and wife, this was also severely impacting our marriage. **Since learning and adopting the strategies contained in this book, we've been able to 10X our monthly revenue in just eighteen months while increasing our net profit margins. Our team has grown from four to fourteen people, all superstars who have been able to give us our time back.** The business now operates and our clients are getting helped when we're not even there. We're so excited for the growth of the business in the years ahead. The sky is now the limit. For any business owner who wants to scale sustainably, get their time back, and secure a financial future for themselves and their business, this book is for you."*

—**ROBBIE AND TAMARA TURNER**, Co-Founders of Axon Property Group

*"Before I came across Elevate, I was playing it safe and small. I was afraid of success and wasn't ready to leap into what the business could really be. Stepping up into being an entrepreneur and CEO who was driving strategy was entirely new ground. **In the six**

months prior to Elevate, I did $250,000 in revenue. In the six months after I did $2,500,000 in revenue. A 10X in six months. I've grown my team from three to fifteen people and put systems and processes in place that mean that I'm not getting involved in things that don't require me. I've leveled up. My energy and attention is now entirely focussed on playing a bigger game and working on my business rather than being stuck in it. I've stepped away from the day-to-day and now spend my time doing what I love best."

—**FRANCIS QUINN**, Founder of Athena Consulting

"*As a personal trainer, I thought I was quite successful. I knew how to get results for people, but I didn't know how to get results for myself in business. Working with The Entourage helped me get out of my comfort zone and the mindset that I was just a PT. I started with thirty members in one small location and was turning over $50,000. Since implementing the strategies and frameworks contained in this book,* **we've scaled all the way to being a global fitness company and franchise network with fifty-two locations and $30 million in revenue.** *The Entourage can teach you the fundamentals of business and the tools to scale profitably and sustainably. If that's what you're after, then this book is for you.*"

—**PETER HULL**, Co-Founder of Fitstop

"*I'd stepped into the director of operations role for my family's business, which had been running for twenty-five years. The Entourage quickly became my go-to so I could master the skills I needed to take over the day-to-day, lead, manage, and ultimately inspire growth in the business. Elevate has since become the most significant changemaker for me and the business.* **During a period where health and fitness clubs were losing on average between 10 and 20 percent of their members, we achieved our best figures ever in the business's twenty-five years: a 20 percent monthly gain in revenue.** *Elevate showed me that growth is always possible, that there is always something that can be done and you can make your mark as a business leader no matter what is thrown your way.*"

—**MONTANA ROSEKELLY**, Director of Operations
of Planet Fitness Newcastle

"*I was working really hard and enjoying my work, but I just couldn't get any traction when it came to making a decent earning. Since applying the lessons contained in Elevate, I've been able to step into myself in a way that I never thought I'd be able to. I now have the confidence to make decisions for my business.* **I've tripled my profit and made more money in six months than I had in the previous eight years.** *I don't feel guilty about taking time off or stepping away from my business now, and that, for me, feels like the biggest achievement. If you're struggling with profit, feeling like you're working really hard but not getting anywhere, or you know you have a passion for* what you do but you're feeling disillusioned and you don't know where to turn, then the strategies in this book are for you."

—**CATE LEIDKE**, Co-Founder of Catherine de Meur Interiors

"When we started our business, we spent so much time on the tools that we never thought about how we'd actually build our business. We were working sixteen-hour days and just thought that to earn more money, we had to keep working longer and harder hours. Elevate changed all that for us. Our roles are now clearly defined, we've learned to delegate and set up processes so that we're only working six hours every day (it could be less than that, but we actually enjoy coming into work now). **Previously, we were turning over $150,000 every month. Within a few months of applying what we learned through Elevate, our monthly revenue was consistently between $650,000 and $700,000.** We're working less and making more profit, which means that now when we go home to our families, we don't even think about work; we can be completely present with them, and that's been the greatest transformation. We never thought we'd be in the position we're in now, but thanks to Elevate, we've found that freedom."

—**STEVE GATTER AND SIMON WELLARD**, Co-Founders of Outdoor Vision Landscaping

"We were a retail business that was forced to shut our doors due to COVID restrictions. This meant that we lost 100 percent of our revenue overnight. Thanks to the strategies contained in this book, we were able to pivot to an online model and put in place the marketing to drive traffic to our site. **That month we did $80,000, our highest month ever.** I had no idea we could ever do this. What we achieved through applying the principles in this book didn't just see us through the challenge; it changed the future of our business forever."

—**CHRIS BERTUCCIO**, Founder of Coco88

"Running a business is a skill. I'm trained technically as a physiotherapist, but I didn't know anything about business—that was until I came across Elevate. Things in the business were fine, but it all felt very comfortable. There was an underlying want to do better, but I knew it was going to be challenging. Elevate helped me lean into and embrace the discomfort. There were systems and frameworks that enabled me to profitably and sustainably grow my business and open a second location within twelve months. **Within just nine months, I'd passed the $1,000,000 mark**, and I'm now hitting numbers that I never thought were achievable. There are people in this world who are better than others at business, and the best of them are at The Entourage."

—**ADAM MONTEITH**, Founder of Evoker

"Elevate is what you need to scale. When we were at the $300,000 mark, it was time-consuming. We were exhausted, at a point of burning out, with five team members and *making big and expensive mistakes.* **With the help of Elevate, we profitably scaled all the way to $3,000,000 in twelve months, grew the team to twenty-five, and stepped away from the day-to-day and got our time back."**

—**MATTHEW MOSELEY AND PETER LISTON**, Co-Founders of Trust The Process

"Before Elevate I was overworked, stressed, frustrated, and burned out. I'd started the business over twenty years ago and felt like we'd reached a plateau. The business hadn't grown for four years in a row. I had no clarity on where exactly I wanted to take the business, let alone how I was going to do it, and the business was so operationally dependent on me that I became a major bottleneck. After implementing the strategies I learned from Elevate, we started seeing immediate and consistent results: where **we were previously doing between $20,000 and $30,000 every month, this quickly doubled all the way to $60,000, and now we're consistently doing months as large as $110,000.** *That's become the norm, so when we eventually did $200,000 in a single month, I would have never previously thought that was possible. I'm no longer operationally involved in the sales or delivery side of the business, and my team is empowered to do great work for our clients when I'm not there. If you feel like you've hit a ceiling and you're burned out or uninspired, feeling lots of self-doubt, or lacking the clarity you need to get to where you want to be, Elevate is for you. It has completely transformed my business and my life above and beyond what I would have ever expected."*

—**BEN MCINTYRE**, Founder of BJM Digital

"My business was ticking along okay. We were growing, but it was slow, and we weren't being strategic. I was blissfully ignorant to a lot of the deficiencies within my business. I was on autopilot, but Elevate flicked the switch for me. I've learned how to bottle magic and scale my business. **We've since increased our revenue by an extra $1,000,000 and doubled the team.** *You get to see what world's best practice looks like at The Entourage. If you want to scale your business but also improve personally and take yourself to the next level, then this book is for you."*

—**JOHN DYER**, Managing Director of Air Adventure Australia

"Before I started Elevate, we'd had good growth and were finding some traction, but the actual management of the business was all over the place. I had no experience in how to actually run the business, and as a result I was wearing all the hats. Without Elevate, I would have struggled to handle the growth of the business. **There were times when I even considered shutting down our website to stop inquiries coming through** *because we just couldn't keep up with the demand and didn't have the systems and processes in place to grow sustainably. Elevate helped me work out what was missing in my business, and there was a huge shift from me being on the tools and doing everything*

myself to stepping into being the business owner and building a team around me. Now, we're in a better position to grow and have a roadmap to get all the way to $2,500,000 this financial year. There's no aspect of our business that Elevate hasn't been a benefit to and no business that wouldn't benefit from it."

—**JARRYD VAN POPPEL**, Co-Founder of Euka Future Learning

*"I was the classic story of the tradie who knew he wanted more and was capable of more, but I was completely stuck in my business. At one point, though, everything was pointing toward the end, and my business was facing imminent closure. With the help of Elevate, I was able to turn it around within a month and ended up **doing my biggest month to date: $150,000 in revenue and $100,000 in net profit.** Elevate gave me the tools and the knowhow to be able to deal with challenges in business properly, and I can honestly say that I'm now the happiest and most fulfilled I've ever been in my life."*

—**SCOTT McLAREN**, Founder and Owner of Scott Electrics

*"While we had a successful business, our biggest issue was that we were the ones doing everything in it. If we weren't there, things weren't going to get done. We were capped at what we could do for a number of years, and we knew something had to change if we wanted to scale. Since implementing the strategies from Elevate, **our profit has doubled, and within four short weeks, we brought on two new clients, both worth six figures each.** This has enabled us to invest in growing the team, which has freed up our time to focus on the future growth of the business. We would recommend this to anyone who is hustling in their business and whose business relies on them to scale, even if it is doing well."*

—**BRIAN AND DANIKA DOWNTING**, Co-Founders of Platinum Building Approvals

*"I was facing so much stress in my business. We were still recovering from the pandemic, which amounted to a $700,000 loss. The Entourage helped me through the chaos. **I've gone from turning over $20,000 every month to consistently doing $70,000, and that's continuing to grow.** My membership base has grown from 250 to 650 people, and my team has grown from five to twenty people. The Entourage helped me see that you can create anything you want and that there is always another way to get results."*

—**LUCY MOLDEN**, Owner of F45 Liverpool

"We were feeling enormous pressures in our business after the pandemic. It had crippled the plans and vision we had for the future of our business. We were in a huge amount of debt, and we had no clear idea of how we could climb out of the hole we'd found ourselves in. It was all so overwhelming, and we didn't think we would make it through.

*Applying the strategies contained in Elevate helped us to navigate these difficult times and stay true to the vision for the business. **We've since had over 450 franchise applications for our business and profitably grown our revenue by an extra $4,000,000 in twelve months**, and now we have the correct systems and processes in place to ensure that we can continue scaling sustainably."*

—**JESS DAVIS AND TYSON HOFFMAN**, Co-Founders of Mr. Potato

*"Elevate showed me how to continue to drive growth and scale, but sustainably and profitably without burning myself out. I've since been able to put into place robust systems, processes, and a structure to support our ongoing growth. **The result? The business's revenues have grown from $40,000 to nearly $5,000,000, and I have no plans on slowing down."***

—**ALEX TATTLE**, Co-Founder of Wild Modular

*"By applying the strategies contained in Elevate, **I was able to increase my revenue from $1,800,000 to $3,500,000 in twelve months.** This was a 90 percent increase in revenue and a 48 percent increase in net profit."*

—**PHILIP OAKMAN**, Founder of Auxilis

ELEVATE

ELEVATE

How to *Accelerate Growth* and
SCALE YOUR BUSINESS BEYOND YOU

JACK DELOSA

AFR Young Rich List
Two-Time Bestselling Author

TIM MORRIS

CEO of The Entourage
Award-Winning Executive

ELEVATE

How to Accelerate Growth and Scale Your Business Beyond You

FIRST EDITION

ISBN 978-1-5445-4287-4 Hardcover
     978-1-5445-4285-0 Paperback
     978-1-5445-4286-7 Ebook

The paper this book is printed on is in accordance with the standards of the Forest Stewardship Council®. The FSC® promotes environmentally responsible, socially beneficial and economically viable management of the world's forests.

We dedicate this book to you,

the business owner doing the work, every day,

to build a better business and a

brighter tomorrow.

CONTENTS

ACCESS YOUR VAULT OF RESOURCES AND DONE-FOR-YOU TEMPLATES

There's a huge amount of substance in these pages, but even so, our biggest challenge when putting together this book was not deciding what to include, but choosing what to leave out.

As such, we've collected together all the resources, templates, and tools that will short-cut implementation and help you install these strategies into your own business. This book combined with these resources will help you grow faster while working less.

You can find them, for free, here:

INTRODUCTION

"There's no way you can trade out of this, Jack."

The insolvency practitioner peered over his glasses like an unimpressed school principal, perusing my financials that were spread out over his desk. His message was the same as my previous advisor's, and the one before them. He was telling me to wind up The Entourage—and, in the process, my life's work. Wherever I turned the message was consistent. "Put the keys on the table, raise the white flag, and exit stage left."

It was October 2016 and I'd barely had time to catch up to the new reality I was sitting in. We were staring into the abyss. Every business owner's nightmare. A previously thriving company, suddenly in danger of falling apart.

Earlier that year, The Entourage celebrated half a decade of unbroken success. At the beginning of 2016, we were a $60 million brand, pursuing a meaningful vision to move the world forward through entrepreneurship. With the capability and commitment of our ninety-strong team, we developed a culture that was named the 4th Best Place to Work in Australia.

The members (clients) of our business coaching program were scaling successful companies at such a rate that when *Business Review Weekly* released their list of "Top 5 Entrepreneurs to Watch," every one of them was a member of ours. The journalist who wrote the story reached out to me and remarked, "What are you doing over there at The Entourage? It seems like every name in entrepreneurship can be traced back to your coaching."

What we were doing was as simple as it was effective. We were coaching business owners to build successful companies that could grow beyond them. In doing so, they became unstuck, achieving a level of freedom in life and business that had previously eluded them. The continued commercial success of our members had attracted a community of over 300,000 highly capable business owners from around the world.

This success brought a lot of parents and students to our door, asking whether we provided any programs suitable for people who wanted an education that would prepare them to *start out* in business. There was, and still is, a rising tide of parents and students rightly dissatisfied with their experience of university. They were concerned that traditional universities wouldn't teach them the tangible business skills they needed to succeed in the real world. They were right.

We saw a huge opportunity to make a systemic improvement to the way traditional education prepared people for the business world, by bringing our programs into an accredited environment and beating the universities at their own game. The space we were poised to enter was the Vocational Education and Training (VET) sector. Early on, we learned that the VET sector was the second-most regulated industry in the country, behind only aviation. Undeterred, we boldly decided to go through the lengthy process of becoming an accredited training provider. After a year of heavy investment, building compliance and product development teams, crafting a marketing engine, recruiting a sales team, engaging boards of advisors, and navigating the minefield of gaining accreditation, we eventually met the requirements placed upon us by the government. We ticked every box and gained the right to issue a Diploma of Business, specializing in Entrepreneurship.

When we launched the accredited arm of The Entourage in 2015, we rapidly met with incredible success. We were inundated with students and their parents beating a path to our door in the hope of receiving practical business training that would set them up for success. The rigor of our programs resulted in student engagement, completion levels, and success rates as much as ten times higher than the traditional education average. The industry soon noticed these results, and shortly after launching we were approached by a tier-one university asking if we'd be willing to partner with them to develop and deliver their cornerstone

MBA program. Even the very institutions we were disrupting recognized the strength we were bringing to traditional education.

That was before everything very nearly fell apart.

Just as we started to move the needle on the quality expected of traditional education providers in the field of entrepreneurship, the ground began to shift beneath us. In early 2016, it emerged that a handful of private providers were abusing the availability of government funding in the sector. This catalyzed two sudden changes.

The first came in March 2016, when the government announced that they would stop paying new entrants to the space for the next six months. Anyone who had become accredited during the previous two years would keep their students and could continue delivering their services, but would not receive payment for doing so until six months later. Six months dragged out to nine months. For us, this meant a cumulative cash-gap of $6 million, which we needed to find elsewhere.

We survived that period by raising money from investors, taking on debt from the banks, invoice factoring from private financiers, negotiating with creditors, and by liquidating many of my own investments. We used every trick in the book to keep the ship afloat.

Unfortunately, that was the easy part. The storm was about to get even worse.

On October 1, 2016, I walked into my office to a newspaper sitting on my desk. "Government to Axe Skills-Based sector. 478 VET Courses Won't Be Eligible," screamed the headline. The second unforeseen announcement had arrived.

In an effort to drive hundreds of thousands of students back to large traditional education institutions, the government was introducing significant policy changes, which would ultimately make it unviable for the vast majority of private providers to continue. The new regulations were due to take effect on January 1, 2017, giving us and everybody else in the industry a mere three months' notice of a reversal that would prove catastrophic. When this second policy change came into effect, we would lose 70 percent of our revenues instantly, bringing us to the brink of collapse.

We were like a sinking ship taking on more and more water. There we were in October 2016, having built an institution around our VET delivery that would become obsolete in three months. We were already carrying more than $4 million in debt due to the government's earlier decision to cut off payments to new entrants, and now, following the announcement of the policy change, we were three months from taking a *monthly* loss of $800,000.

That was when I found myself touring the offices of administrators and insolvency practitioners—people whose job is to help wind up businesses in the least painful way. As they reviewed our financials and researched the pending collapse of the VET sector, they all reached the same conclusion and delivered the same dire warning. *"There's no way you can trade out of this, Jack."*

This was both the single lowest point in my life, and the most catalyzing moment I've ever experienced. Simultaneously, I felt both more defeated and more determined than I had ever felt before. Behind the crushingly awful news I was receiving from every side, there was a deep inner knowing that said, "I do not accept the reality that says we need to quit."

Despite the circumstances, I felt strongly that what we were doing was far too important to simply give up on. Too many people cared way too much about our mission for us to quit on it. Even if we didn't end up making it, and regardless of how hard or painful it might get, not trying was never an option. Sometimes, as all of us in business eventually discover, the only way out is through.

Piling more pressure onto the situation, years earlier I had bought my mother a house to ensure that she didn't need to pay rent or mortgage repayments. It was my way of helping her ease into retirement. Although *she* didn't have a mortgage, I did, and it was cross-collateralized against the business debt. If The Entourage had gone under, my mom would have been homeless, and I would have been in no position to support her financially.

It was the type of nightmare scenario that I hope you won't face too many times during your career.

To save The Entourage from going under, I rallied my COO and CFO into the boardroom to redesign our business and financial model. Our task was to rebuild the business from $4 million in the red, with no products or services that would survive beyond three months, and a cost base that had become significantly too high relative to our revenues. All this, while staring down the barrel of impending and large-scale losses.

We were attempting the impossible. Taking the advice of the experts, giving up and starting again would have been a walk in the park relative to the task we had ahead of us.

For three weeks straight, we spent every day in the boardroom, with countless spreadsheets and computers spread out across the table, drawing up potential play after potential play, only to realize that each one wouldn't work, scrub the whiteboard, and start again. Each night I would go home late, struggle to eat, and snatch an hour or two of sleep, only to return in the early hours of the morning and start architecting more plays on the whiteboard. We had an incredibly difficult problem to solve; even attempting it would involve taking a lot of risks.

After three long weeks of trying to find a path forward, we finally saw a crack of light. A very narrow and treacherous path of a thousand details started to reveal itself. In a distressed scenario like the one we faced, our overarching strategy had to be to "kick the can down the road"—push out costs as far as possible into the future and bring in cash as quickly as possible, to give ourselves a longer runway to survive, in the expectation of eventually becoming profitable again before the company died.

The hardest thing about being in such an extreme position of distress was that every single task seemed almost impossible, and they all needed to be done immediately and concurrently.

For example, to reduce our cost base as much as possible we had to cut our team down from ninety to forty, in a matter of days. While this alone was excruciatingly painful, it wasn't enough to solve all our problems. It was just a necessary first step.

Even after downsizing the team our cost base was still unsustainably high, meaning we needed to strip out every unnecessary cost in the operation. Simultaneously, we needed to design, develop, and deploy a new product suite to immediately take to market, moving away from government accreditation and returning to our original business model of coaching existing business owners. We also needed to restrict everyone's focus to either winning new customers or servicing existing customers—nothing else mattered. Most of all, we needed to care for and lead the remaining members of our team, who had just lost more than half of their colleagues through redundancies. All f this while proactively managing a seemingly never ending list of creditors and financiers, many of whom could have put a bullet through the business at any point, spelling game over.

Deciding to keep fighting began the hardest years of our lives.

However, in those years we achieved something that everybody, including the experts, thought impossible. We navigated through the distress. We continued fighting for our mission to give entrepreneurs everything they needed to build great companies and live meaningful lives. We slowly rebuilt the business to a point where it was healthy again. Most impressively, we repaid *every dollar* to every financier and creditor.

Today, we are in significantly better shape than we were prior to the calamity of 2016. While those years were the hardest we've faced, they forced us to upgrade every aspect of the business. Those improvements mean that today, the successes of our members are greater than ever, our internal culture and operations have sharpened, and our growth rates far exceed those we were registering prior to 2016. Much of the strength we possess today was forged through the fires of adversity.

Another silver lining of our experiences in 2016 was that in 2020, when COVID-19 hit, we knew exactly how to coach our members through their distress. During the tightest year of COVID restrictions in Australia, members of Elevate, our exclusive business coaching program, outperformed average small business growth rates by a massive 310 percent. Over the past twelve months, as restrictions have gradually eased, the same group has collectively generated more than $800 million in revenue.

These results have seen their names, and subsequently ours, adorn the lists of The Australian Financial Review (AFR) Fast Starters, Fast 100, and Most Innovative Companies, the Deloitte Fast 50, Great Places To Work, The Australian Young Entrepreneur Awards, MyBusiness Magazine Awards, Telstra Business Awards, AusMumpreneur Awards, Women In Business Awards, The B&Ts 30 Under 30, and the AFR Young Rich List. With the global media taking notice, The Entourage has become one of the world's most publicized and respected brands in the field of entrepreneurship, propelling our wider community to 1,200,000 of the world's most successful business owners.

In our turnaround story, the comeback was greater than the setback. None of this would have happened had we taken the advice of the experts and decided to *put the keys on the table, raise the white flag, and exit stage left*. Some people call entrepreneurs delusional. But as every business owner knows, taking on insurmountable challenges—and succeeding—requires delusion. Sometimes we owe it to the people around us to draw on the deepest well of delusion we can muster, and use it as fuel to reshape reality.

As entrepreneurs, so much of our maturation is about learning to deeply trust our judgment in the face of other people's rationale and logic. When the voice inside of you is more powerful than the voices outside of you, that's when you've begun to master this journey. That's what it means to be an entrepreneur: not accepting the reality that everybody else subscribes to, and instead deciding to create reality according to the vision we hold. We are not molded by the world; instead we shape it. We must become comfortable insisting on the impossible.

WHY THIS MIGHT BE THE MOST IMPORTANT BUSINESS BOOK YOU WILL READ THIS YEAR

The catastrophe that hit The Entourage in 2016 is very similar to what happened to every business when COVID-19 swept across the globe in 2020. It was an external, unforeseen incident, with no relation to the quality of the businesses it impacted, yet it immediately altered everything. If your business navigated the shifting sands of 2020, you have some appreciation of how we felt when the foundation of The Entourage crumbled beneath us.

While every business was impacted by COVID, however, not every business was affected in the same way. Many were pushed into challenge and distress, fighting to stay alive. All around the world, organizations were forced to shut their doors, reconsider core elements of their business model, and find a path through. On the other side of the coin, some businesses were suddenly catapulted into hypergrowth. A rapidly changing environment dramatically increased the demand for their products or services, forcing them to manage the stresses and pressures that come from a sudden increase in volume. Whatever business you're in, COVID-19 and the pivots it necessitated surely confronted you with one undeniable truth: post-Covid, no business should be operating the same way as it was at the beginning of 2020.

While the lessons of the past few years have been particularly intense, as business owners we experience constant change. At any given time, a business is either **growing**, **declining**, or **plateauing**—and each of these seasons brings its own challenges.

When a company is growing, particularly if it's experiencing hypergrowth, its capacity to meet and manage accelerated demand may be sorely tested. A rapidly growing business faces numerous urgent challenges: recruiting team members quickly, building out the leadership capacity of the team, streamlining product delivery, and sharpening financial management. If your business is growing at a rate that you're struggling to keep up with, you may find that it's all-consuming; the larger the business grows, the harder it becomes to manage.

Alternatively, there are numerous reasons why a company may find itself in decline. A new competitor may enter the market, several key people may leave in a short timespan, or the effectiveness of marketing or sales performance may decrease sharply. You may be hammered by a government policy change, as The Entourage was in 2016. And yes, you may find yourselves caught in the middle of a pandemic or a global recession. These, and many other factors, may tip an otherwise stable business into decline.

Yet another challenging scenario stems not from rapid growth or decline but simply from reaching and remaining atop a plateau. Every business owner goes through periods where they feel like they are bumping up against a glass ceiling. In this scenario, the business remains stagnant, with little or no growth for many years. If this has happened to you, you've probably found yourself losing your spark, no longer enthused by your business and unsure how to break through to the next level. You may think you've fallen out of love with your business. In all likelihood, however, that's not the case. You haven't fallen out of love with your business; you have fallen out of love with the *stage your business is at*.

As entrepreneurs, our businesses are forever going through seasons. Whether we're experiencing rapid growth, are distressed and fighting for survival, or we've hit a plateau that's lasted for years, there is one fundamental truth that underpins each season: at any given moment, we should be focused on *building a great company*.

At The Entourage, we've heard stories of almost every type of business challenge imaginable. Every day, we receive thousands of messages and enquiries from business owners who, one way or the other, feel trapped by what they've created. People who went into business in pursuit of freedom—creative freedom, time freedom, lifestyle freedom, financial freedom—and who are now experiencing everything *but freedom*. The world is full of seven- and eight-figure business owners who might look successful on the outside, but on the inside they are imprisoned by their own business.

This book, and the resources that accompany it, are about taking you on a journey to build a great company, and—in the process—to finally discover the freedom you dreamed of when you first started along this road. The book is about accelerating growth, with less effort, and building a business that can scale beyond you. The journey will take you from being the founder of a reactive and chaotic startup, to being the leader of a well-structured scaleup, a business that achieves more and grows more, even as you personally do less. It will enable you to elevate from being the technician who must personally fix every problem, to being an entrepreneur leading your business from the front. It will take you from being a business *operator*, who spends every day fighting in the trenches because you're needed there, to being a business *owner* with a self-managing company that can grow sustainably without you.

Three months into their journey, we ask our Elevate members for feedback. The most common comment we hear is, "This feels weird. We're growing faster but I'm doing less." If you'd like the same experience, keep reading. The proven strategies contained in this book will spark paradigm shifts and lightbulb moments that will change the way you build businesses for the rest of your life.

Let's break it down, so you can get a clearer sense of what you'll find in these pages. This book is for you if:

- You're not growing at the rate you'd like to. Your business has plateaued and you feel yourself starting to lose the creative spark that once drove you forward.
- You're experiencing rapid growth and feel like you're fighting just to keep up. You find yourself fire-fighting and putting in place temporary solutions to recurring problems. Your growth requires you to build a structurally sound company that can keep up with the demand.
- You're personally doing everything in your business. As the business grows, it doesn't bring you more freedom. It simply takes up more of your time. You're either doing everything, or overseeing everything very closely, neither of which are sustainable.
- You've been carrying the same challenges and goals for some time now, and can't seem to get unstuck. You're ready to scale your business to the next level and play a bigger game, but are unsure *how*.
- You feel like you've reached the boundary of your existing capabilities and want expert guidance on how to break through the glass ceiling you find yourself bumping up against.

WHAT YOU'LL FIND IN THIS BOOK

We've divided this book into four sections: **Part I: The Entrepreneur**, **Part II: The Drive Growth Cycle**, **Part III: The Enable Growth Structure**, and **Part IV: The Future**.

In **Part I: The Entrepreneur**, we uncover the core operating principles of the world's greatest entrepreneurs. These fundamental paradigm shifts will enable you to elevate *your skillset* as an entrepreneur. Installing these operating principles is the first step to exponentially increasing your results in life and business.

Part I consists of five chapters. In **Chapter One: From Startup to Scaleup: The Entrepreneur's Journey**, we outline exactly how to take your business from a reactive, chaotic, and time-consuming startup, to an optimized engine that can run without you. **Chapter Two: The Four Hats: Technician to Entrepreneur**, describes how to go from working *in* your business, to working *on* your business. While you're trapped in technician mode, you'll feel like you're stuck *doing* everything. As you elevate to the role of entrepreneur, you'll become the person *shaping* everything.

Chapter Three: The Six Elements: Business Operator to Business Owner uncovers the blueprint that will enable you to build a structurally sound business that is both scalable and sustainable. In **Chapter Four: Driver or Enabler: Play to Your Strengths**, we will identify your strengths and show you how to build a winning team at the top of your organization. This will highlight the glass ceiling that prevents almost all business owners from growing their business beyond a certain point, and how to break through it. Finally, **Chapter Five: Craft Your Roadmap: Know Your North Stars** shows you how to generate a one-page snapshot that illustrates where you are, where you want to be, and how to get there.

In **Part II: The Drive Growth Cycle**, we focus on the elements that accelerate the growth of your business. These elements will enable you to attract the right customers, keep them, and multiply them. The Drive Growth Cycle consists of the first three of the Six Elements we introduce in Part I. These are the consumer-facing elements, which are visible above the surface and *drive* demand.

In **Chapter Six: Marketing: Construct a Marketing Engine that Generates You Leads**, we outline exactly how to build a marketing engine that grows your brand, scales your audience, and generates the right amount of high-quality leads. In **Chapter Seven: Sales: Drive Growth and Profitability**, we walk you through building a sales process for your business that you can optimize, delegate, and scale. In **Chapter Eight: Product: Develop and Deliver Products That Delight Your Customer**, we reveal the key strategies to optimizing your products and services so that your customers fall in love with them, while outlining how to build-out this function so that it is not reliant on you.

In **Part III: The Enable Growth Structure**, we turn our attention to the remaining three of the Six Elements. These elements enable the growth of your business. If The Drive Growth Cycle makes your business scalable, The Enable Growth Structure makes your business *sustainable*. These are the elements that function behind the scenes to ensure the company is well-resourced and can keep pace with demand.

In **Chapter Nine: Operations: Build a Business That Can Work Without You**, we guide you to install an operating system into your business that ensures each of the functions are streamlined, integrated, and working together. In **Chapter Ten: Finance: Manage and Maximize the Money**, we teach you to develop the financial visibility of your company, how to fall in love with making financially informed decisions, and how you can increase the profitability of your business as it scales. Finally, in **Chapter Eleven: People: Assemble Your A-Team**, we give you a blueprint for developing a world-class culture that is structurally ingrained in the fabric of the company.

As business owners, we will always be faced with new scenarios that challenge us and stretch us. In **Part IV: The Future**, we give you a playbook for every type of situation. The fourth part of this book consists of just one chapter, but it's an important one. In **Chapter Twelve: There's Always a Play: Navigating the Different Seasons of Business**, we describe how to apply the methodologies from the book to any scenario that comes your way. This chapter will equip you with key strategies so that like a chess player who thinks several moves in advance, you always know your best next steps, whatever state your business is in.

There's a huge amount of substance in these pages, but even so, our biggest challenge when putting together this book was not deciding what to include, but choosing what to leave out. As such, we've collected all the resources, templates, and tools you will need to dive even deeper into the strategies contained here, and apply them to your own business. We don't want you to be an armchair reader. We want you to put the guidance in this book to work and reshape your business so it can grow beyond you. The most effective way to do that will be to download these resources and refer to them as you read. You can find them, for free, at our website, www.the-entourage.com/elevate.

WHO ARE WE?

Before we proceed with the rest of this book, we'd like to introduce ourselves, so you understand what qualifies us to write on this vital subject. I (Jack) have been building and investing in businesses my entire life. I made a brief attempt at following a more traditional path by pursuing a commerce and law degree at university, but after three short months my eagerness to develop real-world skills overwhelmed my desire to have some letters after my name, and I dropped out to build my own projects. Instead of higher education, my apprenticeship came through starting businesses and learning from their success and failure. Some of them I loved, some of them I didn't, but each one taught me something. Every success unlocked a new insight into how businesses are built, and every mistake etched into my mind the hazards of an unprofitable path.

In 2007 I co-founded a company called MBE Group, which laid the foundations that would later prepare me to start The Entourage. At MBE, we advised small-to-medium-sized business (SMEs) owners on strategies to raise money from investors, acquire companies, and ultimately build value to exit. MBE enabled our clients to execute over $300 million in transactions, and we became one of Australia's fastest growing companies.

Along the way, I invested in companies spanning the diverse worlds of biotechnology, finance, e-commerce, recruitment, and even aviation, including one that grew into what's known as a "unicorn"; a business that goes from founding $0 to $1 billion within ten years. More recently, I founded a luxury property brand which is building a collection of unique resorts and exclusive hotels around the world, starting with our recent purchase of a beautiful private island here in the Whitsundays of Australia. This brand will provide the ideal destinations for entrepreneurs and executives who want to rejuvenate, reconnect with themselves and their loved ones, or host retreats for their teams.

Since founding The Entourage, I've personally coached and presented live to more than 345,000 entrepreneurs, many of whom have achieved the kinds of commercial results that have attracted the attention of the larger end of town. I've been called upon to develop strategy and boost performance for numerous large-scale organizations, including Fortune100 companies, ASX200 companies, federal and state governments, athletes, the Australian National Rugby League (NRL) and NRL clubs, celebrities, and some of the world's leading entrepreneurs.

This has enabled me to connect with many of the entrepreneurial icons of our time. Over the years I've had the opportunity to work with, learn from, and in some instances become close friends with people like Sir Richard Branson of the Virgin Group and co-founder of Apple Steve Wozniak. People like Janine Allis from Boost Juice, Kristina Karlson, who built a beautiful global brand in Kikki K, Gerard Adams, the co-founder of *Elite Daily*, who went on to sell to the *Daily Mail* for $50 million, Fred Schebesta, the co-founder of $650 million-valued Finder, and Mark Bouris who sold Wizard Home Loans for $500 million to GE Money and went on to start Yellow Brick Road.

By 2015, The Entourage had reached a size that necessitated a more senior executive team so we could operationalize in a way that kept pace with our growth. This is when my co-author, Tim Morris, joined our leadership team.

Prior to The Entourage, Tim had already established himself as a successful business owner and a highly effective executive across the education and technology sectors. His first business, Dynamic Horizons, an innovation consulting company, collaborated with some of Australia's biggest corporations, including banking and utility companies, government agencies, Australia Post, and Cisco, to conceptualize and introduce new products and services. Later, he founded and led Learn Lab, an education development business which was at the forefront of bringing online education into leading Australian universities. Tim has also served as a general manager of Uber, with responsibility for driving the expansion of the ride-sharing business into the Australian market, through Melbourne.

Tim has spent more than twenty years living and breathing entrepreneurial business. In the embryonic days of the Australian startup scene, he launched an e-commerce business, served as a mentor in the country's first startup incubators, and consulted with what are now some of Australia's most successful entrepreneurial businesses on strategy and product development.

In those early days, Tim often met with blank faces and a confused response when he mentioned the term "entrepreneurship." Today, many of the people he mentored back then are emerging as Australia's greatest startup success stories. Whether it's a company raising $40 million in growth capital or achieving a valuation of $1.5 billion, more often than not, Tim has played a part in helping to shape their foundations. Often, he helped them build the very first version of their product, or provided much-needed guidance at a crucial stage of their journey. It's the rare success story that Tim hasn't had a hand in somewhere along the way.

In 2016–2017, while I worked with my team of advisors and met with our bank and other creditors to turn the fortunes of The Entourage around, Tim bore much of the responsibility for managing the internal team, providing much-needed strength and direction to those team members who stayed on when we suffered the wave of redundancies that more than halved the size of the business. While I redesigned the business model, stress testing each play through meticulous financial forecasting, Tim redesigned our programs to ensure they were the perfect marriage between everything we had to offer and exactly what business owners need to sustainably scale their companies. While I focused on driving growth through scaling our marketing and sales engine, which often involved long travel and tours, Tim's management and leadership of the team became even more important as he took on even greater responsibility, ensuring that the fundamentals to *enable* growth were in place and functioning effectively.

Needless to say, Tim's contribution played a key role in bringing The Entourage back from the brink of oblivion. In 2016, when things were at their very worst, Tim was a steadfast and consistent presence. Unbeknown to me at the time, Tim had privately resolved to commit fully to The Entourage and go down with the ship if he needed to. Naturally, Tim and I have developed a strong friendship over many years of growing a successful company, grinding in the trenches together, and then coming out the other side and leading The Entourage back to high growth.

In 2020, Tim ascended into the role of CEO, taking responsibility for operations and the team. This shift has freed me to focus on long-term growth opportunities and amplifying the brand to a position of global market leadership. In collaboration with Tim and other leaders within the company, I shape and direct strategic projects, while they manage the day-to-day operations. As an entrepreneur, developing the leadership capacity of my companies has always been essential to building businesses that can run without me and scale beyond me. At The Entourage, Tim has been a key player in achieving that.

Great businesses are never built by one person alone. One of the most common glass ceilings we see in our members' businesses is that the founder is trying to do everything themselves. As we'll explain in the next chapter, this approach may be necessary in the early stages, but once a company grows to a certain size, a founder who tries to hold on to all managerial and leadership responsibilities themselves will kill the growth of their business.

Tim has been a crucial piece of the growth of The Entourage for eight years, often complimenting my expertise with his. It's for this reason that he and I decided to co-author *Elevate*; to give you a rounded, holistic picture of both the strategic imperatives of becoming a great entrepreneur, and the operational imperatives that will enable you and your team to execute effectively. Although we wrote the book primarily for entrepreneurs, we encourage you to share it with your team and business partners. Thousands of case studies—several of which you'll read about in these pages—have shown that the insights and guidance in this book empower entire teams to operate under one unified methodology.

As co-authors, some of the stories we tell will focus on my experience and others on Tim's. When we share a story that involves both of us, we'll refer to ourselves using the first-person "we." We'll also use the word"'we'" when describing the broader community of entrepreneurs, of which we're all part, and—where necessary—clarify the distinction. When we relate an event from one of our lives, we'll switch to the third person, "Jack" or "Tim," to ensure it is absolutely clear who is at the center of each episode.

A DIFFERENT KIND OF BUSINESS BOOK

There is no shortage of business books in the world. You could walk into your local bookstore—or look online—and find dozens of books that will tell you how to start a business or how to scale a billion-dollar tech company in Silicon Valley. There are also plenty of academic textbooks attempting to apply old theories to a new world, and even books that take strategies from the corporate world and attempt to apply them to a small business environment.

The problem is, none of them focus on what to do when you've built the foundation of a business, feel like you're bursting at the seams, and want to grow in a more scalable way. None of them focus on how to build a structurally sound business that can grow beyond you. You're not starting a new business, you're not raising millions of dollars to build the next billion-dollar tech company, and you're certainly not a corporation looking to become a slightly larger corporation. Small businesses are *not* smaller versions of big businesses; they are a unique, entirely different ball game.

What's particularly frustrating about this gap in the literature is that small- to medium-sized business is the engine room of the economy, yet these businesses are horribly overlooked by a world obsessed with who's creating the next Facebook. In the grander scheme of things, the Facebooks of the world represent a tiny proportion of the business landscape, and not the most useful proportion. It's small businesses that make the world go around. Most of the products and services that we use every day are brought to the world by small business owners striving to make a valuable contribution. Yet, we see a huge discrepancy between how important small- to medium-sized businesses are to the world, and the level of support they receive. We wrote *Elevate* to close that gap.

This book focuses on one very important phase of the business journey that is ignored pretty much everywhere else: you're running a small business, maxed out beyond your capacity, and looking to accelerate growth in a way that relies less on your personal input and exertion. Maybe you want to go from doing a million dollars a year working sixty hours a week to a million dollars a month, working six hours a week. Maybe you're doing $10 million a year but, because everything relies on you, you are seriously burnt out.

Despite these challenges, you love being in business. You want to continue to grow your company while working less *in it*, and more *on it*. This combination might sound counterintuitive, but these are the exact results we help real-world, business owners just like you to achieve everyday. We call this process of turning your small business into a finely tuned engine that can scale beyond you, *going from startup to scaleup*. This book is written for you, the business owner who wants to grow beyond the ceiling you have now reached.

Here's what you'll find in these pages:

- Real strategies to build a scalable company, coming from people who've been there, done that and understand the challenges.
- Tried, tested, and proven frameworks to help you implement every step of the way.
- The blueprint for how different parts of a scaleup-stage business fit together and interact.
- Honest, unflinching descriptions of challenges we've faced along the way, outlining how we've overcome them, so that you can shave years of struggle off your learning curve.
- Case studies from members of our Elevate coaching program, breaking down how they've successfully put the principles from each chapter into practice. All the case studies come from real Elevate members and full-length videos of them telling their own story, in their own words, can be found on our website. For the most part, we use the actual names of the people and businesses we describe. Occasionally, for reasons that will be obvious, we've omitted their names.

Here's what you won't find:

- Fluffy advice about how to start a business. This book is written for owners and managers of existing companies who find themselves working harder, doing more, and earning less.
- Wild strategies aimed at raising hundreds of millions of dollars. While raising money from investors is absolutely something this book will help with, more often than not businesses at this stage of the game can fund their own growth by simply increasing profit and generating more cash.
- Strategies more appropriate for big corporations, that attempt to hammer your small business into an unnatural shape, like a square peg through a round hole.
- Academic theories about how to build a business. This book is a distillation of more than forty years of real-world business

experience, starting, scaling, and investing in businesses at this very stage of their growth curve.

- A get-rich-quick cheat sheet. This book is about the long game and the specific skills and strategies that will enable you to develop into a world-class entrepreneur.

How do you know whether this book has something valuable to offer you? You might be an accountant who's built the foundations of a strong accountancy practice, yet you still find yourself entrenched in the doing, putting in sixty hours a week. Maybe you run an e-commerce business that has reached seven figures but is bursting at the seams operationally and financially. Alternatively, you could be a personal trainer who's built a fledgling team but feels stuck when it comes to removing yourself and scaling to the next level. The founder of a construction company who's developed a great team and is running several projects, but can't see a clear path to taking on anymore without succumbing to burnout. A retailer working around the clock, wondering how you could ever scale beyond your current size because you couldn't possibly work any harder. A coach who's created a great brand that people love, but wants to build out your operation, and ultimately reach more people and maximize your impact.

Whatever your story, if you're a real business owner doing the real work, this book is for you.

PART I

THE ENTREPRENEUR

W hy does the first part of this book concentrate on you, the entrepreneur? Because, as an entrepreneur, your business is a reflection of you. You've already built a company that is successful in many ways, but you know it has the potential to become much better. You're right. The starting point to building a great company is to elevate *yourself* as an entrepreneur.

A business will never outgrow the internal software of its founder. The vast majority of business owners have an ineffective operating system; a way of approaching their business that keeps them playing small. Therefore, the business is limited by the skillset of the entrepreneur. Conversely, dedicated study of the world's best entrepreneurs reveals an underlying pattern to the way they build companies. There is a common *archetype*, which all great entrepreneurs harness.

While most business owners spend their lives trying to run faster and work harder, seasoned entrepreneurs know how to build an engine that enables them to get far more done in less time. When most business owners are laboring tirelessly to keep the plates spinning, great entrepreneurs are playing the long game, to transform their company into an asset that can run without them. As most business owners rush from one fire to the next, great entrepreneurs install an operating framework that enables them to drive performance at scale. While most business owners exhaust themselves trying to be all things to all people, the world's best entrepreneurs understand how to play to their strengths, and hire their weaknesses. Instead of thinking of their role in the business as a mechanic or a technician, diving under the hood whenever something goes awry, they think of the business as something they design, lead, and shape. Business is never a solo sport, and great entrepreneurs understand this fundamental truth. Therefore, they build a team, knowing that the team will build the business.

Part I: The Entrepreneur, is about upgrading your software so that you're running the same internal operating system as the world's best entrepreneurs. These simple, foundational principles have been the unlock for the hundreds of thousands of business owners we've coached and trained, allowing them to break free of where they were, and ultimately build a self-managing company that reflects their potential. Our aim in this part of the book is to introduce you to the fundamental paradigm shifts you'll need to make to operate like the world's greatest entrepreneurs, and indeed—if you consistently apply the principles you find in these pages—to become one.

I

STARTUP TO SCALEUP

The Entrepreneur's Journey

Even across a diverse range of industries, the glass ceilings that keep businesses stuck are remarkably similar. Years of hard-fought experience in starting, building, and scaling our own companies, combined with the direct insight we have received through working with tens of thousands of businesses, has revealed to us a pattern in the core challenges that cause businesses to plateau or to grow rapidly without the necessary foundations in place. The journey of the entrepreneur contains some remarkably common elements. Usually, it goes something like this.

You start out with a good understanding of the market opportunity and a deep empathy for the consumer. Instinctively you're able to join the dots. You know what sort of product or service will address the existing market demand and fulfill the unmet consumer need, and you start bringing together the resources to make this happen.

As entrepreneurs, this is what we do. We are alchemists. We intuitively understand how to take an opportunity others can only glimpse, and turn it into something real. We are not constrained by doubts and limitations, because we understand that entrepreneurship is never about resources; it is always about *resourcefulness*. What starts out as an inspired thought in our mind or feeling in our heart, eventually blooms into something very real.

In the startup phase, the business is small enough for you to wrap your arms around it. You're excited to manage all the moving parts yourself. You work directly with every person on the team, communicate informally, make decisions based on gut feel, and pursue opportunities as quickly as they arise. When the business needs more sales, you can personally step in and drive the numbers up. When a customer complaint arises that your team can't handle, you step in and help solve the problem.

Sure, the early years are challenging, but you love them. You're in your element. You feel alive. You're building your business with drive, tenacity, creativity, resourcefulness, and grit, not policies and procedures. You're an entrepreneur in your natural state, leading from the front.

Then, something changes. The business grows to a point where it becomes too large for you to lead alone.

Your customer base, once small and manageable, has grown to a point where delivering in a way that upholds your brand promise is beyond your capacity to manage by yourself. Your company's reputation has risen to the point where customers expect a consistently high standard. Delivering your product or service is now an entire function in and of itself, requiring more management than what you're able to offer.

As the business has grown, so has the number of sales you are making. Like many founders, you are still the main revenue generator, meaning that as sales increase so does the time you personally need to dedicate to them—another glass ceiling you find yourself bumping painfully up against.

Meanwhile, your growing business has more moving parts than it used to. Managing your growing team has become yet another full-time job you don't have time to do, and the *ad hoc* approach to decision-making that served you so well in your company's early years now means that the company lacks a unifying direction. With your company's increased size, company culture—once full of camaraderie and understanding—has become dispersed and chaotic. Operational complexity has grown too, and no one is taking ownership of getting the right things done. With higher wages, greater expenses, and bigger tax bills, it's becoming increasingly difficult to stay on top of week-to-week cash flow, let alone forecast the future performance of the business.

The business has reached a size no one person can possibly wrap their arms around, and its demands have outpaced your capacity to handle them all yourself. For you, the entrepreneur, the consequences of hitting this brick wall are profound. Instead of your business serving you, you feel as though you're pouring endless time and energy into it, with diminishing returns. The freedom and impact you once dreamed of now feel further away than ever. Instead, you find yourself buried in spreadsheets, putting out daily fires, dealing with HR issues, writing policies and procedures for your team to follow, trying to keep up with the sales, optimizing your CRM and—in your spare time—doing your best to manage the cash, all while wondering why you're not as profitable as you'd hoped to be.

What was once a vision that excited you has become an all-consuming machine that drains your energy. The entrepreneurial vigor that catalyzed the early success of your business is diluted, if not extinguished. No longer leading from the front with drive and creativity, you're now playing the role of operations manager at best, or admin assistant at worst.

This is not why you started the business. You're not even that *good* at most of the day-to-day operational work. As an entrepreneur you're naturally a visionary, a big-picture thinker who can lead a business to great heights. Burying yourself in the day-to-day operations of the business isn't where you want to be, and it's not how you contribute the most to your team, your customers, and the business itself. If that was your zone of genius, you'd never have started the business in the first place. A genius in the wrong position looks like a fool, and you're in the wrong position. You desperately want your business to succeed, so you keep grinding. Meanwhile your sense of fulfillment continues to diminish. As you continue along this path, you find yourself working harder, doing more, and earning less.

However hard you try to put on a brave face, your dissatisfaction and frustration seeps into the rest of the business. Growth starts to plateau.

Despite your best efforts, running your business is like driving a car with the handbrake on. It's going nowhere fast. Welcome to the Seven-Figure Ceiling. The inevitable point where your business has outgrown the startup stage, yet you continue to manage and lead it the same way you did in the startup days.

When you sit down and reflect on the trajectory of your business, one thing becomes very clear: what got you to where you are is not going to get you to where you need to be. The strategies you know how to execute have served you well up to now, but they are no longer fit for purpose.

There's good news, too, however. You're not failing as an entrepreneur. You're exactly where you need to be. Hitting the Seven-Figure Ceiling is not an optional step on the path of the entrepreneur, yet no one's talking about it, or how to smash through it. We're here to tell you that to get to where you're going, you need to pass this checkpoint. There's no avoiding it. In fact, it holds a number of key lessons that will be fundamental to your future success as an entrepreneur.

The core paradigm shift we want you to absorb from this chapter is this: as entrepreneurs, it's not our job to market, sell, and deliver a product. It's our job to *build a business* that can market, sell, and deliver a product. Until now, you've had to do everything yourself to get the business up and running. That way of operating got you this far, further than many businesses ever get. Now, it's time to elevate. The next phase is about building a business that can operate without you, enabling you to transition from being the person *doing* everything to being the person *leading* everything.

While this journey takes time, it is not about running faster or working harder—quite the opposite. It's about beginning to work smarter. It's about preserving the entrepreneurial dynamism that has brought you this far, while underpinning it with the fundamentals necessary to build a self-managing company. On the other side of this journey, you will find yourself working less, achieving more, and making exponentially greater profits.

A JOURNEY EVERY BUSINESS NEEDS TO TAKE

In this chapter, we'll identify the key differences between startup and scaleup. From there, we can start to examine how some of the practices that helped you achieve your success during the startup stage are now a hindrance as you grow toward scaleup. We'll share a case study that illustrates how shifting your approach to your business will unlock the next stage of growth, and finally we'll share Jack's personal experience of struggling with, and ultimately transcending, the ceiling we describe.

Startup stage is where every entrepreneur begins. It's where the business takes shape, and where we as founders lay the foundations for every development that follows. The problem is that as most businesses grow, how they operate doesn't mature in line with that growth. They never transition to the scaleup way of operating, which keeps them small forever. Herein lies the number one glass ceiling that we see in seven- and eight-figure businesses: no matter how much they've grown, no matter how much they're doing in revenue, they still function like a startup.

If we could summarize the journey we'll take you on in this book in a few words, it would be this: we're going to teach you how to make the transition from startup to scaleup. The vast majority of entrepreneurs don't understand that there are potent operational differences between these two modes of doing business. As they grow, they move from building a small startup to building…a bigger startup. Disillusioned by the additional work this brings them, and the degradation of their quality of life, they resign themselves to the idea that their business will never fulfill its true potential. If only they knew how to turn their burgeoning startup into a scaleup, the story could be very different.

The first step toward a cure is diagnosis. Let's begin this chapter by diving into the characteristics of the startup stage in more depth.

WHAT MAKES A STARTUP

In startup, while you've built some good revenues and a foundational customer base, the operations of the business are still nascent. You're yet to develop a business model that can scale beyond your daily, personal exertion. Which is fine; at this stage, it's par for the course.

Startup is a dance with the consumer; it's about getting *attuned* to your customer. Therefore, one factor matters above all others: interaction with the market. Your primary focus will be figuring out what the customer wants, so that you can market, sell, and deliver to them in a way that makes them want to come back. You will decide what to build in response to what the market likes, and what to discard according to what the market doesn't appreciate. Make no mistake, no amount of business planning, financial modeling, or academic theory can provide a substitute for direct contact with the customer.

At this stage, you are not yet concerned with the internal operations of the business. Your focus on the market, and on winning new customers, should border on the obsessive. This obsession will give rise to an agile operational style. You will be constantly responding and reacting to the lessons you learn through marketing, selling, delivering, and listening to your customers. Every lesson learned is an invitation to improve. This type of rapid testing and iteration may feel chaotic, but for now it is necessary. Startup is about rolling with the punches. When you reach the scaleup stage, you will need to operate to a framework. In startup, the punches *are* the framework.

In the early years of your business, startup is exciting. Everything you do is infused with optimism and a vision of what the future will bring. You can see your dreams coming to life, and your close-knit team shares a strong camaraderie. This energy and enthusiasm gives rise to an "all-hands-on-deck" approach, where everybody rolls up their sleeves and does whatever is necessary to edge your company closer to fulfilling its vision.

You can't remain in this stage forever, however. It serves a purpose—getting you from zero to a burgeoning company—but as the business reaches the seven-figure mark and beyond, your focus—and the focus of your entire company—needs to shift. What were once your greatest strengths start to become the very characteristics that hold you back.

OUTGROWING THE STARTUP PHASE

During startup, your relentless focus on acquiring and satisfying new customers meant that everything else was genuinely unimportant. As you grow into the scaleup stage, however, this translates into a lack of operational rigor and limited cohesion across the company. As the company expands, cracks start to show.

You've arrived at the dilemma that we see so many members of The Entourage face. This is both a huge challenge for a growing business, and an enormous opportunity. The capacity to navigate this challenge determines which businesses mature into successful companies, which plateau, and which fade away.

In startup, your agile and adaptive nature was a strength. When you spend every day absorbing and responding to lessons learned in-market, there isn't much point developing a planning cadence or operating principles and processes. As you mature into the scaleup stage, however, you start to see the inherent weaknesses of this approach. You lack any scalable infrastructure. Without structure to guide and gauge the performance of your team, what do you do when your business grows and there is more to be done? As the founder, your initial response is likely to put the company on your back and personally do more.

This is where your business begins to stagnate or even spiral downward. The "all-hands-on-deck" approach that once served you so well means that every task is accomplished manually, often on an *ad hoc* basis by whoever notices the problem first. Nothing is automated, measured, or managed. The eagerness of your well-intentioned team means that people often overestimate their capabilities. With more people fulfilling more functions, what was once a strength has now mutated into a lack of clarity around each person's role and a distinct lack of coherent workflow among the team. The "everybody-just-does-everything" approach has long passed its use-by date and is becoming a real problem.

Suddenly, it seems like your business has flipped on its head. Previously, the sense of camaraderie that was a hallmark of your startup culture meant that you were able to monitor performance informally. With such a tight-knit team, you had a visceral understanding of who was and wasn't performing. Now, your business has grown and there are more people on the bus, which translates into a lack of visibility around performance. You don't have any targets, scoreboards, or other methods of measuring accountability, so this way of doing things has become unmanageable.

Perhaps the greatest indicator of an enduring startup culture is that you, the founder, are still doing everything—or at least overseeing every-thing very closely. In the startup phase, whenever something needed to be done, you stepped up to the plate. On the odd occasion where you delegated, you needed to monitor the task very closely to ensure it was completed to the required standard. At the time, this was okay. As the business has grown and demands on your time have grown, however, you have become the bottleneck for what the business can accomplish. As the entrepreneur, you have moved from being the company's greatest asset to the company's biggest liability.

The fire in your belly that drove your initial expansion is burning you out. Sure, startup is fun for a period of time—it's exciting, dynamic, and impactful—but eventually it becomes completely exhausting. The world's greatest entrepreneurs are single-minded about creating one thing: lever-age. In any given system, leverage is the ratio of inputs to outputs. Because startup requires your constant oversight and exertion, there is no leverage in the startup way of operating. In startup, when your business needs to generate one unit of output—implementing a new marketing campaign, making more sales, delivering on a promise to a customer, writing a new system, recruiting a new team member, or even getting the books up to date—your response is to personally contribute one unit of input. As the demands of the business increase, this strategy becomes increasingly unsustainable. Before long, you find yourself working sixty- to seventy-hour weeks, just to keep your head above water.

As such, startup is a great stage to move through but a terrible place to live for an extended period of time. Around the world, the single most damaging problem in small-to-medium-sized businesses is that they continue to operate like startups even when they pass the startup stage. The world is full of founders failing to live up to their true potential, because they're exhausted and buried in operational detail. If this sounds like you, don't worry. It's completely normal. Every entrepreneur passes through this threshold, and we see people in your position every day. As entrepreneurs, no one ever teaches us how to build a structurally sound company. In the next section, we're going to break down the differences between a startup and a scaleup, so you can finally get your head above the parapet and begin to imagine what lies ahead.

EVOLVING INTO A SCALEUP

As a business owner, maturing from startup to scaleup is one of the most rewarding journeys you'll ever go on. This is where you will ascend from being a business *operator* to becoming a business *owner*. There's nothing more empowering than seeing something you have built start to grow into itself and take on a life of its own, enabling you to elevate into the position of a true entrepreneur.

What exactly *is* a scaleup? Our definition is a business that is growing sustainably, without your operational involvement. You will still be crafting the vision, charting the direction, shaping the company, and leading the team from a strategic level, but you won't be bogged down by the day-to-day activities that are better off delegated to others. Whereas in startup, everything is done manually and is reliant on your personal exertion, a scaleup business is a finely tuned engine that runs without you.

Startups lack one core ingredient that is fundamental to scaleups. Once you identify this ingredient and start to make it an essential part of your business, you will be able to elevate into an entrepreneur leading a scalable company. That core ingredient is **structure**. What is structure? An effective structure comprises the right **people**, **principles**, and **processes** to drive your next stage of growth. The right people—especially senior people—to develop the company without you. The right principles to guide the operations of the business. And the right processes to capture and communicate how things get done.

Structure unlocks scalability. When you embed structure throughout an organization, everything changes. You adopt a planning rhythm and a framework that helps you capture the best strategies, point them in one unified direction, and communicate that direction vividly to your team. You develop an operating model for the team, so that everybody knows where they sit inside the organization and how they can maximize their contribution to the bigger vision. You learn to identify the core inputs that drive successful outcomes, and you turn those inputs into metrics that can be measured and managed. When these pieces are in place, everybody knows when you're succeeding and when you're not.

You begin to document optimal processes, so that everyone can readily follow them—until someone finds a better way of doing something, and then *that* becomes the way it's done. You gain complete visibility over the financial performance of the business over time, so you can understand where money will come from and where it will go. Armed with this information, you develop the confidence that comes from making financially informed decisions. And, ultimately, as this structure starts to enhance the performance of the entire organization, you find yourself growing faster, working less, and earning more.

In startup, everything is improvised. In scaleup, everything is orchestrated. The key benefit of structure is that *it enables you to capture best practices, so that they become infinitely replicable.* Scale is not about doing more things, it is about doing fewer things better. Great businesses are great because they do the fundamentals, at scale.

From structure comes the leverage you need to continue growing the business. When you have built a company with a scalable infrastructure, no longer does every task and project require your personal exertion. Once you've turned your startup into a finely tuned, scalable engine, you will be able to contribute one unit of input, and the organization will produce 1,000 units of output. The first time this happens is one of the most empowering moments of an entrepreneur's career.

SCALEUP MAKES EVERYTHING WORK BETTER

Many entrepreneurs worry that fundamentally altering the dynamics of their company will kill what makes it beautiful. However chaotic the startup environment can be, there's something beautiful about chasing a dream, building a business from nothing, and powering it all with a vision to make the world a better place. Sure, you may sometimes feel as though you're running on nothing more substantial than hope and caffeine, but you're doing something meaningful, and there's no better feeling than knowing you're making a difference.

This is why it's so important to emphasize that when we talk about elevating into a scaleup, this does not mean shedding the entrepreneurial dynamism that has brought you this far. It is about combining the business's existing entrepreneurial nature with structure, in a way that enables you to do infinitely more. Moving into scaleup is not about diminishing your entrepreneurial spirit, but about adding serious firepower to it. Moving to scaleup isn't about diminishing your dreams, but about putting in place the machinery to expand and fulfill them to a far greater degree than you ever could in startup. It was Albert Einstein who said, "A mind once stretched to a new dimension can never return to its original form." Once you realize that you can achieve exponentially more by being the architect instead of the carpenter, it will change the way you do business for the rest of your life.

At this stage of the game—when you're chafing against the limitations of startup culture and exhausted by trying to oversee every aspect of your growing business—it is structure that will set you free. And that's what this book will give you—every principle, every paradigm, and every practice you need, to build a structurally sound business that can grow beyond you.

CASE STUDY: FRANCES ELEVATES OUT OF SERVICE DELIVERY

To bring the journey from startup to scaleup to life, let's explore the story of Frances Quinn; how she struggled to break through the Seven-Figure Ceiling, and what happened when she finally succeeded.

Frances is the founder and CEO of a consulting company. Her business works with medium- to-large-scale organizations to optimize their customer journey, ensuring their customers are happy and coming back for more. She also helps them to create an environment of operational excellence, to save money and maximize their resources.

Prior to discovering The Entourage, Frances had been running her business for four years. This is how she described it to us: "The first part was just about hustle. I found myself succeeding, yet not fully harnessing how big it could be. Before joining The Entourage I was playing it safe and small. I had a fear of success." Like many consultants, Frances started her business believing that it was about *being a consultant*. It wasn't. It was about building a consulting business—a very different thing.

This experience probably sounds familiar. It mirrors the journey described above, along with the experience of so many entrepreneurs. Frances brought what she had learned from her previous job into her own business, believing that owning a business was about being *in it* and doing everything herself. "I had my fingers in every pie and believed I was the only person who could do everything as well as it could possibly be done. I found a certain level of security in hanging on to the details, and that was a safe space for me."

Startup had become Frances's comfort zone. And yet, it was keeping her small. When stuck in startup, it's very common for founders to spend most of their time developing and delivering their product or service—and this is exactly what Frances was doing. This meant that she didn't have any capacity to strategize the growth of her own company, or to build out a team. Being entrenched *in* her business meant that she didn't have any time to spend *on* her business. She simply sold and delivered jobs. Although she was brilliant at this, she intuitively understood that she was essentially working a job rather than building a business.

Frances recognized that this "do-it-all-yourself" approach, which had served her well until then, needed to change if she was going to take her business to the next level. She wanted to ascend into being a CEO in the true sense of the word; building the team that would ultimately build the business. Taking this step required strategy, know-how, and courage. As Frances put it: "Stepping up into being an entrepreneur and a CEO was less familiar and more scary."

For Frances to elevate how she was operating, her first step had to be delegating the service delivery that was taking up the vast majority of her time. To do this, she needed to build out her delivery function in a way that enabled *other* people to deliver the service—to at least the same standards as she was hitting. There was a catch, however: she lacked the spare cash flow to confidently employ a senior person to fulfill this delivery role. As we'll examine in the next chapter, this position of being caught between a rock and a hard place is a situation almost *every* business owner finds themselves in at some point in their career: wanting to build a team to free themselves up, but unable to afford the extra salaries.

The unlock here for Frances was to improve the quality of her marketing and sales process, integrating case studies that quantified the results her existing clients were achieving (we cover *all* these strategies in Part II: The Drive Growth Cycle). In doing so, she was able to increase her prices, winning larger contracts more often. The revenue uplift from this increase in price and clientele gave her the cash flows she needed to start recruiting great people. One by one, she built out her delivery team in a way that was commensurate with the extra work coming through the door.

Each time she won more business and built out her team, she inched closer to being a full-time CEO directing and orchestrating the business, rather than being entrenched in it. Although she'd always had the title of CEO, in retrospect, Frances had been behaving more like an employee. Finally, her activities matched her title.

With Frances driving sales and marketing, her delivery and administration teams started to develop the scalable infrastructure needed to enable the continued growth of the business. "This," she told us, "means I'm not involved in the details I don't need to be involved in. I've stepped away from delivery completely, and I'm playing a bigger game, focusing on driving the strategy and the culture of the business, while supporting the team, which has grown from three people to fifteen."

Reflecting on the growth of her business, Frances told us: "In the six months since joining Elevate, we've seen our leads go from 1.5 per month to 6.5 per month; our sales conversion rate has gone from 44 percent to 66 percent, and new client contracts have gone from four to seventeen. My average contract has jumped from $65,000 to $150,000. Overall, we've gone from doing $250,000 in the six months prior to joining Elevate to $2.5 million in the six months since."

As Frances discovered, perhaps the most empowering part of going from startup to scaleup is the identity shift that comes with it. She started to see herself differently. "What this journey has done for me is help me realize my own magnificence. It's helped me to break free of the small place that I used to play in."

Like every business we have taken through this process, the journey from startup to scaleup for Frances started with shifting her paradigm around how she saw the business and her role in it. If there's one thing we can say for sure after working with thousands of entrepreneurs, it's that the solution is *never* about running faster or working harder. It is about developing a strategy that enables our members to reach their goals in the most effective way. As Frances's story highlights, the counterintuitive outcome of executing this strategy is that the company grows faster and the founder works less. In Frances's case, her only regret was that she didn't start sooner. "I asked myself, 'Why the hell have I never stopped to work on my business and not just my clients' businesses before?'"

HOW JACK DISCOVERED THE BLUEPRINT
FOR SCALING COMPANIES

In each chapter of this book, we want to share with you some of our own history. We're not perfect; we've made mistakes and learned many lessons along the way, and we think it will help you to read about some of those scenarios.

When Jack started out in business in 2004, he was young, ambitious, and—like every new starter—highly inexperienced. In his first three years of entrepreneurship, he founded two businesses. While this was a great apprenticeship period for Jack, the businesses never broke out of the startup stage, and certainly never achieved the level of traction that his later companies have done. Like so many entrepreneurs around the world, Jack was stuck in the cycle of believing that if he just *worked harder*, his businesses would eventually break through to the next stage. He was yet to understand the importance of creating structure and building a team to create leverage.

The turning point occurred in 2007, when Jack co-founded MBE Group. MBE trained and advised companies on how to raise money from investors, increasing the value of their business and facilitating an exit. Jack's co-founder, Reuben Buchanan, had a track record of advising businesses on these types of deals, and wanted to turn what he was doing into a scalable company. As such, he approached Jack with a proposal: Reuben would bring the expertise, while Jack would build, manage, and drive the business. Jack flew to Sydney to meet Reuben, and after a few days of strategizing, MBE was born.

It was evident early on that although Reuben brought considerable experience, MBE would require more expertise than he could deliver alone. For MBE to scale, Jack would need to develop a team of advisors who could service their clients as demand increased. Jack's relative inexperience meant that he wasn't in a position to be an advisor himself. He simply didn't have the core skillset. Initially, he was frustrated by his inability to jump into technician mode and do the work himself. Like many business owners, Jack felt inadequate, believing that his capabilities weren't where they needed to be. He didn't realize that this obstacle was actually the greatest gift he could have received. Lacking the skills to become the technician meant that Jack *had to* build out a panel of advisors who could deliver the services at scale. Being the carpenter was never an option; what he *could* do was become the architect, building the game plan, developing the team, delegating the core deliverables, and driving the business. At an unusually young age, Jack was forced into learning how to become a real CEO.

As the person who emceed the seminars, hosted the trainings, and often participated in any way he could during the advisory process, Jack gained a visceral and firsthand insight into how scalable companies are built. Through obsessive observation, Jack learned early that whether a business owner wanted to raise money or sell their company, the preparation period was largely the same. Investors and buyers looked for two crucial indicators: low risk and high-growth potential. These factors significantly increased the valuation of the business, ensuring that it was ready to take on investment capital or exit at the right price. Whatever the business's leaders wanted to achieve, the underlying objective was always the same: build a great company.

Early on, Jack also identified the number one block preventing investors from buying or investing in a business: "key person dependency." Put simply, the more reliant a business is on its founder, the riskier it looks as an investment proposition. Understanding this, a core part of MBE's work was advising their clients on how to build a structurally sound business that didn't rely on any one key person. In line with their appeal to investors, Jack also noticed that companies that reduced their reliance on the founder experienced an uplift in performance, because the business no longer had a bottleneck constraining its throughput. When a business went through the process of reducing their key person dependency, they grew faster, got more done, and made more money. As we discussed earlier in the chapter, in most cases the founder believed themselves to be their company's main asset. In fact, they were its biggest liability.

Years later, Jack heard the same message from one of the world's most successful and renowned entrepreneurs. After developing the curriculum for The Branson Centre of Entrepreneurship in Johannesburg, Jack received an invitation to visit Sir Richard Branson's home of Necker Island. Now a more mature entrepreneur, Jack was encouraged by his host's viewpoint on the subject. Throughout the week they spent together, Branson's core message was consistent: "If you want to build a great brand, you must develop the leadership within the company. It can't be reliant on you."

NEXT UP...

As we've mentioned throughout this chapter, the first step in moving from startup to scaleup is to stop being the person doing everything, and start being the person leading everything. Before you can do this effectively, you need to understand how the roles you play in your business affect your capacity to generate leverage.

If you're constantly solving small, day-to-day problems, you will quickly find that your calendar looks absurdly packed, and—worse—the problems themselves continue to mount. The solution is not to work harder, or to get more deeply involved in the details, but to plot a path out of the minutiae, so that you can oversee, lead, and direct your business, instead of constantly trying to fix what's going wrong. We call this the transition from technician to entrepreneur, and in the next chapter we will explain precisely how you can make this journey in your business.

2

THE FOUR HATS

Technician to Entrepreneur

In the early years of any venture, it's all about how much you, the founder, can get done on any given day. You start with a blank canvas and an empty calendar, and work your way through everything that needs to be done. Starting from scratch, you don't have customers, team members, or deadlines to force you into action. All momentum is dependent on your personal input and output.

As your business grows, however, so do your commitments. At this stage of the game, as the needs of the business increase, your workload increases proportionally. Everything that needs doing needs to be done by you. You're stuck in the role of technician, taking a hands-on approach to every problem and every opportunity. Before long, you reach a point where you can't possibly do anymore, or fit additional hours into the week. Over time you learn the hard way that this way of operating is not only unsustainable, it can't possibly scale. If everything that needs doing requires your time and attention, and you're *already* stretched beyond capacity, then how can the business possibly grow any further?

As we discussed in the last chapter, although it becomes painfully obvious that something's got to give, you feel stuck between a rock and a hard place. You want to build out a team, enabling you to take your hands off the tools, but you lack the time, the cash flow, the know-how, *or all three*, to make this ambition a reality. Welcome to where most business owners spend their lives: trapped in perpetual technician mode for years, or even decades, without knowing how to break the cycle. Much as you want to reclaim your time to work on more meaningful tasks, you don't know how to make this happen. At this point, you realize that without a fundamental shift in how you operate, you and your business will be stuck in this frustrating place forever. The bad news is that you're absolutely correct. The good news is that this awareness can be the catalyst for a much-needed change of gear.

When your business depends on you to such an extent, everyone feels the consequences. When your team needs your input at every stage, it causes workflow congestion. This bottleneck impacts you, your team, your business, and ultimately how well you serve your customers. The solution here isn't for you to figure out how you can personally work harder, it's for you to build an ecosystem that enables *other people* to contribute great work under your leadership.

WORK *ON* YOUR BUSINESS, NOT *IN* IT

For our Elevate members, the material in this chapter represents one of the most powerful paradigm shifts in the entire book. When they come to us, they know from hard-fought experience how to take a business from zero and get it off the ground. That in itself is a monumental act of faith and will, and they're proud of what they've created. As their business grows, however, they continue to dip into their reserves of will and faith, until they're exhausted. They understand that they can only carry the company on their back for so long, but they don't know what to do differently.

As a result, they risk grinding to a halt, burning out, or staying small forever. They haven't yet made the transition from technician to entrepreneur, and—as a result—their business hasn't become everything it could. This is the *number one* misconception we see in the field of entrepreneurship: people think being a business owner involves working *in* their business. Instead, becoming an effective business owner means working *on* your business. When a business owner doesn't understand this, they spend their days doing, doing, doing, and never experience the leverage that comes from moving from the role of technician, with their hands on the tools, to the role of entrepreneur, leading and directing a fully functioning operation. As soon as you understand this paradigm shift and start moving in this direction, you will set yourself apart from the vast majority of founders. This is the unlock that will allow you to build a self-managing company that can scale far beyond what you alone could have ever achieved.

The crucial point is that as entrepreneurs, at any given time we can be wearing one or more of the Four Hats, each of which describes a fundamental relationship to the business. These Four Hats are technician, manager, leader, and entrepreneur. If the startup stage is exhausting, it's because you're constantly wearing all four hats. Learning how to elevate from technician to leader and entrepreneur is a critical step in the transition from startup to scaleup. In this chapter, we'll explain the features of each of the Four Hats, the most common pitfalls of getting stuck wearing each one, and how to clear a path to move all the way from technician to entrepreneur.

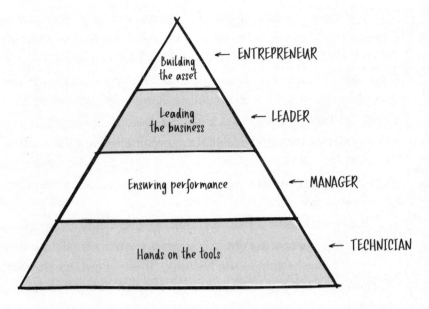

Figure 2.1: From Technician to Entrepreneur

TECHNICIAN: HANDS ON THE TOOLS

The first hat is that of the technician. Whenever you are personally doing the work, with your hands on the tools, you are in technician mode.

To help you identify exactly what that looks like, you're wearing the technician hat when you're:

- Developing marketing copy, campaigns, and ads
- Selling to prospective customers
- Delivering your product or service
- Responding to customer inquiries
- Performing administrative tasks
- Reconciling accounts or doing the bookkeeping
- Implementing a new tool or piece of technology

Technician mode is synonymous with doing. In early-stage businesses, it's inevitable that you'll wear the technician hat across all the different functions of your business. In many cases, this is actually useful. You gain firsthand experience of the different elements of the business, so you know exactly what needs to be done and how. As your team grows, this early hands-on experience will make you a better manager and leader.

The problem occurs when wearing the hat of the technician becomes your comfort zone, and you stay there longer than you need to. Should this happen, you become a serious bottleneck on the productivity and growth potential of the company. As your business grows, it's critical that you employ people you can delegate to, and build the structures that will set them up to succeed. While it's highly likely that as a founder, you'll start out wearing the technician hat most of the time, your ultimate goal should be to gradually put in place the people and processes that will enable you to elevate to the next level.

Even later in the evolution of your business, once you've built a company that can operate without you, we still encourage you to spend around 5 percent of your time wearing the technician hat. Why? Because living in an ivory tower is bad for business. As you grow your team and develop the scalable infrastructure of your company, you still need to stay connected to your consumer and to the inner workings of your business. Continuing to spend 5 percent of your time in technician mode achieves this. Great entrepreneurs stay connected to their team, aligned with ground-level company operations, and keep their fingers on the pulse of customer needs.

How Do You Get Stuck Wearing the Technician Hat?

Some business owners are addicted to operating in technician mode because running from one thing to the next *feels* productive. The adrenaline rush from putting out fires every day can be intoxicating. For a business owner always looking for the next dopamine fix, the company becomes their amusement park, where they ride roller coasters all day long, oscillating between terror and ecstasy.

Exhilarating as this may be, however, it's not good for business. The single most expensive belief business owners routinely subscribe to is,

"I need to do everything myself." In the early stages, this may be true, but many entrepreneurs continue this habitual way of operating long after it ceases to be necessary. The first step to becoming a great entrepreneur is making the mental switch from "me" to "we" and realizing that your business—and your mental health—will improve significantly once you get out of the trenches.

For many business owners, however, this is easier said than done. Once a business owner decides they've had enough of being trapped perpetually in technician mode, there are three barriers to elevating out. The first is **time**. This applies to you if you find yourself thinking: *I don't have the time to think strategically or to recruit other people, I'm too busy doing things.* The second is **money**. You'll know you're struggling with this if you tell yourself: "I'd love to start building out the team, I just don't have the spare cash flow to employ anymore people." The third is **expertise**. If this is you, you'll be thinking: *I have the cash flow and could make the time, I just don't know where to start.*

How to Remove the Technician Hat

Archimedes said, "Give me a lever long enough and a platform strong enough, and I shall move the world." In other words, his solution to moving the immovable was *leverage.* As we discussed in the last chapter, when your business requires your involvement in everything, but you yearn to rise above daily operations, you feel like you're caught in a catch-22. You want to spend more time working *on* the business, but you're so bogged down *in* the business that you don't have the time or cash flow to build out the team.

So, when you're in this position, what is the first step in breaking free of this pattern? As we saw in Frances's story in the previous chapter, you start by placing an emphasis on revenue generation. We're deliberately using the word *revenue* here, not *profit*, because this move is not about trying to create short-term margin. It's about generating more cash that can be reinvested in recruiting the right people to grow the business.

To elevate from technician to entrepreneur, you need to develop your team incrementally, in a way that is proportionate to demands of the business. Think of it this way: you build the team and the team builds the business. To begin building the team, however, you need to drive more cash flow into your business. Therefore, elevating from technician to entrepreneur usually occurs at the rate at which you can sustainably grow revenue, a subject we'll cover at length in Chapter Six: Marketing, and Chapter Seven: Sales.

For now, how do you generate more cash without spending more money you don't have? By improving the *quality* of your marketing and sales. As the case study we'll highlight in a moment indicates, improving conversion rates through your marketing and sales process enables you to generate more revenue from your existing activities. This then provides the surplus cash flow that can be used to start building out your team.

All growth comes from marketing and sales. One of the core reasons companies plateau or see slow revenue growth is that the business owner is spending too much time doing low-level tasks that should be delegated, and not enough time in revenue-generating activities—namely marketing and sales. While this *whole book* is about how to elevate from technician to entrepreneur in the best possible way, the starting point is to ensure you have the cash flow to build your team. The precise strategy for each business will be different; the most common path, however, can be summarized in these five steps:

1. **Drive revenue.** Improve the quality of your sales and marketing to generate more leads, convert more sales, and drive more cash into the business.

2. **Build your operational teams.** Use this surplus cash flow to hire people and incrementally delegate the work that can be fulfilled by others. This will often start with delegating your roles in product delivery, operations, and anything administrative. Each person hired should contribute either directly or indirectly to increasing the profitability of the business, freeing you up to spend more time driving your sales and marketing function.

3. **Focus even more on sales and marketing.** By backfilling yourself in product delivery and anything administrative, you free up extra capacity for yourself. Use this capacity to drive sales and marketing. Initially, dive into this as a technician. As the functions take on a more definite shape, start to build out your sales and marketing teams.

4. **Build your revenue-generating teams.** Build your sales and marketing teams, increasing the business's capacity to drive further growth.

5. **Lead the business.** Now that you've got teams of people both driving growth (sales and marketing) and enabling growth (delivery, operations, admin), orchestrate the development of the business wearing the hats of leader and entrepreneur.

We're summarizing a multiyear journey from technician to entrepreneur here. As you can see, the crucial first domino is to ensure your business has the cash flow to start building out your team—something this book will help you with. This will enable you to break free from the painful position of being stuck between a rock and a hard place.

MANAGER: ENSURING PERFORMANCE

You're wearing the hat of manager when you are assigning and overseeing technician-level work; in other words, when you are managing the people who have their hands on the tools. The startup stage is often devoid of management, as founders opt instead for a gut-feel approach to monitoring and improving performance. As your company grows, however, you will need more rigorous management practices to create the visibility needed to achieve scale.

In terms of specific activities, you're wearing the manager hat when you're:

- Assigning and overseeing technician-level work, such as deploying marketing tactics, making sales, and responding to customer inquiries

- Developing and managing team members, and conducting one-on-ones with them to check on their well-being, provide feedback on past performance, and offer direction for the future
- Navigating hard conversations, managing under-performance, and hiring and firing employees
- Developing and updating your organizational chart to provide clarity on your company structure
- Crafting position descriptions that outline key responsibilities and performance measures for each role
- Developing project plans, including budgets and managing people to milestones and deadlines
- Organizing and allocating resources that balance competing priorities

Management is about ensuring that people have the proper training, direction, processes, tools, support, and accountability to perform at their best. If you've started to expand your team, but feel like the business isn't achieving more, the problem is often a deficiency in management. This is an indication that you haven't yet put in place the management framework that provides the necessary clarity and direction so your team can orient themselves and perform at their best.

In our experience, about 20 percent of business owners are highly proficient managers. This means that 80 percent—the vast majority—are not. While most founders are much more talented leaders than managers, good management is an essential element of a scalable company, and we need to hone our appreciation for the conscientious rigor that management brings. What gets measured gets managed, and what gets managed, improves.

Although management doesn't come naturally to most entrepreneurs, the ladder from technician to entrepreneur inevitably passes through manager. There will be a stage in the journey where you are building out your team of technicians, and yet you are the only senior person capable of providing managerial oversight. As such, it will be necessary to wear the hat of manager until you begin building out a team of senior managers and leaders. This is particularly true in startup, because when you're in startup, you are limited by employing the people you can afford. When it comes to people, you either pay in money or time. As such, be prepared to balance startup wages with a high price in management time, such as inducting, training, instructing, and monitoring.

Wearing the hat of manager may be necessary for a period of time, but as your business grows and you can afford to start building out your management team, this, too, is a hat you will eventually delegate. Just like the technician hat, however, you'll need to continue to spend some of your time in management, overseeing the performance of the business and each function within it. With the right management framework in place, you want to reach a point where you're spending just 5 to 10 percent of your time in company management. In Chapter Eleven: People, we outline the exact management framework you can install into your business to ensure performance is measured, managed, and continually enhanced. This structure also enables you to delegate the management of different functions when the time is right, giving incoming senior managers an established operating rhythm with which to work.

How Do You Get Stuck Wearing the Manager Hat?

As business owners wrestle with the journey of ascension from technician and manager to leader and entrepreneur, one of the most common fears we hear from them is: "I'm a control freak. I don't want to lose control." This is a *very* important point: if scale causes you to lose control, you are *not doing it right.*

As your business grows, so should your team, your systems, your specificity around roles and targets, your precision around measuring results, and the scoreboards that give you (and everyone on the team) complete visibility of performance. If the fear of losing control is rearing its head, it's an indication that you don't yet have these things in place. When you grow with structure, scale gives you *more* control, not less.

If you've been operating like a startup, chances are you're the only senior person on your team, having built a team of technicians who report to you. You'll know if this is true for you because every time you go into the office or participate in a remote meeting with your team, everyone is pulling at *you*. When you live like this, it's very easy to develop the misconception that you're the only person who can fulfill the managerial responsibilities in your company. This is how you will get stuck in manager mode.

How to Remove the Manager Hat

While it's likely that you are the only person in your *current* team who can successfully wear the hat of manager, as an entrepreneur your entire world will change when you realize that there are executives in the workforce who can manage the operations of your business *better* than you. They may not be better entrepreneurs than you, they may not be better CEOs than you, but they should bring years of experience in their particular field of expertise, which makes them highly effective at managing *that specific function.*

Additionally, when you bring on a senior person to manage and lead a particular function of your business, for example the marketing function, they will spend 100 percent of their time there, whereas—due to the breadth of your responsibilities—you may only have been spending 20 percent of your time there.

Over time, your goal should be to gradually hire senior managers who have the experience and expertise to manage all the company functions. In Chapter Eleven: People, we outline exactly when and how to build out your senior management team. As a rule of thumb, in a startup you will wear the manager hat 40–60 percent of the time. However, as we indicated earlier, once you've created structure and developed your management team, you should aim to drop this to no more than 5–10 percent of your time.

LEADER: LEADING THE BUSINESS

Leadership is about ensuring that each member of your team is intrinsically motivated to perform. Leaders know how to inspire people toward a compelling vision and highlight the role each person plays in actualizing that vision. You're wearing the hat of leader when you're creating an environment that inspires high performance.

When you're wearing the leader hat, you will focus on:

- Creating a clear and compelling vision for the future and enrolling people into it
- Capturing values that define and communicate your unique company culture
- Setting the standard and expectations for excellence and holding others accountable
- Translating vision into strategy, often inviting input and collaboration from the broader team
- Developing, coaching, and encouraging your team to step up to new challenges
- Tackling big problems and big opportunities
- Exploring new frontiers without a roadmap, including new countries, territories, markets, and consumer and product categories

One core factor that differentiates founder-led companies from larger corporate organizations is the ability to create a meaningful culture that is centered around a shared vision. Our favorite quote on leadership comes from the French writer, poet, and pioneering aviator, Antoine de Saint-Exupéry, who once said, "If you want to build a ship, don't drum up the people to gather wood, divide the work, and give orders. Instead, teach them to yearn for the vast and endless sea." Great leaders have a claim on the future and inspire other people toward creating it.

Management and leadership are equally important and to scale sustainably, your company will need both. Traditional business thinkers often conflate management and leadership, but they're not the same. In fact, other than the fact they both center around people, they have very little in common.

Management deals with what's measurable. It's about managing people's performance, implementing key metrics and monitoring results, developing operations and detailed plans, and assessing resources and timelines. Good management ensures that people feel supported and accountable in their day-to-day activities.

Leadership is less tangible. It deals with the *human* aspect of the business. It's about ensuring people care about and buy into the company's vision, mission, and values. Leadership communicates what everyone must contribute to the realization of that vision, imparts a sense of mission that drives discretionary effort, and inspires values and standards that permeate the culture. While leadership may appear to be less measurable than management, it is every bit as real.

In short, management works with the head; leadership speaks to the heart.

When a company has strong leadership, but underdeveloped management, it may be inspiring and well-intentioned, yet ultimately lack substance, and consistently fail to execute on the promise of the future. When a company is proficient in management but devoid of proper leadership, employees will work efficiently toward muddled or meaningless priorities. In Stephen R. Covey's words: "Efficient management without effective leadership is like straightening deck chairs on the Titanic."

Management is doing things right; leadership is doing the right things.

Together, management and leadership create an ecosystem that turns people's talents into performance. For this reason, every great company must excel in both management and leadership. Most founders shine—and add the greatest value to their team, business, and customer base—when they wear the hat of leader. When navigating the startup stage, however, most business owners only spend around 10 percent of their time wearing the leader hat, because the demands of the technician and manager roles are all-consuming. As you delegate more of those responsibilities and develop your team, you should aim to spend the majority of your time in leader mode, going where vision is required.

How Do You Get Stuck Wearing the Leader Hat?

Founders can usually add the most value to the business, their team, and therefore their customer, when they wear the leader and entrepreneur hats. This is a good thing because most business owners *want* to spend the majority of their time wearing these two hats. As an entrepreneur, you were born to lead. Think back to the startup stage of business, when you felt most alive; what was it that inspired you? Probably it was that you were leading from the front, guiding your people, and shaping your business. By wearing the hat of leader, you can now reclaim this role. Once you've built an effective structure, team, and system of reporting, you can confidently lead from the front, while staying completely attuned to performance at a company level, team level, and individual level.

Spending your time wearing the hats of leader and entrepreneur is not about abdicating responsibility, it's about *delegating* responsibility. Effective delegation requires you to have the right people, systems, controls, and reports in place, to ensure that while you are not *doing* the tasks, you always have visibility of *performance*. As your business grows in structure and functionality, you *delegate to elevate*.

Although most business owners want to spend the majority of their time switching between the hats of leader and entrepreneur, a percentage aim to solely wear the hat of entrepreneur. There are a number of factors that will influence this decision, such as lifestyle preferences, age, and stage of life, along with whether you aim to sell your business anytime soon. Ultimately, none of us will be able to run our businesses forever, and when we reach this point, the business needs to be operating in such a way that it is not dependent on us. It is worth remembering as we stated in the last chapter, if you do ever want to sell your business or even raise capital, the number one factor that destroys the valuation of private companies is key person dependency; a business that is too reliant on the owner to operate successfully is not attractive to potential investors.

When you do reach the point where you want to solely wear the hat of entrepreneur and hang up the hat of leader, the crucial limiting factor is that you will need a very strong 2IC (2nd in command) in place. This could be a COO, general manager, or CEO. To elevate beyond the level of manager, you required senior people to manage each function. To take the next step and ascend out of the function of leader necessitates that you have somebody those managers report to. Your 2IC must be a trusted leader, who can assume critical management and leadership responsibilities and take full P&L accountability.

The journey from technician to entrepreneur is one that takes several years and is *the* most important investment you can make as a business owner. By its culmination you will have a GM or CEO leading a team of managers who are leading teams of technicians. This is how you create a business that can grow sustainably without your operational involvement.

ENTREPRENEUR: BUILDING THE ASSET

As entrepreneurs, we build assets that can work without us. When you're wearing the entrepreneur hat, you are building an asset that can work without your active involvement. This comes as a surprise to most people, who don't realize that the role of entrepreneur is operationally removed from the business. Far from being involved in every detail, many iconic entrepreneurs that we look up to are at a stage in their careers where they no longer consider playing an active role in their companies.

In practice, you're wearing the entrepreneur hat when you're:

- Starting the company, including taking on the financial, legal, and reputational risks inherent in funding and growing a business
- Developing the vision and long-term direction for the company
- Reviewing and contributing your experience and direction to the company strategy

- Ensuring the company has the capital, resources, and senior team to execute its growth plans
- Connecting the business and its management with networks that may be useful to the company's growth
- Monitoring overall performance against the company strategy and forecasts, and appointing, developing, or removing senior leaders accordingly
- Attending and chairing board meetings to guide, shape, and direct the company

Take someone like Sir Richard Branson, for example. Branson can have a controlling stake in over four hundred companies without losing control, because he's extraordinarily good at choosing highly effective CEOs for every one of them. In doing this, he actively frees himself up to exclusively wear the entrepreneur hat.

How Do You Get Stuck Wearing the Entrepreneur Hat?

You don't. This is the goal that the founders we work with are shooting for—a fully functional, scalable business that operates without them. It's a multiyear journey, but incredibly fulfilling. When you reach this point, you can do what you want, how you want, when you want, safe in the knowledge that you have the financial freedom to support your choices.

Stay involved, step away, found an entirely new business. Once you're wearing the hat of entrepreneur, the choice is yours.

USE THE FOUR HATS TO RECLAIM YOUR TIME

Now that we have dug deep into every one of the four hats, it should be clear that one of the main reasons the startup way of operating is exhausting is that you're wearing all the hats. You're wearing the technician hat, because you're still the best at everything. You're wearing the manager hat, because you employ the people you can afford, paying in time rather than money. You're wearing the leader hat, because startups are high-demand

and high-change environments that require your guidance. Finally, you're wearing the entrepreneur hat, because as the business is maturing, it's like a teenager figuring out who it wants to be when it grows up, and you need to shape the long-term vision of this asset you're building.

The journey from startup to scaleup, and from feeling harassed by constant demands to regaining control of the hats you wear, is a journey of reclaiming your time. While this entire book is about getting your freedom back, in this section, we'll show you where to start.

Everyone's goals are different, and yours will depend on your current stage of life and business. Your first step on this journey, therefore, is to get a feel for how you are currently allocating your time, and how you want to allocate it in the future. How frequently are you currently wearing each hat? How much time do you want to spend wearing each of them? You can use the diagram below to map this transition out for yourself. Customize your triangle by adding your own percentages, filling in your current estimates on the left and, on the right, your desired balance two years from now.

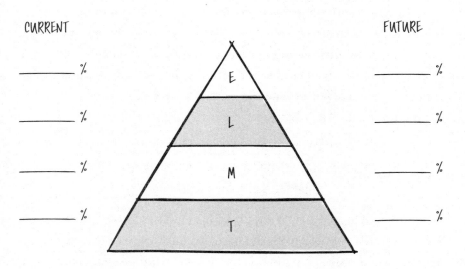

Figure 2.2: Your Current and Desired Balance

When business owners first consider discussions with their team about stepping back from operations and elevating from technician to entrepreneur, they often feel guilty. *Won't my team think I'm trying to get out of doing the real work?* Remember, you're not moving into an ivory tower, never to be seen again. You are reallocating your time and brain power for the highest good of your company, your team, and your customers. The leader who stays buried in operational detail becomes the bottleneck not only for the productivity of their team, but also the potential of their company.

As you ascend the Four Hats, it not only gives others permission to do the same, it necessitates that they do. Your example literally pulls your team up, to continually develop *their* skills and expertise, so your company and people can grow together. This is how teams excel, and extraordinary businesses get built.

As company founders, the journey from startup to scaleup, and from technician to entrepreneur, is one of the most rewarding we can travel. Once you start elevating to the next level, you will discover new opportunities and challenges that reinvigorate you and remind you of your love and passion for what you do. You'll rediscover the joy of applying your unique abilities in service of your business. You no longer *have* to do things—you *get* to do things. One of the reasons this journey is so rewarding is not just the freedom it generates, but the capabilities you develop along the way. Building a business is a skill; once you see the real-world results, you realize you're free to apply these competencies to any venture, as Jye Bohm's story below illustrates.

CASE STUDY: JYE BOHM SCALES HIS BUSINESS AND BRANCHES OUT WITH A NEW ONE

Jye Bohm and his partner, Justin Bliss, run a busy painting, sandblasting, and industrial coatings business. Like every business owner, they eventually reached a crunch point: they wanted to grow further, but they couldn't possibly work anymore hours or take on additional responsibilities. In

Jye's words: "Before starting the Elevate business coaching program, we worked a lot in the business. Although we had a mentor previously, teaching us everything he knew, things were still crazy. We had so much to do. It was frantic. We didn't have time for ourselves or to do the things we wanted to do, because we were always "in" the business."

Jye and his business partner had their technician hats glued firmly to their heads. They were consistently putting in sixty- and seventy-hour weeks. Even as they were trying to drive company growth, they were still operating in startup mode, which was totally unsustainable. Like so many business owners, Jye and his business partner knew there had to be a better way; the problem was, they couldn't see it yet.

As Jye put it: "I was doing all the quoting and estimating, and my business partner covered all the product delivery. We were working crazy hours. We'd start at 5:00 or 6:00 a.m. every morning and work until 5:00 or 6:00 p.m. every night. That was just the labor component. Then we'd have to go into the office at night to quote more work to keep this seesaw of win work and deliver work going. We had no plan, no future, and until we found The Entourage we couldn't see ourselves getting out of it. They told us we needed to build operational structures and hire people who could do everything we were currently doing."

Like many businesses, for Jye and his partner, the first step in elevating from technician to entrepreneur was generating more money from the same amount of work. They needed more cash flow to invest in the resources that would enable their growth. Jye explains, "The first thing we worked on through the Elevate program was our sales cycle and process. One of the things they taught us was that for the business to grow, we needed to start with revenue. We learned from Jack how to structure our sales process to generate more leads, convert more of them, and increase the average price per sale. We've gone from closing 40 percent of deals to 70 percent, and that process has given us the stability to focus on our operations, finance, and people. This has steadied the ship; now, we're winning work, delivering work, and making money from it."

These changes generated the cash flow necessary for Jye to build his team and develop a proper CRM to manage the different components of his customer journey. Additionally, Jye and his partner finally developed the processes necessary to ensure that everybody knew what part of making the production line work was their responsibility.

As Jye and his business partner began to build out both their team and the company's operations, they created *leverage*. Their ratio of inputs to outputs increased exponentially. The business was no longer entirely dependent on them, because they had figured out how to convert one unit of their input into a thousand units of output. They turned their startup into an engine that didn't require their constant supervision and involvement and, in doing so, unlocked their company's scalability.

Reflecting on the journey, Jye says with amazement, "When we joined Elevate, we had ten people working in the business. We now employ over a hundred people, and we've been able to scale our revenue from $1.5 million to $20 million."

Since elevating out of technician mode, Jye has gotten pretty comfortable wearing the entrepreneur hat more often, utilizing his capabilities in his core business to launch and scale new ventures. On his latest step, he says, "It enabled me to join and help scale a clothing business called Front Runner and, using the lessons I've learned from The Entourage, we've been able to grow that business to seven figures in just twelve months."

Jye understands that there is always a next level in business, and each new level requires a new version of himself. It may seem counterintuitive that the more successful an entrepreneur becomes, the more they engage in developing themselves, but it's a universal truth. Jye puts it like this, "We've been with The Entourage for four years now. We continue to work with them and will do so in the future because there are *so* many different elements to running a company. Every time you grow and reach a new level in your business, there are new things to learn. You go from managing technicians to leading managers and finally being an entrepreneur focusing on bigger ticket items."

If you're growing as a person, your business is growing. If you're plateauing as a person, chances are your business is stagnating too. Jye understands that as an entrepreneur, he must consistently level up so that his businesses can also grow. At The Entourage, we are thrilled to watch Jye integrate his new skills with his entrepreneurial drive and vision. We can't wait to see what he'll do next.

JACK AND TIM ELEVATE THROUGH THE FOUR HATS

At The Entourage, we have our own storied history with the Four Hats. Initially, Jack filled every role to first build the company, then save it from total collapse, and finally to rebuild it with Tim and a renewed executive team. Today, he spends most of his time wearing the leader and entrepreneur hats, but that doesn't mean he has completely abandoned the roles of technician and manager.

Ascending from technician to leader and entrepreneur is not always a one-way progression. Situations will arise that require you to return to roles that you had once delegated. It's important to understand that as you elevate, gaps might appear in the levels below you. As a founder, you are responsible for filling these gaps and ensuring the workload doesn't get dropped in the meantime.

When Jack started The Entourage in 2010, he had already demonstrated a capability to drive strong growth and build businesses that could operate without him. By 2015, The Entourage was a team of ninety, with a senior executive team managing and leading each business function, freeing up Jack to spend most of his time wearing the leader and entrepreneur hats. At this point, The Entourage was a profitable, high-growth company with efficient management.

That was before the 2016 regulatory changes we described in the introduction. When the fateful newspaper landed on Jack's desk bearing the headline, *"Government to Axe Skills-Based Sector. 478 VET Courses Won't Be Eligible,"* he knew right away that things were about to get ugly. In the space of one day, The Entourage had gone from peacetime to wartime, losing 70 percent of our revenue and entering a rapid tailspin.

While the senior executives The Entourage had in place were exceptional at running an accredited education company, most had little experience managing and leading a company through distress. And The Entourage was beyond distressed. While the company would still need strong leadership, the *style* of leadership that would be required was more reminiscent of a street fighter than a professional executive. Jack decided to take back the reins and dive into a role that was a hybrid of leader and manager.

To say that the following months and years were an uphill battle would be an understatement. The Entourage had to fight legal battles, closely manage financiers, provide confident leadership to the team, and aggressively downsize personnel, all while achieving rapid growth to stem the losses. Every single day, for years, Jack, Tim, and the remaining executive team were managing existential risks. Their entire agenda consisted of making fast and imperfect decisions, always knowing that just one of these choices could determine whether the company survived or died.

Step by step, day by day, the company slowly clawed its way out of trouble, and took on a new shape. The increased demands on the business meant that Tim started fulfilling two roles. In addition to his original director of education role, Tim's performance earned him the general manager position. For years, Jack *drove* the company's growth as CEO, and Tim *enabled* the growth as general manager and director of education.

In 2017, when Tim stepped into the role of general manager, the executive team reported to Jack. As part of a multiyear plan for Tim to assume full operational control of the business, however, the reporting structure was about to change. For the first month, Tim sat in on the one-on-one meetings Jack conducted with his direct reports on the executive team. For the second month, Jack sat in on Tim leading the discussions. Then, from the third month onward, the executive team reported solely to Tim.

There's a lesson here. As you are changing hats in your organization, it's crucial to design a transition process that factors in new reporting dynamics and responsibilities. The most common mistake we see people make when elevating their role is trying to rush the process. Because

Tim had been in the business for several years and worked closely with each member of the executive team, Jack and Tim were able to engineer this transition much more quickly than they could have done if Jack had brought in a general manager from outside the organization.

The complexity and nuance of implementing a proper handover between executives requires thoughtfulness and patience. For top roles such as GM or CEO, this transition can easily take three to six months, even as much as a year. You must allocate this time to adequately transfer multidimensional knowledge and experience, ensure proper structures are in place, and implement measures that will monitor the performance of the direct report. Often, when a founder appoints a 2IC, the 2IC will wear the hats of manager and leader, with the founder predominantly wearing the hats of leader and entrepreneur. In Chapter Four: Driver or Enabler, we outline how to harness this relationship to create maximum impact for the organization.

Over two years, Tim drove strong operational development as general manager. Then, on July 1, 2020, five years after he began as The Entourage's director of education, Tim ascended into the role of CEO. This move saw Jack delegate operational control and P&L responsibility to Tim. Tim's new role included a greater breadth and depth of responsibility, meaning he needed to wear the hat of leader more often, a transition which began when he developed a renewed leadership team to operate under him.

This, in turn, enabled Jack to further reduce his operational involvement, focusing once again on what he does best: wearing the hat of leader and entrepreneur. Jack now dedicates a good portion of his time to macro-level projects that structurally elevate the entire company. Wearing the leader hat, Jack can focus intensely for months at a time on strategic projects, such as developing the sales process that enables us to impact more people, exploring new territories to work out how we can best enter and contribute to new markets, or even co-writing a book to share The Entourage method with many thousands of entrepreneurs! He also develops strategy with Tim and the broader executive team. To shape the business and communicate with the team, Jack meets with Tim fortnightly for a one-on-one. He also holds monthly one-on-ones with key executives and delivers a quarterly founder's address to the entire team (more on this in Chapter Eleven: People: Assemble Your A-Team).

These cadences enable Jack to provide high-level leadership and direction, which Tim, the executives, and the broader team can then operationalize with clarity and confidence. By wearing the hat of entrepreneur, Jack performs the role of chairman of the board, directing the company from a board level.

NEXT UP...

Creating a company that can work without you allows you to focus on high-level projects without operational distraction. It enables your senior leaders to elevate to their highest potential, and necessitates constant progress for your entire team. As you break new ground as a leader and entrepreneur, so must everyone else. When one elevates, all must elevate.

To move from startup to scaleup and elevate from technician to entrepreneur, you must create a structurally sound company. Your company needs to operate like an engine, becoming both scalable and sustainable. In the next chapter, we'll uncover the blueprint for doing exactly that.

3

THE SIX ELEMENTS

Business Operator to Business Owner

In a founder-led company, your business is quite literally a reflection of you. Its strengths and weaknesses arise from yours. For many founders, this dynamic comes with another challenging element; like most of us, they lack full awareness of their strengths, weaknesses, and unconscious preferences, often blinding them to the areas of their business that need improvement. This causes certain functions to remain underdeveloped and constrain overall growth.

When deciding which areas to focus on, some business owners naturally gravitate toward activities they enjoy. For example, many founders are growth oriented. They feel comfortable and confident in sales and marketing, so that's where they direct most of their attention. This often results in strong top-line growth and effective sales and marketing, weighed down by inadequate product delivery and internal operations. They may achieve a spike in revenue in the short term, but it's unsustainable over the longer term, meaning it doesn't translate into bankable profit.

Other business owners love taking care of existing customers and tinkering with internal operations. For them, the positive results are often great relationships with their customers, strong word-of-mouth referrals, smooth internal operations, and high employee retention. The marketing engine and sales process, by contrast, are usually deficient, causing slow growth or stagnation. Their ship may be steady but it's going nowhere fast.

THE SIX ELEMENTS BRING BALANCE TO YOUR BUSINESS

Clearly, the areas we've described above are all important to the expansion and smooth running of a company. Just as clearly, none of them are optional. If sales comes naturally to you but you loathe operations, your business will grow in a lopsided fashion, the undeveloped element dragging it down like an anchor. If you could happily spend hours tinkering with spreadsheets but you balk at marketing, the reverse will be true. The internal workings of your business may look impeccable, but it's doubtful you'll have many customers to impress with them.

The primary message of this chapter is that it's not enough for your company to excel in one of these areas to the detriment of the other. If you aim to build a truly successful company, you absolutely must design your business to be both scalable and sustainable. Therefore, it's critical to develop a blueprint for assessing your company and its requirements in their entirety, rather than looking solely through your own partial lens.

Attempting to approach your business as a series of disconnected parts is exhausting and time-consuming. Conceiving of it as an interplay between the Six Elements described in this chapter requires far less mental energy, because you can easily fit everything that happens into one of the categories, and quickly understand what you need to do to improve it. Saving mental energy is a key part of entrepreneurship.

To help you ensure that you're looking at your business from every angle, we've developed a model that can be applied to any company in any field. It's a model we've identified by working with tens of thousands of companies across 150+ industries. Through The Entourage, we coach our members on this core framework for sustainable growth. Whatever field you're in, whether you're online, offline, business-to-business, business-to-consumer, or a product or service-based business, every company comprises six key elements. These Six Elements are the foundation for building a high-growth, cross-functional company that is both scalable and sustainable. Later in the book, we'll dive into each of these Six Elements in depth. In this chapter, we'll introduce you to each one.

THE SIX ELEMENTS: YOUR BLUEPRINT FOR SUSTAINABLE GROWTH

Often, when we first ask business owners to explain how all the parts of their business work together, they're at a loss for words. Sometimes they manage to describe the elements they're most intimately involved with, but it's extremely rare for us to hear a coherent description of the functioning of the business as a whole. When asked to define a framework that links all components together, most people blank. Many entrepreneurs exert much of their mental energy conceptualizing and carrying their entire business in their head, which becomes an increasingly heavy mental load to bear.

Perhaps you're familiar with this experience. Before adopting the Six Elements, your business might seem similarly chaotic and confusing. There are a thousand moving parts and no unifying structure to make sense of it all. The good news is that the Six Elements comprise a fundamental framework that will enable you to rise above the detail, so you can clearly see the distinct components that fit together to form the engine of your company. This blueprint will allow you to build a structurally sound business.

What are these Six Elements? In the order we'll discuss them in this book, they are:

- Marketing
- Sales
- Product
- Operations
- Finance
- People

Harnessing the Six Elements will enable you to transition from business *operator* to business owner. Imagine your business as a production line. The Six Elements elevate your perspective: instead of being the mechanic working underneath the car, you become the engineer scanning the entire operation to ensure the entire assembly line is functioning smoothly. You transition from being the person "in it." focusing on one specific aspect after another, to being the person "on it," surveying the entire process from start to finish.

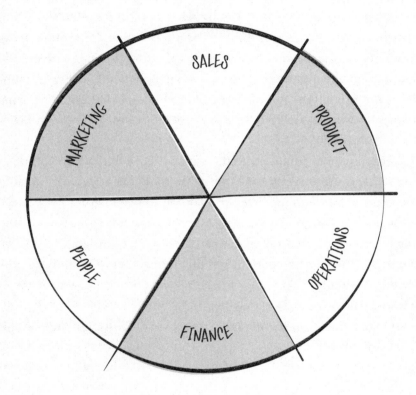

Figure 3.1: The Six Elements

At The Entourage, we approach every company through the Six Elements, whether we're working on our own businesses or advising members and investee companies. We do this because every individual area of a business is interrelated and interconnected, and they should rarely be viewed in isolation. A change anywhere causes a chain reaction everywhere. A loss in any area is a loss in every area. Similarly, a win in any area is a win in every area. Return to this framework whenever you're strategizing, building structure, making a change, growing your team, or thinking through future scenarios. Now, let's visit each of the Six Elements in turn.

1. Marketing: Design a Marketing Engine that Generates Leads

In your company's production line, marketing is the first element, because everything starts when you capture the attention and interest of your prospective customers. Most businesses, particularly those operating in startup mode, market reactively, as and when needed, or not at all, instead of marketing proactively to build a consistent lead flow. Marketing is the genesis for everything else that occurs in your business. As such, it's crucial to create an engine that builds your audience, then nurtures and converts that audience into leads that can be passed through to sales.

2. Sales: Drive Growth and Profitability

This is the element where you harness the attention and interest generated by marketing. Sales turns prospects into paying customers. This conversion can happen in person, over the phone, digitally, in social media chats, through an event, or on a landing page. Most founders sell intuitively; they do it their own way, and allow everyone else who sells to do the same. While this tactic may work initially, especially when the founder is the primary salesperson, it doesn't scale. The founder ends up being the main revenue generator for far too long, placing a glass ceiling on the growth of the company. To break through this limitation, you need a defined company sales process that can be trained, delegated, managed, and ultimately scaled.

3. Product: Develop and Deliver Products That Delight Your Customer

The next element is the realm of product development and delivery. In your customer journey, everything that happens to your customer once they've bought from you, happens here. In most businesses, the product or service is delivered manually, which requires much of the owner's time. This presents a massive impediment to growth because there is a limit on what one person can accomplish, even if they deliver product around the clock. Additionally, while the founder is snowed under handling product delivery, they are not developing other elements of the business. Becoming a consumer champion starts with building a product function that continually improves your product development, grows through consistently delivering on your promises, and expands through capturing the stories of happy buyers and feeding them back to marketing to amplify customer happiness.

A note here on terminology: when we describe products and services in a business context, we almost always prefer the term product. We certainly include services under this umbrella. Why then do we uniformly use the term product? Because if you run a service-based business, you should look to modularize, systemize, and productize your offering in a way that bottles the magic and allows it to scale. The Entourage is a service business, as are about 55 percent of the businesses in our Elevate program. But we all create consistent service-based *products* that can scale, and therefore refer to them in those terms.

4. Operations: Build a Business That Can Work without You

The fourth element grows in importance as your business scales. Operations, or the internal workings of your business, are built first of processes, second of technology that helps enact those processes, and third of communication between each of the Six Elements, to ensure each function is aligned with the others. In high-growth businesses, operational concerns often get left behind, causing chaos, confusion, and carelessness. As a result, many founders spend a lot of their time tinkering with operations. As we often tell our seven- and eight-figure members: "If you don't have an operations manager, you are one." Developing streamlined operations is critical in building a business that can work without you.

5. Finance: Manage and Maximize the Money

Like operations, the importance of a strong financial component to your business increases as the business gets bigger. An effective finance function provides meaningful reporting on your company's past performance, along with forecasts to give you visibility into the future. Founders, focused on their vision and on bringing in new business, rarely pay enough attention to this area until they've felt the pain of financial mismanagement or under-performance for an extended period of time. Financial performance does not happen by accident. Business owners who have been running a successful company but neglect to focus adequately on financial performance frequently tell us: "We're still not making the profit we want after being in business for seven years. Maybe we're in the wrong industry. Maybe we've got the wrong business!" They're not in the wrong industry and (usually) they don't have the wrong business; they just need to adopt a greater focus toward the financial fundamentals of their company.

6. People: Assemble Your A-Team

This sixth and final element brings the first five to life. No business can succeed without a team of skilled, enthusiastic people. Initially, most company cultures rely fundamentally on the energy of the founder. Without constant supervision and leading by example, both culture and performance would plateau and eventually decline. Like so many of the dynamics we detail in this book, this setup is workable at the startup level, but it isn't scalable. If you put yourself in this position, you will exhaust yourself and frustrate your team. Instead, the key to building a world-class culture that grows *with the business* is to structurally ingrain leadership principles and management practices into the organization's fabric. To this end, the people element focuses on the composition of your team, defining your leadership practices, and instilling your management cadence.

THE SCIENCE OF SCALE:
COMBINING THE FOUR HATS AND THE SIX ELEMENTS

Together, the Six Elements forge a foundational framework for building a structurally sound business that enables you to elevate above the day-to-day. The real gold, however, comes from combining the Six Elements and the Four Hats to create a detailed holistic map of your business's progress. This is how great entrepreneurs and CEOs design their companies.

How does this work? Think of it like this. When you started out in business, and throughout the early stages, you likely wore the technician hat across all Six Elements. When you wanted to design and deploy a marketing campaign, you completed most or all the tasks hands-on, while overseeing the process from start to finish. You made the sales, delivered the product, wrote the systems, and managed the numbers. Across the Six Elements, you were closely involved in every aspect of your business.

There's no way you can sustain this level of involvement throughout the business as it grows, but you don't want to put your attention in one area only to neglect others. We'll show you how to design a roadmap enabling you to elevate from technician to leader in every one of the Six Elements. This is not a quick fix that happens overnight, but an actionable map to building a great company over time. The medium-term goal here is to set up every element such that they each grow sustainably without requiring your direct involvement in the day-to-day.

The Business Growth Profile (BGP): The Myers Briggs of Business

You'll generate your custom roadmap through our world-first business diagnostic tool, the Business Growth Profile (BGP). In as little as twenty minutes, the BGP will enable you to take a deep dive into every function of your business, identifying your most pressing challenges and biggest opportunities for unlocking growth. Dubbed "The Myers Briggs of Business," the BGP is a new benchmarking and analysis tool that is applicable to any industry. It offers an insightful 54-point diagnosis of your company's health and performance, distilling the science of scale to advise you on what *exactly* you need to do to grow from where you are to where you want to be.

Figure 3.2: The Business Growth Profile

We suggest you complete your own personalized BGP before reading on. As a reader of *Elevate*, this is yours absolutely free. You can find the BGP at www.the-entourage.com/elevate.

To illustrate how the BGP works, we collected real, aggregate data from numerous members in different industries who have completed their BGP. As the example below demonstrates, sustained growth is never achieved solely by making more sales. Instead, as a company scales, it structurally builds out *each* of the Six Elements, resulting in sustainable growth across all business components.

CONSULTING COMPANIES AT DIFFERENT REVENUE STAGES

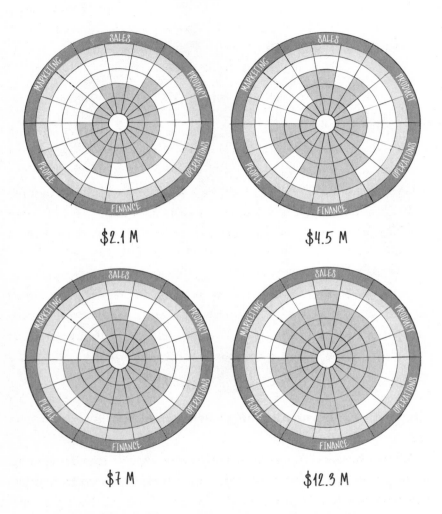

$2.1 M

$4.5 M

$7 M

$12.3 M

Figure 3.3: Consulting Companies at Different Levels of Revenue

Your fundamental objective should be to become a well-rounded business owner, building a well-rounded company, and the BGP will give you crucial insights into how best to do this. It's not that you will consistently divide your time equally between each element. At times you'll need to devote a lot of attention to marketing. At other times, you'll zero in on improving your people strategy. The BGP will help you identify which components to focus on at each stage to drive maximum business growth, so you know exactly how *and when* to build out each element in a way that is both structurally sound and optimized for scale.

SOME ELEMENTS DRIVE GROWTH, OTHERS ENABLE GROWTH

The Six Elements fall into two distinct categories: those that *drive* growth, and those that *enable* growth. Founders usually favor either driving or enabling growth, mostly—around 80 percent—driving growth. In the next chapter, we'll explore the characteristics of drive-growth and enable-growth founders, and how to balance these styles. For now, it's important to understand that businesses that scale successfully have mastered not just one, but both of these two distinct yet synergistic aspects.

The first three elements—marketing, sales, and product—are the areas that *drive* the growth of your business. These elements ensure you attract the right customers, keep them, and multiply them. The drive-growth elements are external and consumer-facing, generating customer demand.

The second three elements—operations, finance, and people—are the areas that *enable* the growth of your business. These elements function behind the scenes to ensure the company is well-resourced and smoothly run. The enable-growth elements are internal and allow the organization to keep up with the demand.

When a business is young, it usually swings wildly from being excessively focused on driving growth to being excessively focused on enabling growth. In startup, most businesses err on the side of driving growth, because that's what it takes to get them off the ground. After a while, however, this leads to the company's back end struggling to keep up with expansion on the front-end, resulting in poor delivery and disgruntled customers.

Founders who recognize this often swing to the opposite extreme, diverting their energy and attention to focusing solely on the internal operations of the business. However, this often leads to neglecting the activities that brought in customers in the first place. Years later, the founder realizes that putting all their attention on enabling growth means they no longer *have* a steady flow of incoming customers, and the business is stagnating.

You've probably experienced this seesaw yourself, without being able to fully articulate it; a multiyear cycle, where your business swings between being too drive-growth-heavy to being too enable-growth-heavy. Either you develop the drive-growth-focused elements at the expense of your company's internal processes, or you focus on the enable-growth elements, without developing a marketing and sales engine to acquire new business. Let's take a look at the strengths and weaknesses of these lopsided scenarios to give you an idea of where you might currently fall on the spectrum.

First up, here are the strengths and weaknesses of a drive-growth-focused business, lacking enable-growth-focused elements.

DRIVE GROWTH

ABOVE THE SURFACE
DRIVES SCALABILITY

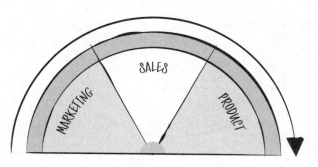

STRENGTHS

■ Winning new business

   Founder and business have
   an impressive skillset when
   it comes to marketing & sales

■ The outside looks great

   Branding, marketing & sales
   collateral, winning awards,
   testimonials

■ Revenue is growing

   So focused on sales and marketing
   that business appears to be growing

WEAKNESSES

■ Delivering to customers

   Not enough attention given
   to the product delivery;
   there is a growing base of
   unhappy customers

■ Operationally very weak

   No processes, people, or
   thought given to the inner
   workings of the business

■ Profit is not growing

   A lack of financial
   understanding and
   management means there
   is no profit

Figure 3.4: A Drive-Growth-Focused Business

Conversely, here are the strengths and weaknesses of an enable-growth-focused business, lacking drive-growth-focused elements.

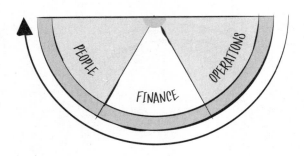

ENABLE GROWTH

BELOW THE SURFACE
ENSURES SCALABILITY

STRENGTHS	WEAKNESSES
■ Looking after existing customers	■ Winning new business
A strong care for product delivery means that their reputation and referrals are strong	Because all of the attention is on existing customers and operations, there is no firepower in marketing sales
■ The inside looks great	■ The outside looks "blah"
Systems are good, things get done reliably, people are happy, employee retention is strong	The branding, marketing & sales process is not attractive, appealing, or scalable
■ Revenue & profit are stable	■ Revenue & profit are not growing
There is a small foundation that is being looked after well	A lack of drive behind marketing & sales means growth is incremental and slow

Figure 3.5: An Enable-Growth-Focused Business

We group the three drive-growth elements under the heading the *Drive Growth Cycle*, because, when set up correctly, this process becomes self-perpetuating. On the other hand, we categorize the enable-growth elements under the heading of the *Enable Growth Structure*, because they provide a bedrock for sustainable growth. As a rule of thumb, the drive-growth elements will make your company scalable, whereas the enable-growth elements will make it sustainable. To grow your business successfully, you need both working synergistically.

There's no such thing as a pure drive-growth-focused business, or a pure enable-growth-focused business, but many, if not most, are excessively skewed toward one or the other. Over time, you'll want to find a balance between the two and create a well-rounded business.

USING THE BUSINESS GROWTH PROFILE

The Six Elements provide a foundational framework that applies to every business, across all industries. In our member community, we see the universality of this structure play out every day in conversations and daily interactions. While most founders understand the similarities they share with businesses in their own industry, very few are able to extrapolate lessons from other industries and apply them to their business. This, however, is where the most powerful innovation occurs.

The Six Elements gives our members a shared language they can use to understand the common patterns in every business, and to learn from each other, no matter how superficially different their industry or activities. Psychologists learn from financial planners, construction companies apply wisdom shared by franchises, and accountants adopt strategies they see being deployed in public relations firms.

Using the Four Hats model, combined with the Six Elements, as your blueprint for growth will continually remind you and your team that to be successful, you must *combine* scalability and sustainability. Marketing, sales, product, operations, finance, and people are components of every thriving business. To rise above technician-level activities and guide your business toward achieving your vision, you must be addressing the right elements at the right time, according to where you are along your growth journey.

If you haven't yet completed your company's custom Business Growth Profile, we highly recommend you do so before reading further. It will allow you to pinpoint the existing strengths and weaknesses of your business, identifying whether you skew heavily toward either driving or enabling growth. Armed with this knowledge, and an understanding of how you may have slanted too much toward either external, consumer-facing components (marketing, sales, product), or internal elements (operations, finance, people), you'll finally understand exactly what you need to do to improve neglected aspects of your business.

CASE STUDY: DANIELA AND NATALIA SUPERCHARGE GROWTH

Sisters Daniela and Natalia had built their business, Verge Girl, into a successful seven-figure e-commerce fashion business, but it was bursting at the seams. They had so many orders that their warehouse and dispatch was messy and disorganized. Their buying wasn't systemized, meaning they usually had either too much stock on hand, or not enough. In months that could have been big months for them, their growth was depressed because they didn't have the product to sell. They worked too many hours in the week, and their team was scrambling to keep up with many competing and often confusing demands, as they tried to manage the unmanageable.

Overwhelmed, they didn't know where to turn or how to take their business to the next level. The company was successful and well-staffed, but a lack of structure forced them to spend their days running from one thing to the next, putting out fire after fire. "Our business was doing well, but we had hit a plateau and didn't know how to scale it. We felt we had taken Verge Girl to the furthest point we could by ourselves," Daniela reflected.

When they applied the Business Growth Profile to their business, it became clear that Daniela and Natalia were stuck in technician mode across each one of the Six Elements. While they both had the talent and skill needed to excel at their core business, the company was not set up to grow beyond what they could contribute each day. They didn't have the confidence to *drive growth*, and they hadn't built the structures to *enable growth*. Like many business owners who are stuck at this stage of the game, they were plagued by self-doubt and paralysis, believing that the roadblocks they encountered were symptomatic of their shortcomings.

To unlock growth for Verge Girl, Daniela and Natalia first needed to focus on developing their Enable Growth Structure. While most entrepreneurs naturally gravitate toward driving growth, often a period of enabling growth must come first, to set the business up to scale confidently.

We started by clearly delineating the roles of each founder, clarifying —for them and for everyone else—who was in charge of what. Daniela and Natalia then developed an organizational chart with position descriptions for each role, bringing structure and definition to the team's composition. No longer were they operating under the "everyone-does -everything" approach. Right away, every team member knew their exact role, where they sat in the context of the broader team, who they reported to, and where to go when they needed something from different parts of the business.

They also captured the core performance drivers of the business by implementing key targets within each of the six elements, and for every individual. Progress against these targets was displayed throughout the office for everyone to see, providing complete visibility of performance and driving accountability throughout each team. This step meant that, every day, everyone on the Verge Girl team knew whether they were ahead of target or behind target, instilling a performance-oriented culture. Finally, the sisters enhanced the technology that underpinned the business, streamlining every function and giving the business a platform for more effective collaboration.

Implementing these structures to enable growth gave the business vital visibility, structure, and unity. At this point, Verge Girl was ready to push forward, driving growth with confidence, knowing the back end was in place to handle increased volume.

The Verge Girl drive-growth strategy began by defining the different stages of the marketing funnel, so the team could tailor communication with prospects depending on which stage of the buyer's journey they were at. This meant their marketing messages were more targeted and increased conversions at each stage of their marketing funnel. After this, Daniela and Natalia developed their marketing attribution model (a process we'll reveal in Chapter Seven: Marketing). This model tracks every dollar of revenue back to the exact marketing tactic that generated it. By correctly attributing their income to specific marketing efforts, the team discovered the confidence they needed to scale their marketing profitably. Thanks to this one strategy alone, today every dollar that Verge Girl spends on marketing returns $3.50 to the company. With this kind of ratio in place, Verge Girl can allocate an unlimited marketing budget to winning new customers—a superpower for any business that wants to drive growth.

Natalia explained the change in perspective like this: "It's given me confidence, and it's given the girls confidence. We're just excited about the future in a way that we weren't before, because we felt there was potential, but we didn't know how to unlock it. Now we've got the keys and know what to do."

Like many six-, seven-, and eight-figure businesses, Verge Girl had buckets of talent and potential, but hadn't yet understood how to construct the strategy and structure necessary to grow the business beyond their day-to-day efforts. By implementing the advice from their Elevate business coach, they hugely accelerated their growth while personally doing a lot less. Finally, Daniela and Natalia broke the cycle of perpetually living in technician mode. The results speak for themselves. Verge Girl turned even its worst months into million-dollar months, and, "In the last six months of working with The Entourage, we've already gone from a seven-figure to an eight-figure business," they explained. Even better, with the bedrock of a strong Enable Growth Structure and a high-functioning Drive Growth Cycle, their continued growth is both scalable and sustainable.

THE ENTOURAGE BALANCES OUT A LOPSIDED GROWTH TRAJECTORY

At The Entourage, we certainly haven't been immune to focusing too much on some elements of the business, to the detriment of others. Like most of the tools we develop and coach our members with, we initially designed the Six Elements' framework to solve our own problems. In the company's first five years, like most high-growth companies, we zeroed in on driving growth. Inspired by the success stories of the businesses participating in our programs, we were intensely driven by a deep sense of mission to help as many people as possible.

By 2015, however, we reached a point where our growth was so steep that we often needed to make fairly large decisions quickly. Inevitably, we would make a change to remedy an issue that was screaming at us in one area of the business, only to realize months later that we'd created problems in other areas of the business. We didn't yet fully appreciate the interconnectedness of each of the different elements, nor the importance of communication among different departments, so we were making decisions in isolation.

When introducing a new product, for example, we thought about it simply in those terms: "we're going to introduce a new product." We didn't recognize that there is *so* much joined-up thinking behind this move: What will the marketing funnel be? How will the sales process flow? How will we ensure product delivery happens in a streamlined way, complementing our existing product delivery system? Operationally, how do we bake these new systems into the business? How much is all this going to cost? What is our breakeven point, and when will the move be profitable? And from a people perspective, how are we going to communicate with the team and train them on everything they need to know about the new product? Will all this distraction even be *worth it*, or are we better off simply doubling down on our existing activities?

Not fully thinking through these considerations meant that every time we solved one problem, we unknowingly created three more. The result? The busier we got, the busier we made ourselves—a spiral you might relate to. We felt like we were always chasing our tails, often cleaning up the mess from shortsightedness of our previous decisions.

To make better decisions, with a more comprehensive view of the overall business impact, we needed a framework that enabled us to trace the knock-on effects of a decision in one area. This framework needed to be something we could come back to whenever we wanted to make any strategic or structural moves. In summary, we needed to systemize how we would think through decisions holistically.

To do this, we created the Six Elements architecture by simply sketching out the different functions of the business, and how they needed to work together, onto a piece of paper. Thereafter, whenever we needed to make a structural decision, we had to train ourselves to literally reach into the top drawer, pull out that crumpled piece of paper with the Six Elements sketched onto it, and think through the different dimensions of the situation. Immediately, we were amazed at how much angst this strategy removed from the process, and how much easier it became. No longer were we carrying every element of the business in our head, attempting to mentally map the flow of consequences. This profoundly simple model did the heavy lifting—all we needed to do was think into it.

Over the years Jack has developed a principle that an entrepreneur's worst enemy is a blank piece of paper. As entrepreneurs, we exert enormous mental energy on thinking through complicated scenarios and trying to reinvent the wheel. Having frameworks that we can pull out of the metaphorical top drawer in different scenarios, accelerates decision-making and ultimately moves the business forward faster.

Today, whether in our own businesses or those of our members, we always employ the Six Elements whenever we're developing strategy, creating an operations plan, defining core targets, mapping out how we will grow the team, or making *any* important decision. It has become the bedrock for making considered decisions and building structurally sound companies that scale to eight figures and beyond.

NEXT UP...

If you're a little overwhelmed right now, thinking that you must immediately master all Six Elements to build a successful company, don't worry. While this framework is essential in understanding how to elevate yourself from technician to leader, nobody is exceptional at every single element. Our intention is not to overwhelm you with the idea that you must be brilliant at everything, but rather to encourage you to create the time and space to double down on your circle of genius and attract people with talents who complement yours.

To help you do this, we want to give you the tools to identify what *kind* of entrepreneur you are, an essential next step to building a great company. Now that we've outlined the Six Elements, the Drive Growth Cycle, and the Enable Growth Structure, it's time to understand which elements of your business light you up personally, and which ones feel like a drag, so you can place people—including yourself—in roles that match their passions and capabilities.

4

DRIVER OR ENABLER

Play to Your Strengths

Experience tells us that right now you're spending too much time doing things you're not good at and don't enjoy. This is holding you back, bottlenecking the company and acting as a glass ceiling, limiting how much your business can grow. At your current stage of business, this is probably the number one factor inhibiting your growth.

As business owners, we tend to confuse entrepreneurship with management. We think it's our job to hold onto everything, do everything, and manage everything ourselves. It's not. As we've discussed in previous chapters, while this may be inevitable for a period of time in the beginning, as the company grows, it is absolutely critical that you, the founder, get very clear about where you're highly skilled and where you suck, and start to hire people whose strengths match your weaknesses.

Great entrepreneurs develop a high level of honesty and self-awareness around what they're great at, and what they're not. They understand that building a scalable company is about building the right team, with the right people occupying the right seats. Knowing how to build a team that exponentially amplifies your strengths and covers your weaknesses is a core part of entrepreneurship. If you aspire to join the ranks of great entrepreneurs, it's a skill you need to master.

How can you do this? The first step is to find total clarity around the roles you should and should not be playing. In this chapter we're going to introduce you to the two very distinct types of leadership every founder-led company needs: the **driver of growth**, who sees the future and focuses on the outside, and the **enabler of growth**, who turns the company's vision into reality by managing the inside.

The driver of growth is a dreamer with a pioneering spirit. As a founder, there's an 80 percent chance you fall into this category. If so, you excel at seeing the future and leading the company toward seizing big opportunities. These are the characteristics that inspired you to start a business in the first place, and which keep pushing you to grow further. Your counterpart, the enabler of growth, looks at the world through a very different lens. Instead of seeking the future, they focus on how things are today, and what needs to be done to deliver on the business's promises. The enabler of growth is a realist. Their superpower is to manage the organization in a way that ensures internal structures are solid, performance is consistent, and targets are met. In most cases, the enabler of growth excels as a second-in-command.

These two different ways of thinking and operating are diametrically opposed, and there's an inherent tension between drivers and enablers of growth. In poorly managed businesses, where the relationship dynamic between the driver and enabler is not well understood, these competing perspectives bubble up into arguments and ongoing conflict. If you come to appreciate the importance of the driver/enabler combination, however, and put strategies in place to effectively manage the relationship, you'll find that the interplay between these different perspectives is exactly what makes this dynamic so incredibly powerful.

This dynamic often plays out before our eyes when we're facilitating a strategy session for two business partners, or a founder and their second-in-command. Almost always, there is an unresolved tension between them. Both feel stuck, misunderstood, and frustrated by a relationship that is clearly not working. Prior to the strategy session, they usually interpret this tension as an indication that they are not the right fit for working closely together. When we share the Driver and Enabler Framework with them, however, and explain the key principles behind making the relationship work, they start to see that their differences are precisely the reason why they *are* suited for collaboration. Far from being a weakness to be avoided, their opposing perspectives are a powerful strength to be harnessed.

Another dynamic we see regularly is the driver who is yet to fully appreciate the importance of enablers, and instead surrounds themselves with people whom they have a natural rapport with—other drivers. They build their team in their own image, and then wonder why nothing ever gets seen through to completion. In the startup phase, operating with a team of drivers may be somewhat effective, because pursuing growth at all costs can be valuable. As your business scales, however, it is imperative that you counterbalance the tendencies of a drive-growth-heavy team with enablers who can ensure that resources are managed, deadlines are hit, and deliverables are achieved.

BUILD YOUR STRENGTHS, RECRUIT YOUR WEAKNESSES

Reading the content in this chapter should feel like talking to a friend who really gets you, and sometimes sees you more clearly than you see yourself. Whatever your natural tendencies, there's no doubt they're already shaping your business. By bringing them to light, you can work consciously with them, recognizing where they serve you and where you need to collaborate with those whose strengths complement yours.

Understanding and implementing the driver and enabler of growth concept has already transformed the businesses of thousands of our seven- and eight-figure members. They now understand their zone of genius and spend their time doing what they enjoy. This alignment between their strengths and their role has turbocharged their business growth. These breakthroughs have fundamentally changed how they live their lives. They feel like they know themselves again and can build their businesses accordingly.

If you know where to look, the stories of great companies are littered with famous pairs of drivers and enablers: Walt Disney and his brother Roy; Henry Ford and James Couzens; Ray Kroc and Fred Turner; Steve Jobs and Steve Wozniak; Mark Zuckerberg and Sheryl Sandberg, and Sir Richard Branson and the CEOs and COOs of his many Virgin companies, to name a few. Great entrepreneurs know that to build a great company, they need someone pioneering scalability—a driver of growth, a role they usually fulfill themselves—and someone ensuring sustainability—an enabler of growth.

In the previous few chapters, we've introduced the idea that a company should be both scalable and sustainable. Integrating these two different styles of leadership is key to achieving this goal. Understanding this dynamic and how to make it work helps drivers unshackle themselves from the day-to-day details, focus on the big picture, and play the pioneering role they are naturally so great at. Similarly, it helps enablers to have free rein creating organizational harmony, enabling commercial performance, and maintaining a cohesive and synergistic relationship with the driver. Let's explore the different styles in greater depth.

THE DRIVER OF GROWTH: WHO YOU ARE

As a driver of growth, you have an unbridled passion for life and for shaping the world to match your vision of the future. You see things that don't yet exist, in a way that most other people simply can't. You have big dreams, and sometimes you love the dream of what your business *could* be more than the business itself. This is a gift, because this tension between how things currently are and how you see them is constantly pulling you toward your vision. As we mentioned above, in our experience, about 80 percent of founders are drivers, so there's a high probability this profile matches your personality type.

If so, you're a big-picture person. The greater the problem or opportunity, the more you are in your element. When you're buried in detail, you get bored very quickly, but hand you a huge problem to tackle, one that most would see as insurmountable, and you'll relish the opportunity to rise to the occasion. Secretly, many drivers see their business as a way to demonstrate their brilliance to the world.

This big-picture perspective only heightens your capacity to see the future. You have a deep sense for industry trends, where the market is going, and what your business needs to become to be in a commanding position—and you love to connect these dots, creating a strategy that stretches out into the future.

Many people find the visionary approach of drivers highly inspirational. As a driver, you're a classic entrepreneur, someone who builds with tenacity and creativity. You stake a claim on the future, and see it with such clarity that those around you can't help but be emboldened by your certainty. You're an innovator, a business builder, a change maker. Drivers represent only 3 percent of the population—they are the classic entrepreneur archetype. Because the driver of growth is such a unique personality, you may have spent most of your life feeling misunderstood.

Despite this sense of alienation, drivers are often highly empathic. As a driver, you deeply understand the goals, challenges, aspirations, wants, and needs of your consumers. This means you likely have an intuitive sense of how to brand your business and what messaging will resonate with your customer, making you a natural marketer and salesperson. This empathy also translates into the way you connect with your team, making you a great coach and companion. Your inherent connection to the future, along with your empathy for what might be keeping someone stuck, makes you influential in guiding others to see beyond their problems and recognize possible solutions.

Your visionary style means you're full of ideas, obsessively brainstorming ways to make things better. You don't operate within processes; in fact, you take pleasure in breaking apart existing structures to create something new. Your superpowers are tailor-made for the beginning of a project, when the key skills are obsessive focus on the problem at hand, the ability to march forward in the absence of a roadmap, and a high degree of tenacity. In A *Hunter in a Farmer's World*, John F. Dini says that entrepreneurs possess "the ability to navigate in the fog, knowing how to keep moving in the right direction when you don't have a compass and there are no signposts. Entrepreneurs hunt. They don't manage. They explore rather than analyze. They build companies with vision, creativity, and tenacity; not with policies and procedures."

Indeed, you relish the opportunity to start from nothing and create something, however imperfectly. This out-of-the-box thinking and obsession with making things better means that you are a wellspring of new ideas. Put you in an uncertain situation, and you will either find a path forward or make one.

THE DRIVER OF GROWTH: YOUR WEAKNESSES

As a driver, you are a unique character with special gifts to offer the world. As with every personality type, however, there is another side to the story. Inherent and extreme strengths are often offset by their corresponding weaknesses. The good news, however, is that these weaknesses are only a problem for as long as they remain unconscious. Once you understand them, this self-awareness becomes one of your greatest strengths.

When you understand your gifts, you also understand where you *don't* excel. You become laser-focused on the places where you add tremendous value, and build a team around you to handle the things you should *not* be doing. Picture a one-person band. However talented the person is, they will sound far less impressive than a talented orchestra playing in harmony. Similarly, the one-person band will never reach their full potential at any particular instrument, because they're trying to play *all* the instruments.

Entrepreneurship is less about being great at everything, and more about knowing how to amplify your strengths and cover your weaknesses. When you clearly identify what you're *not* good at, you can surround yourself with people who *are* brilliant at those things and, in so doing, bring together a team that is collectively capable of achieving so much more than any one individual. Therefore, please interpret this section as constructive direction, not criticism. Our intention is to help you see behind the curtain of your own personality, and thereby put in place strategies to maximize your impact and minimize your struggles.

As a driver, your lust for the future may distort how you see the present. Your vision is so strong and clear in your head that it may override your ability to see things as they *are*, right now. While everyone else is looking at what *is*, you are focused on what *could be*, which may lead those around you to perceive you as delusional. People may accuse you of having your head in the clouds, and they're right. You do. That's what makes you brilliant.

Your sense of the future may be so clear in your head that you under-communicate with those you need to enroll to help make that vision a reality. You think through a change or new direction for weeks, map out the different scenarios thoroughly in your head until you're convinced you've found the right move, and eventually settle on a decision. When you communicate this change in direction to your team, however, you greatly underestimate how much ground you have covered, and therefore how much detail you need to convey for them to catch up. While you've been living, breathing, and dreaming the new idea for weeks, your team has been devotedly doing their jobs, entrenched in the minutiae of their day-to-day routine.

There is a huge gulf between the high-definition picture in your head and what your team is seeing as they undertake the routine tasks that make up their days. If you don't yet understand your natural proclivity to skip the details and assume that others can automatically see what you're envisaging, you simply won't appreciate how much communication is required to change your team's mind. For you, it is *so* clear. "Why don't they get it? I've told them three times now!" You will proclaim. "It's so obvious!"

This is the catch-cry of the driver who doesn't yet realize that under-communicating ideas that are clear to *them* is part of their inherent nature.

Another archetypal driver weakness is a disregard for detail. You may be so married to the future that you genuinely believe something is real, or has already been done, even when it has only progressed 10 percent. If so, you will fall short when it comes to executing your brilliant ideas. Unless you become aware of this trait and build a team to cover it, your disdain for detail, process, and proper implementation will create a culture where many things get started and few things get finished.

Compounding this issue, your inability to focus on detail may lead you to greatly underestimate how much work, and how many resources, are required to successfully complete a project. In your mind, everything is achievable by tomorrow, without allocating any additional resources. Again, this clarity of purpose is your greatest strength, enabling you to surmount obstacles others would deem impossible. If you remain unaware of the shadow side of that strength, however, you will bring additional chaos to an already chaotic environment.

Your natural empathy is a similar double-edged sword. On the positive side, it makes you a great coach and companion. On the other hand, it also manifests as a tendency to befriend your team rather than *manage* your team. We often work with drivers who form such close friendships with their team members that hard conversations about necessary performance indicators and accountability are simply not happening. As long as you're unaware of this tendency, you will likely shy away from initiating those conversations, opting instead to be liked by everyone. Too often, the empathetic driver's measure of culture will be, "it *feels* good, and people don't *not* like me." This is a limited way to assess a company culture, seriously discounting the importance of strong and clear management. Ultimately, if left unchecked for too long, this type of culture will cause a lot more issues than one built on clear accountability, and a commitment to addressing issues head-on.

Another driver of growth tendency is to act as a fountain of ideas without ever truly capturing and pursuing individual paths. This will cause organizational whiplash, changing direction at a speed that leaves everybody around you disoriented. Drivers love chasing shiny things. Unless you find ways to moderate this characteristic, it can have serious consequences: for example, your business running in one clear direction for ninety days, before you determine that it needs to change tack. At this point, all momentum will be halted as you point somewhere new and yell "that way!" Your team will grind to a halt and head off on the new trajectory, only to experience the same jarring shift of focus a few months down the line. This inconsistency will mean that the company never truly has time to get its feet under itself, instead constantly shifting and rearranging according to your latest and greatest idea.

The good news is through The Entourage, we have worked with thousands of drivers who exhibited most or all the tendencies above. We've seen them go from allowing their natural tendencies to rule their business, to becoming powerful and impactful company leaders. If you winced in recognition at some of the descriptions in this section, understand that your weaknesses can be mitigated, and your strengths powerfully enhanced when you operate in alignment with them.

Most drivers live their lives trying to be something they're not—a manager. Or they are being completely themselves, but are confused as to why their business isn't progressing at the rate they expect. Here, understanding the driver/enabler dynamic is a fundamental unlock. When you bring awareness to who you innately are, you will be able to craft the perfect role that amplifies your strengths, and begin building the perfect team that covers your weaknesses.

Enter, the enabler of growth.

THE ENABLER OF GROWTH: WHO YOU ARE

Enablers of growth are the essential counterparts to drivers of growth. You'll either need to work with enablers of growth, or you are one. By virtue of what it takes to start a business and build it from nothing, most founders are big-picture people without a high attention to detail. A few, however—approximately 20 percent—fall into the category of enablers.

Businesses founded by enablers of growth are most common in professional and technical fields, where one or more founders leave a large corporation to start their own business. If you're an enable-growth-focused entrepreneur, you lead differently. Instead of crafting a vision of the future and mobilizing others toward it, you focus on putting one foot in front of the other and leading by example. You are far less focused on your dreams of the future, and more focused on day-to-day execution.

As a result, you will likely be much slower to embrace marketing and sales as a route to drive up revenue, meaning that you eventually bump up against slow or stagnant growth rates, causing the business to plateau or gradually decline. To succeed, you will either need to embrace and enhance your inner driver, or hire one or more key drivers to fulfill vital roles such as marketing and sales.

On the other hand, your superpower is making things happen. While the driver of growth lives in the future, you obsess about day-to-day operational clarity. Whereas the driver is in their element when it comes to inspiration, you are in your element when it comes to application. The driver wants everything done by tomorrow. You know how to prioritize, allocate resources, and manage deadlines, thereby ensuring that grand visions actually translate into reality. In short, your unique ability is running the organization. Highly diligent, consistent, and conscientious, you value implementation above anything else.

Whereas drivers inspire people by painting a vision of the future, you enjoy diving into the details, and prefer to let your results speak for themselves. You aren't easily seduced by far-reaching dreams—if anything, you view them as a distraction from the real work of building step by step. Pragmatism is your watchword, and you prefer to lead by example than stand at the front of the room and talk about what you're going to do. Big dreams are great, but you know the path toward them is paved with day-to-day performance.

To this end, you love to tinker with the nuts and bolts for as long as necessary to make the machine sing. You get excited about *executing* the business plan, and enjoy being accountable to the profit and loss statement. Whereas drivers are brilliant at generating a vision and charting a course, you love playing where results are measurable.

Unlike drivers, you are not romantic, you are highly rational. You see things mechanically, which is the perfect counterbalance to a driver's empathetic nature. Whereas a driver sees the business in poetic terms, as a living, breathing organism, enriched with a soul unto itself, you view it as a force for productivity, and you know how to harmoniously integrate each of the Six Elements to ensure they are working together in a cohesive fashion. This rational streak also makes you brilliant at management, holding people accountable, and having the hard conversations drivers prefer to avoid.

Your love of operational perfection makes you brilliant at sustaining and maintaining a business, a steady, implacable force that anchors the wide-ranging focus of the driver of growth. If you're mature enough to recognize your abilities and their limits, you will be able to influence the driver, helping them to see when an idea does not fit the business, when now is not the right time to pursue it, or frankly—and this is often the case—when it's just not very good. In this way, you act as a filter between the driver and the rest of the team, preventing the organizational whiplash that would occur if the driver gave their ideas completely free rein. While the driver has their head in the clouds, you keep your feet firmly on the ground, anchoring the organization long enough to build a robust foundation and record measurable results.

THE ENABLER OF GROWTH: YOUR WEAKNESSES

Just like the driver of growth, your enabler of growth powers come with their own kryptonite. The flipside of your clear strengths are their corresponding weaknesses.

Your focus on tasks, projects, and outcomes makes you a powerful contributor to your organization. On the other hand, this focus on making things happen can lead you to neglect the human element of both your interactions and your overall business goals. This is especially true when you have too much to do and not enough time in which to do it. As stress and tunnel vision kick in, your focus on efficiency can cause you to become militant in your management of people, tasks, and even yourself. An enabler under stress can become a demanding perfectionist.

Another risk is that your stringent focus on excellent performance may cause you to lose sight of the big picture. Even while driving day-to-day execution, it is important that you stop every so often and take the time to reflect on the milestones you and the team have already achieved, and where the organization is headed. This breathing space will help you ensure that the day-to-day is lining up with the long term, something that is often forgotten when an enabler has their head down working on tasks. This will also help you to stay connected to the positives, not merely problems, and energize you to fulfill your role with a sense of vigor and purpose.

Drivers are more focused on maximizing the upside than minimizing the downside. Conversely, unless you strive to become consciously aware of your natural disposition, you may become excessively focused on minimizing the downside, causing you to hesitate instead of seizing positive opportunities. The more stressed you are, the more likely it is that you will become obsessive about avoiding mistakes. At an extreme, you may implement measures guaranteed to prevent mistakes, such as micromanaging your sales team to be so focused on administrative accuracy that it detracts from the time they are able to allocate toward making sales. In your mind, this may feel justified because it reduces administrative errors, but this benefit is more than offset by the degree to which it limits the performance of the team. Although you may satisfy your need to avoid mistakes, the end result is net-negative.

A final risk is that as the person who holds others accountable and initiates tough conversations, you may get a reputation as the villain. While you grapple constantly with driving performance and the demands of executing flawlessly for the sake of the business, you may struggle with the feeling that others don't always like you. This may lead you to feel underappreciated, even unseen. Should the demands of your role become all-consuming—a frequent occurrence in a fast-growing business—you may become irritable and impersonal, further exacerbating the distance between you and other team members.

As with the driver, however, none of these weaknesses are insurmountable. When you team up with a driver who understands their personality type, and learn to work together effectively, your partnership can enhance your undoubted strengths and turn the volume down on your respective weaknesses.

DRIVER AND ENABLER: WORKING TOGETHER

As we've described above, the driver and the enabler provide diametrically opposed skills. When managed well, this partnership will generate a unique blend of magic, ensuring that your company is both scalable *and* sustainable. If either of you is yet to learn about the dynamics of the driver/enabler relationship, however, or you're unsure how to set the relationship up, your collaboration can be a source of unhealthy tension, and eventually fracture. Even when you set up and manage this relationship well, you will still experience challenges. By bringing a driver and an enabler together, you are essentially creating disagreement by design, in the knowledge that the fruits of your connection will spark an alchemy neither of you could generate alone.

First, let's talk about how things can go awry. As the driver, the one with the vision, you may start to believe the enabler is there purely to do what you ask of them. They are not. There is a very important reason why we describe this function as the enabler *of growth* and not simply the enabler: they are not there primarily to enable *you*. In the early days of the typical startup, when you were bootstrapping based on the picture in your head, your relationship with your assistant or still-junior-team was authoritative. You instructed, they executed.

Once you bring in a senior executive who is an enabler, however, that dynamic should mature. They should have a high level of experience and commercial capability, and therefore informed opinions about how to operationalize the business and increase performance. As the seniority of the enablers you work with—and, for that matter, your entire team—increases, you need to give them more autonomy, and more ownership.

By the time you have a CEO in place, their voice should carry a lot of weight in the decision-making process, particularly when discussing elements of the business—such as operations—that are not your strengths. It was Steve Jobs who said, "We don't hire smart people to tell them what to do, we hire smart people so they can tell us what to do."

If you're a senior enabler, however, particularly if you come on board early in the company's development, you may start to believe your role is to disillusion the driver of their wilder ideas. Allow this tendency to express itself unchecked, and there's a risk that you will expend a lot of energy pouring cold water on the driver's creative vision and stifle the growth of the business.

You are not there to undertake every wild goose chase that enters the driver's head, but you *are* there to bring the best parts of their vision to fruition, through putting in place the structures that enable it to find traction. Because that vision is based on how things *could be* instead of how they *are*, it is inevitably fragile. If you arm yourself with enough facts and figures, it is possible to shoot down almost any idea the driver comes up with. The problem with this approach is when doing so, you will throttle the entrepreneurial life out of the company. If you're a driver/enabler business partnership, the driver may defer to you based on your apparently realistic version of events, but see their verve for changing the world ebb away, until the business becomes staid and boring. This may fracture the relationship, as the driver loses faith in your ability to execute on the direction of the company.

To counter these scenarios, it's important to clearly delineate how the relationship between driver and enabler will function. We have achieved this by giving Jack the louder voice when it comes to vision, strategy, consumer-facing brand and messaging, and key expansion initiatives and their timing. Meanwhile, Tim is closer to the action, so his view holds more weight than Jack's on anything internal and/or operational, and on questions of driving immediate performance. While Jack will offer Tim direction and support when it comes to achieving short-term P&L performance, the ultimate decision must rest with Tim. Similarly, while

Jack will solicit and consider Tim's input on expansion initiatives and brand building, the final call in this area must be made by Jack.

In Chapter Eleven: People, we'll dive deeply into how to structure your entire team. For now, however, let's address some of the key ways you can set your driver/enabler relationship up for success.

- **Develop and maintain a deep understanding of the driver/ enabler dynamic.** As soon as you bring conscious awareness to the driver/enabler alliance, and the strengths and weaknesses of each person, it will change the relationship on a fundamental level. If you are already in a driver/enabler dynamic, and you weren't previously aware of it, simply reading this chapter will transform how you show up in that relationship.
- **Clearly outline each role, using detailed position descriptions.** You must divide and conquer. Failure to do this will sow confusion, both between the two of you and among your team. Whenever you have senior people working together, it is *critical* that you draw up clear lines of responsibility that delineate who owns what. Two or more strong personalities operating without clear definition will certainly butt heads in an unhealthy fashion. Position descriptions should include the core role, targets, reporting lines, direct reports, and cultural expectations. To download plug-and-play position descriptions, head to www.the-entourage.com/elevate.
- **Develop a deep appreciation for one another's perspective.** Time in this dynamic will teach you to appreciate the viewpoint of the other. If you're the driver, you will most likely learn through experience that the practicalities an enabler puts forward are in fact, important considerations for you to take into account. There may be times when you learn this the hard way: in your haste, you choose not to take the enabler's input on board. As the project progresses and cracks start to form, it turns out that the exact scenarios the enabler pointed to are coming to pass.

If you're self-aware, you will be able to reflect and realize that you should have taken the enabler's feedback on board. If you're the enabler, you may initially worry that the driver has their head in the clouds. Are they crazy? As the relationship progresses, however, and you experience firsthand the driver's power to create things of tangible value, you will learn to appreciate this capacity, and harness it in a way that translates to improved company performance.

- **Meet one-on-one on a regular basis.** One-on-ones are sessions where you develop and maintain alignment in areas critical to the success of the relationship. For this reason they should be scheduled and rarely missed. As a general rule of thumb, the driver will want to discuss big-picture strategy, whereas the enabler will contribute more tactical and operational agenda items. These one-on-ones are regular check-ins to ensure everything is moving forward optimally, so they should lean more toward the tactical and operational. The best time for the driver to discuss big-picture strategy and structure is usually the monthly advisory board meetings, and biannual strategy sessions, which we'll cover below. At the beginning of your relationship, one-on-ones should take place weekly. After a year or two, if it serves you both better, you can move them to fortnightly. When we realized that coming together weekly didn't give Tim enough time to really implement and make progress between meetings, we moved our one-on-ones to a fortnightly cadence.

- **Schedule regular meetings with your advisory board.** Again, in the beginning these should be monthly. Once you've created a strong performance rhythm, they can be moved to bimonthly. These advisory board meetings should include you, your key driver/enabler partner, and your advisors. This is how we work with our Elevate members: their monthly coaching session serves as their monthly advisory board meeting. The purpose of these meetings is to review performance, assess how the company is tracking year-to-date, and discuss future strategy and initiatives that are going to maximize growth. This provides an important opportunity to examine and manage company performance, and to ensure that everyone is on the same page going forward. These meetings should ensure alignment between the long-term strategy of the company and the short-term initiatives.

- **Every six months, undertake multiday strategy sessions.** These sessions are an invaluable method of aligning you and your counterpart on important business questions. As we introduced previously, one of the core dynamics that *will* form between every driver/enabler team is that the driver will frequently want to discuss the big picture, the earth-shattering ideas, and the overarching direction, whereas the enabler managing the business simply won't have the mental bandwidth to fully digest these concepts. When you integrate these strategy sessions into your annual rhythm, it gives both of you the opportunity to download your thinking and discuss big dreams and major moves. This not only helps you to achieve complete alignment, it also creates a dedicated space to talk strategy every six months, soothing the driver's constant desire to discuss the big things every week. For the enabler, the disconnect from daily responsibilities represents an opportunity to rise up out of the detail, allowing for the space and capacity to truly *hear* and engage with the big ideas, which the enabler actually enjoys and appreciates when they have the time to do so. These sessions should run for two to three days. They may involve just the two of you, or you can choose to bring in key advisors or leaders of specific areas of the business for relevant parts of the session. While the weekly one-on-ones are mainly tactical, and the monthly advisory board meetings are a combination of strategy and tactics, these sessions are reserved for high-level strategic conversations. While they may conclude with the development of an operational roadmap, the conversation mainly leans toward the big picture.

Between them, these cadences will greatly ease the tension between your preferred style of operation and your key collaborator's. Nonetheless, it's important to understand that even when you do all the above, the first six-to-twelve months of a driver/enabler relationship may still feel tense at times. This is normal and natural. View this time as a teething period, where the relationship is forming, and you are learning how best to work with each other. Like any relationship, this will involve disagreements, along with periods where you fall out of love with the idea of working together and need to work on the relationship. If you truly believe you're in the right driver/enabler relationship, commit to doing what is required to build a healthy partnership, based on mutual respect.

Think of the spectrum of potential activities as a scale from one to ten, with one representing the most routine tasks and ten representing the biggest picture, most blue-sky thinking. The driver may be most comfortable operating between seven and ten on the scale, whereas the enabler's preferred territory may fall between four and eight. Neither, however, will get to live exclusively within their ideal range, focusing purely on their natural areas of expertise. Different scenarios and business stages will require both driver and enabler to move up and down the spectrum.

A good analogy here is vocal range. Every singer is most comfortable within a specific part of the musical scale, and no single performer can cover every single note. On the other hand, we can all broaden our range and, in time, become comfortable in areas that previously felt inaccessible. Challenging each individual to explore and expand their range is an important part of a fulfilling career.

In the early days of a new driver/enabler relationship, you may both need to pay considerable attention to the lower end of the scale, overseeing the day-to-day elements of the business. While the enabler will always have their finger on the pulse of daily activities, the driver may need to get involved at a manager level, or even a technician level, on occasion. This is especially true if you're only just entering the scale stage, and still in the process of making the transition from startup mode to a scalable organization.

Equally, it's natural that as the business evolves, both the driver and the enabler will move up the scale, spending a greater portion of their time addressing strategic concerns—where the business is headed over the next one, three, or even five years. The driver will push this process forward and spend more of their time here, but the enabler will also have an essential role to play.

Despite your best efforts, it's important to realize that not every driver/enabler combination is going to work. This is okay. When an important driver/enabler relationship in your business breaks down, the key is to reflect honestly on what didn't work in that particular scenario, so you can build more wisely in the future.

There are two components to this reflection. The first is what we all focus on when a relationship doesn't work: What was it about your partner selection that failed? What incompatibilities or red flags did you ignore when entering into the relationship that you can rethink next time? The second is the type of self-analysis that most people avoid their entire lives: What was it about my behavior and communication style that caused the relationship to fail? This question demands that you reflect only on the components of the breakdown that are your responsibility. Consider all your historic and current relationships and you'll quickly realize there is only *one* common denominator: you. As such, the ability to wrestle with uncomfortable questions about how *you* can improve in relationship with others is an absolutely fundamental aspect of becoming a better leader.

In the table below, you'll see a summary of both the driver's and the enabler's superpowers, along with an explanation of what happens when these powers clash, and what happens when they combine to generate the alchemy that characterizes the best driver/enabler relationships. You can use this table to pinpoint your own strengths and weaknesses, along with those of your key driver/enabler business partners, and to understand what you need to do to elevate the effectiveness of the relationship.

Driver	Enabler	When Not Managed	When Managed Well
Sees the future, obsesses over the dream of the business and what it can become	Makes things happen, obsesses over organizational perfection today	The difference of perspective will be an ongoing source of unhealthy disagreement, stalling the business. If the rubber band stretches too far, it will break.	A synergistic relationship that gives the business a clear vision and strategy, translating to operational performance.
Sees the big picture, loves big problems and big opportunities	High attention to detail, enjoys tinkering with the nuts and bolts	Both will believe that the other, "just doesn't get it." The driver will think the enabler doesn't understand what drives the growth of the business. The enabler will think the driver has no clue about the work required to get things done.	A synergistic relationship that unshackles the driver from the day-to-day details to focus on the big picture, and gives the enabler autonomy to create organizational harmony.
Has many ideas and can be impulsive	Filters ideas and is a good anchoring force	Each will feel that the other wants them to work against the grain of who they are. The driver will err more toward organizational whiplash, and the enabler will dig their heels in and remain stagnant.	Both feel they are working to their strengths. As a result, the company is working toward compelling goals, with adequate resource planning and timelines.
Focuses on the outside	Manages the inside	There is a disconnect between the drive-growth functions and the enable-growth functions of the business. This is a nightmare for the team, the customer, and yes, you guessed it, each other.	The business is driving growth at the rate at which it can enable it. The company is scalable and sustainable.

Empathetic	Rational	The dynamics of the business are disconnected from the mechanics of the business. Feels like organizational psychosis—the business says one thing but does another.	The dynamics and mechanics work together. The company is clear on its intent and operationalizes accordingly. There is strong heart/head alignment.
Impactful leader	Effective manager	The driver underestimates the importance of immediate performance; the enabler neglects the human side of the business. Soon, a good cop/bad cop dynamic will form.	The company has a culture that is inspired toward a compelling future, while achieving performance targets.

DRIVERS NEED ENABLERS, ENABLERS NEED DRIVERS

We trust this chapter has made it very clear that both drivers and enablers are gifted with unique talents, essential to the creation and maintenance of a successful, sustainable company. Whichever direction you lean, you have something vital to contribute. If you're a driver, you possess the vision, enthusiasm, and sheer determination to conjure a company out of thin air—a rare and extraordinary talent. If you're an enabler, you understand what it takes to bring solidity to a fledgling business, making it undeniably real and lasting.

Equally, you now understand that you can't do without your counterpart—or, at least, you'll be making your life much harder than it needs to be if you attempt to go it alone. The person who can successfully straddle the skillsets of both driver and enabler is vanishingly rare. The person who can do so while growing and shaping their business, through the transition from startup to scaleup, is even rarer.

We encourage you to take the content in this chapter and use it to understand your entrepreneurial archetype, then take that knowledge back into your business and apply the strategies you've learned in this chapter to surround yourself with people who complement you. Don't be too quick to dismiss people with whom you don't see eye-to-eye—they may hold a missing piece of the puzzle that lies outside your line of sight. On the other hand, make sure the partnerships you form are productive, not destructive, with everyone ultimately pulling in the same direction.

Before we wrap up, let's take a look at a husband-and-wife team who were beginning to think they were totally incompatible, until they discovered their entrepreneurial archetypes and realized they were perfectly suited.

CASE STUDY: ROBBIE AND TAMMY BREAK THROUGH THEIR GLASS CEILING

Robbie and Tammy are a husband and wife team who run Axon Property Group. When it comes to caring for their business and those they serve, they wear their hearts on their sleeves. Robbie served as a high-ranking officer in the military for twenty-four years, and today he and Tammy run a heart-centered company that helps military veterans to achieve financial freedom through property investment.

Years ago, they kept bumping up against the phenomenon we discussed in the introduction, the Seven-Figure Ceiling; they had done all the right things to reach seven figures, but struggled to grow beyond that mark. Although they were doing around $1 million each year, they, like many businesses that reach that point, couldn't seem to transcend it. "We were wearing all the hats, doing everything ourselves," Robbie would later remark.

They felt stuck. They were investing in training programs, working with several business coaches, and engaging in self-driven learning online, yet nothing they tried seemed to unlock the next stage of growth for them. With every passing month, their plateau was becoming increasingly frustrating, and the frustration was beginning to impact their marriage.

As Robbie explained, "There were no boundaries. There were no lanes we could operate in. Best friends, husband and wife, and then we'd come into the business and we were at loggerheads all the time. We almost didn't even remain together. It got that dire. It got to the point where we were like, 'we really do need some assistance.'"

That was when, in 2018, they attended an exclusive boardroom session we held in Brisbane, Australia, for a limited number of seven-figure business owners. Throughout the session, the lights going on in their eyes were visible, and the breakthroughs they experienced were palpable. One by one, they recognized each of the factors keeping them constricted, how the behaviors that once served them had begun to hold them back, and what they would need to change to unlock the next stage of growth.

They committed to the Elevate program with the intention of working through their blocks and finally breaking through the Seven-Figure Ceiling. Initially, however, there were some bumpy times ahead. When Robbie and Tammy started their Elevate journey, during their first one-on-one strategy session with Jack, Jack could see that years of tension had rendered the partnership fractured. On key questions such as how they thought the business should be run, and how to grow it further, Robbie and Tammy were diametrically opposed.

Prior to the session, Robbie and Tammy had not defined their roles, which meant they both owned everything. Married couple or not, this overlap is enough to strain any partnership. They lacked position descriptions, KPIs, meeting rhythms, and shared communication principles. They didn't yet have a full appreciation of the strengths each person brought to the relationship, or an understanding of one another's weaknesses, and how to complement them. Robbie thought Tammy was trying to slow him down, and Tammy thought Robbie was crazy. Turns out we had found the root cause of Robbie and Tammy's plateau: *Robbie and Tammy.*

As they debated hotly, both tabling their seemingly irreconcilable viewpoints, Jack did the last thing they were expecting him to do—he sat there watching the back-and-forth tennis match with a beaming smile on his face. After a few moments, Robbie and Tamara noticed Jack's delight. This broke their pattern, and they both looked at Jack, confused and intrigued. "Why are you smiling?" Tammy asked, as she burst out laughing.

"This is the perfect partnership," Jack responded. This was the last thing they were expecting to hear, but it was true. Robbie and Tammy were a driver and an enabler who hadn't yet learned the language of their different styles and priorities. Robbie wanted to swing for the fences, and Tammy wanted to move diligently. Robbie wanted to take the lessons from the boardroom session and drive growth through sales, marketing, and building their team. Tammy wanted to take the exact same lessons and use them to develop greater operational rigor and organizational clarity. With exactly the same information at their fingertips, they were in complete disagreement. It was perfect.

Enthused, Jack leaped out of his seat and started sketching the driver/enabler dynamic on the whiteboard, explaining both the challenges and the magic inherent in the relationship. As they began to understand that their fundamental disagreements, if harnessed, could become their greatest strength, Robbie and Tammy's entire energy shifted completely. At one point they both paused, looked at each other, laughed, and simultaneously said, "This is like marriage counseling." They were starting to see how a partnership like this could work, both inside and outside of the business.

As Robbie would later reflect, "What Tamara's really good at in the business, I'm not good at. And what I'm good at isn't her speciality either. The coaching from The Entourage allowed us to understand that it's okay to think differently about the business. I would come in with an idea and Tammy would say, "Why do you think we should do it that way?" and my response would always be, "Why are you being so negative?" I couldn't quite realize she wasn't being negative. She was just being a reality check for what I was trying to do."

Through defining their roles, playing to their strengths, covering the other person's weaknesses, and most of all truly working together as a team, they were able to unlock the next stage of their growth. In this new configuration, Robbie drove the growth, Tammy enabled the growth, and together their differences became their strengths. They captured a synergy they hadn't previously imagined was possible.

When Robbie and Tammy embarked on their Elevate journey, their company employed four staff and had done $960,000 in the preceding twelve months. Over the following twelve months, they achieved $1.5 million. The next year that figure rose to $2.8 million, then $4.3 million, and in their fourth year of the Elevate Program, Robbie and Tammy achieved revenues of $7 million. They have built their team to eighteen people, established a position of market leadership in Australia, and accomplished all this while significantly increasing their profit margin and reducing their stress levels.

The frustration that once kept Robbie and Tammy stuck has transformed into excitement. Reflecting on their journey, Robbie says, "When you've started from nothing and put your own capital and so much energy into the business, [it feels great] to get to a point now where we have certainty about the future of the business and we know the future is going to be good. We have this feeling of excitement about what the next few years are going to hold for us."

Tammy acknowledges the same shift, saying, "We've gone from the business being key-person dependent and Robbie not being able to leave the business or take a holiday, to a point where we can go on an overseas holiday, and our clients are now getting served when we're not even there. It's amazing."

For Robbie and Tammy, the fundamental difference was the shift in their driver/enabler relationship. As she explains, "When your relationship is on track, it ripples out to every other area of your life and business. There's a path ahead, and we're not playing small anymore."

JACK AND TIM WEATHER THE STORM

For most of his career, Jack has deeply appreciated the value of building teams that complement and counter-balance his strengths and weaknesses. Earlier in his career, this meant hiring the right assistant, or bringing on board team members who could help him execute in areas that weren't the highest and best use of his time. For the last decade, it has meant surrounding himself with exceptional leadership and executive teams, general managers, COOs, and CEOs.

Despite this commitment, he knows how challenging it can be to get the driver/enabler dynamic functioning fluidly. As we discussed earlier, the first year will be turbulent even in the best driver/enabler relationships. This is because bringing together a driver and an enabler involves deliberately creating disagreement by design. The key is to move past this stage and reach a point where both driver and enabler can disagree well.

Turbulence certainly raised its head for Jack and Tim during Tim's first year as general manager, reporting directly to Jack. We were two strong personalities, both highly intelligent, with almost-always-opposing views on pretty much everything. Arguments often arose, as Jack had one viewpoint on an issue, Tim had a different viewpoint on the same issue, and we both dug our heels in, defending our perspective in an almighty attempt to be *right*.

Usually, when two people disagree, both parties walk away, giving their egos free rein to justify throwing in the towel and blame the other person. In this instance, both of us refused to do that. Our commitment to the relationship, and our unwavering belief in each other, gave us the resilience to sail through the stormy seas of the first year. Throughout this period, Jack recalls making a conscious choice to reflect on his own behavior rather than decide the relationship wasn't working. He clearly remembers thinking, "Tim has been a great friend and contributor for many years. I know he is highly intelligent, I know he is deeply committed to what we're doing here, and I know he is as trustworthy and high-integrity as they come. If there are areas of friction, I must examine my own thinking, my own behavior, and my own communication, rather than pointing the finger."

This approach was the best thing we could have done, because it bought us *time*. Time to learn and *deeply* appreciate the other's perspective. There's a reason we pinpoint the crucial importance of developing a deep appreciation of one another's perspective—because we've done it ourselves, the hard way. There were times when the tendencies we

describe in that section came to pass. For example, Tim flagged considerations early in the development of a new project, which Jack, in full-on
driver of growth haste, chose to ignore. Further down the road, problems
sometimes arose with these projects, just as Tim predicted. While Tim
never said, "I told you so," when Jack reflected honestly he remembered
Tim had flagged the relevant issues earlier, and it would have been quicker
to take them into consideration at the time.

Similarly, there were times where Jack shared his conviction about a
new direction for the business, and Tim didn't see where Jack was coming
from, or understand the potential benefits. As time passed, and Jack's
vision began to take shape, Tim recognized that Jack's prescient insights
often held real power, and unlocked great value.

These revelations came primarily from staying in the relationship long
enough to develop a deep and genuine appreciation of one another's perspective. Now, when we discuss anything, we are genuinely eager to *truly
hear* the other person's viewpoint, so we can integrate the two to create
much stronger outcomes. If our conversations in that first year sounded
like nails scratching down a classroom blackboard, today they are more
like jazz: improvised exploration, progressing in exciting, unexpected
directions as we build on one another's contributions.

NEXT UP...

Whether you're a driver of growth who has many grand plans for the future,
or an enabler of growth who needs to think forward more often, the end
result is usually the same: the absence of a clear, concise plan that gets
everyone on the same page. While planning in your head and through
conversation may have been fit-for-purpose up until now, it's time to bring
more structure to your plans for the future. This will bring alignment to
the business and propel you toward becoming a much more impactful
leader. In the next chapter we'll uncover why this becomes increasingly
important as your business grows, and how to get you and everyone else
in your business on the same page—literally.

5

CRAFT YOUR ROADMAP

Know Your North Stars

As we covered at the outset of this book, throughout the startup phase of your business, there's no need for a lot of planning. Startup is about execution and iteration; you're making it up as you go along, and at this stage, that's a good thing. You need the flexibility to continually respond to market feedback.

As your business grows, however, strategy becomes increasingly important. The number of moving parts grows, and this becomes an increasingly heavy mental load to carry. As a business owner, you don't have a roadmap until you create one. In the absence of a defined strategy, you expend a lot of energy agonizing over the decisions that need to be made on a daily basis, because you don't have a baseline plan against which to assess each one. This slows you down, causes stress and anguish, and ultimately grinds the business to a halt.

This lack of clarity ultimately permeates your entire team. As your business becomes larger it employs more people, which translates into greater operational complexity. As the founder, you are overseeing the use of significantly more resources. This creates a disconnect. In most scaleups, the founder continues to store whatever plans they create only in their head, communicating them haphazardly whenever an acute need arises. There's no defined plan, only a vision that may be clear in the mind of the founder but is opaque to everyone else on the team.

In the absence of a shared strategy, your people and resources will be running in different directions. You, in turn, will feel as though everyone is grabbing your time and attention, and they just don't seem to be able to problem solve without your constant supervision. As a founder, the way to channel your people and resources toward common objectives is to document where the business is today, where it is headed, and the core initiatives that are going to get you where you're aiming to go. Moving these things out of your head and into a concise format that you can confidently share with others is both highly effective and incredibly cathartic.

When the plans in a founder's head have not been translated into a clear roadmap, every member of your team will have different ideas about what's important, how to make effective decisions, and what to prioritize. This can lead to a nightmare scenario where, as your team grows, every additional person simply adds to the chaos because everyone is pulling against each other.

One of the core differences between a startup and a scaleup is that as your business evolves into a scaleup, you need to add structure to your planning. At any given moment, you should be operating with a defined strategy. This is not to say the business loses its entrepreneurial dynamism, or you can't veer from the plan when circumstances demand. It is simply to say you need to create and maintain north stars that help everyone make the best possible decisions and move in a unified direction. One of the most potent superpowers you can have is to always know your best next step, and to take it with confidence.

GOOD LEADERSHIP REQUIRES STRUCTURE

What is leadership? Simply put, it is the capacity to meet people where they are and take them to where they need to be. Until you determine the destination you plan to reach and the path to get there, you cannot possibly lead effectively. As your business matures, you will need to hone your leadership skills. The Growth Roadmap we describe in this chapter is a crucial tool for doing this, and the most fundamental starting point is asking and answering these three questions:

- **Where are we now?** This is a way to audit the business, using the Six Elements framework to get an objective sense of where it is today.
- **Where are we going?** This question identifies what is possible for the business, and where the future growth potential lies.
- **What are we going to do, and not do, to get there?** Once you understand your current baseline, and your potential for the future, what core initiatives do you need to focus on to get there in the most effective and efficient way?

Establishing the answers to these questions not only enables everyone to get clear on what their core focuses *are*, it also helps everyone understand what their core focuses *are not*. That's why we're introducing you to the Growth Roadmap. In a founder-led company, particularly one headed up by a driver of growth, the tendency will be to always pursue the next shiny thing. A defined and concise roadmap helps remind everyone, *especially* you, what is important and what isn't. This is your key to avoiding the kind of organizational whiplash we discussed in the last chapter.

It's important to understand we're not trying to lock you into the kind of rigid, process-driven monotony that characterizes many large organizations. Some founders balk at the idea of planning, believing it will lock them into a specific course of action. They think of planning as a straitjacket, in opposition to the freedom they currently enjoy—even if this version of freedom comes at the cost of their sanity. It's important, therefore, to be clear that the type of planning we're outlining here is not intended to be constricting and inflexible. We do not build a strategy to set things in stone—plans can and should change. In fact, whenever we are presenting plans to our team, we often precede them by saying, "This is the plan, we are not going to stick to it." Whenever a potential change emerges, it's exceptionally useful to have a concise tool that enables you to assess the situation within an established framework. This removes the guesswork and angst from making adjustments along the way.

This is not to say tht the plan doesn't carry weight; it does. Having a strategy is exceptionally valuable. When an opportunity or challenge presents itself, it gives you a baseline against which to assess it. You're always free to determine if the new opportunity is better than the initial plan. If so, great, make a change. When a new challenge rears its head, making it unwise to continue down your existing path, take a new one. On the other hand, your core roadmap will enable you to honestly and rapidly assess whether the existing plan is superior to the new opportunity. If this is the case, or if you decide the new opportunity will be too distracting, you'll want to stick to your established game plan. The desired outcome is always to bring all your people and resources together to move in one common direction.

There are two reasons why most companies don't have a defined strategy for the future. If you're a driver of growth, you probably believe the organization's strategy is clear; and maybe it is, *in your head*. The problem is no one else really knows about this strategy or, worse, everyone *thinks* they know, but actually each person has developed their own independent version of the plan. Alternatively, if you're an enabler of growth, you probably don't have a clear vision or strategy. You're more focused on deliverables. Whichever situation you find yourself in, whether you're a driver with a plan that no one knows about, or an enabler without a plan, the problem is the same: you lack a shared understanding of a path forward that will unify your team.

In either case, you need a framework that enables you to develop a compelling strategy and to *effectively communicate* that strategy. This will make it possible to create an impactful plan that actively moves your team forward. That tool is what you'll find in this chapter. Your Growth Roadmap is a simple, one-page summary of where your business is right now, where it's going over a defined period of time, and how you're going to get there. Over the coming pages, we're going to explain how you can create your Growth Roadmap and how to use it.

YOUR GROWTH ROADMAP

Most businesses either don't plan at all or immerse themselves in convoluted, impractical planning that adds complexity rather than resolving it. Neither is ideal: a complete lack of a plan breeds obvious hazards, but an overly detailed, academic approach is the enemy of effective planning. It's important to understand we don't plan for planning's sake. We plan to capture the core fundamentals of where we are, where we are going, and how we're going to get there. The more clearly and concisely we can capture these fundamentals, the more memorable and impactful they will be. Everything else is irrelevant. In any written document, one of our core principles at The Entourage is to fight for brevity; we aim to make each document as short as it can possibly be while maximizing its impact.

As we discussed, as an entrepreneur, your worst enemy is a blank piece of paper. When you're asked to create a strategic plan, or *any* other tool for your business, you need a framework to think into. Without one, you may spend years or even decades trying to reinvent the wheel. Models are a key to shortening your development and accelerating your results. That's why developing your Growth Roadmap is a vital first step away from drowning in the day-to-day of the business to having a clear bird's-eye view of what's going on, and what needs to be done to get to where you want to go.

Through developing and refining our planning framework with thousands of high-growth companies, we have fought hard to distill the core fundamentals onto one page. While we also help our seven- and eight-figure members develop a more detailed operational plan, which we'll outline in Chapter Nine: Operations, and a meaningful financial forecast, which we'll cover in Chapter Ten: Finance, every planning exercise *starts* here: with this one-pager. This tool includes everything necessary and nothing more. It's time to create your Growth Roadmap.

3-YEAR NORTH STAR

	CURRENT	3 YEAR
Revenue	_____	_____
NPBT	_____	_____
Team	_____	_____
Hats	_____	_____
Hours p/w	_____	_____

12-MONTH CHALLENGES

1.
2.
3.

12-MONTH OPPORTUNITIES

1.
2.
3.

MARKETING

Current Score: —/10 12 Months' Time: —/10

CURRENT
1. _____
2. _____
3. _____

12-MONTH GOALS
1. _____
2. _____
3. _____

TO-DO's
1. _____
2. _____
3. _____

SALES

Current Score: —/10 12 Months' Time: —/10

CURRENT
1. _____
2. _____
3. _____

12-MONTH GOALS
1. _____
2. _____
3. _____

TO-DO's
1. _____
2. _____
3. _____

PRODUCT

Current Score: —/10 12 Months' Time: —/10

CURRENT
1. _____
2. _____
3. _____

12-MONTH GOALS
1. _____
2. _____
3. _____

TO-DO's
1. _____
2. _____
3. _____

OPERATIONS

Current Score: —/10 12 Months' Time: —/10

CURRENT
1. _____
2. _____
3. _____

12-MONTH GOALS
1. _____
2. _____
3. _____

TO-DO's
1. _____
2. _____
3. _____

FINANCE

Current Score: —/10 12 Months' Time: —/10

CURRENT
1. _____
2. _____
3. _____

12-MONTH GOALS
1. _____
2. _____
3. _____

TO-DO's
1. _____
2. _____
3. _____

PEOPLE

Current Score: —/10 12 Months' Time: —/10

CURRENT
1. _____
2. _____
3. _____

12-MONTH GOALS
1. _____
2. _____
3. _____

TO-DO's
1. _____
2. _____
3. _____

WHAT HATS ARE YOU WEARING?

	CURRENT	12 MONTHS' TIME
ENTREPRENEUR – building the asset	%	%
LEADER – leading the business	%	%
MANAGER – ensuring performance	%	%
TECHNICIAN – hands on the tools	%	%

YOUR QUARTERLY PRIORITIES

Q1	Q2	Q3	Q4

Figure 5.1: Your Growth Roadmap

This is how the Growth Roadmap looks in practice. For the rest of this chapter, we'll take you through each individual section, explaining its purpose and utility.

Three-Year North Stars

This is our starting point. Think about the current state of your company, and ask yourself: What can I envision the business becoming in three years? How much will we have grown? What do I want the team to look like? What role do I want to be playing in three years?

Getting clear on the answers to these questions is crucial because so many founders get stuck operating reactively and forget they actually have the power to *choose*. Even if you've felt trapped for years, the strategies you are reading about in this book, and the resources that accompany it, can put you back in the driver's seat. The first step is to decide: How do I want my life to be? How do I want my business to be? As a rule of thumb, your Three-Year North Stars should both excite you and scare you.

The reason we want you to start three years in the future is to ensure that when you develop a plan for the next twelve months, it aligns with where you're aiming to go over the longer term. We see too many business owners create short-term plans, in pursuit of vanity metrics that are actually in opposition to their long-term goals. By starting at the three-year mark, we can ensure that every subsequent piece of planning lines up to your long-term direction.

Next, let's dive into the different categories, not to simply outline what they are—you already know that, otherwise you wouldn't have built your business to the size it is now—but to discuss how to approach them like a seasoned entrepreneur. For maximum value, we want you to apply a specific lens to each of these areas.

1. **Revenue.** How much revenue did you do over the last twelve months? Implementing the marketing and sales strategies that we'll cover in the next two chapters, how much revenue can you envisage bringing in three years from now? We've heard a lot of

people condemn a focus on revenue as vanity, and often it can be. When approached with a strategic eye, however, revenue numbers can be extremely important. The reason we want you to drive revenue is so you can afford the team and resources required to build a self-managing company. Revenue that is reinvested in building your engine does not translate to immediate profit, but it is very meaningful in securing the future profitability and freedom you seek. Once you have that team and those resources in place, your business will be capable of producing a far greater profit than if you had gone straight to maximizing margin. It's not a question of *revenue versus profit*, it's a matter of generating the revenue you need to build a company that will operate without you *and* deliver significantly more profit.

2. **Net profit before tax (NPBT).** What was your NPBT over the last twelve months? With everything you're going to absorb throughout this book about driving revenue, building highly productive teams, and maximizing operational efficiency, what do you envisage your annual NPBT could be three years from now? We drive revenue to build a great company that can ultimately deliver strong profits. Getting clear about what sort of bottom line your business can achieve is critical in determining how you shape the business.

3. **Team.** How many people are currently on your team? With the scale that you'll be able to achieve over the next three years, how many people do you expect to be on your team three years from now? As your plans evolve, this number may change, but from where you sit right now, what size team do you envision leading in three years' time?

4. **Hats.** Here you define *your* role in terms of the Four Hats we described in Chapter Two: technician, manager, leader, and entrepreneur. As we've discussed in previous chapters, most business owners spend their entire careers wearing the hats of technician and manager, forever limiting both the growth of

their business and their personal freedom. The primary reason for this stagnation is they are simply unaware of the Four Hats concept. They never make a distinction between being a technician doing the work, and becoming an entrepreneur building a business that does the work.

First, write down which hats you are most often wearing right now. Then, assume that over the next three years, you will successfully drive revenue, increase profit, and build the team you desire. At *that point*, what hats do you want to be wearing? Many founders want to spend the vast majority of their time in the roles of leader and entrepreneur. If you love the practical elements of business, you may even want to include some time spent in the technician role. The key distinction is even if you *love* wearing the hat of technician, your goal is to take the business to a point where you are doing so because you want to, not because you *have* to. Further down the roadmap we'll go into more detail about this concept. For now, simply capture what hats you are wearing, and what hats you want to be wearing in three years' time.

5. **Hours per week.** This is a very important and overlooked section. As we've discussed in previous chapters, if your business is still operating like a startup, it will feel all-consuming. Founders of chaotic businesses often tell us they're trapped, drowning in the unceasing demands of the monster they've created. The first step to taking back control of your time is to identify how many hours you would eventually *like* to spend in and on the business. Right now, how many hours per week do you spend working in and on the business? Now, fast-forward three years. Let's assume you've built a self-managing company that gives you *choice*; how many hours would you love to spend in and on your business each week? It's important to understand there is no right or wrong answer here. Some people *love* working sixty-or seventy-hour weeks, while others build their company to operate with only

one hour a week of input from them. Remember, this is about *choice*. So the only question is, what do *you* want?

Challenges

Right now there are inevitably challenges holding you back. You may have been carrying some of them for months or even years. To unlock your next stage of growth, you need to start by identifying the core challenges that are holding you back. In business, clearly identifying the problem is the most important step in arriving at the optimal solution.

Take a second to think and feel into this question: what are my three biggest problems right now, that if resolved would make the largest difference to my life and business? Then, write them down.

Opportunities

When you dream about what your business could become, what opportunities would you love to seize if only you had the time, expertise, and resources? Narrow these down to the three biggest opportunities you could capitalize on in the next twelve months, with the potential to make the biggest impact to your life and business. Add them to the roadmap.

Auditing the Six Elements of Your Business

As we've discussed, to be both scalable and sustainable, great entrepreneurs build companies that are cross-functional across all Six Elements. To do this, you need to get very clear about your current position in each of the Six Elements, identify where you want to be, and focus on the core decisions or actions that will get you there.

To do this, score each element's current state out of ten, and then give each element a score out of ten based on where you would like it to be in twelve months' time.

When you've done this, list three characteristics that best describe what's happening in that element of your business right now. For example, these might be words like:

- Nonexistent
- Reactive
- Manual
- Declining
- A black hole
- Messy
- Strong
- Improving

Next, outline the three characteristics you'd like to describe that element twelve months from now. For example:

- Streamlined
- Profitable
- Fully developed team

The words themselves are less important than choosing terms that capture what is most important to you.

Finally, the three to-dos at the bottom of each element represent core actions you can take in the next seven days to begin moving in your desired direction. These to-dos can be as big or as small as you'd like. The key is not how large they are, only that they get you started.

What Hats Are You Wearing?

This section of your roadmap is where you take the information about which hats you're wearing—and which you want to wear—from your Three-Year North Stars, get more specific in terms of current percentages, and work out exactly how you want to spend your time twelve months from now.

The first step toward elevating from technician to entrepreneur is auditing how you're currently spending your time, and how you *want* to be spending your time twelve months from now. In the Four Hats section of your roadmap, write the approximate percentage of time you are currently spending wearing each hat, and then set a goal defining how you'd like to spend your time twelve months from now.

Your Quarterly Priorities

Once you have completed every other aspect of your roadmap, the final step is to translate the company's most important priorities into quarterly objectives that define which initiatives you will take on and when. Most businesses make the mistake not of doing too little, but of attempting to do too much—they spread themselves too thin and nothing gets finished. Effective planning and clarifying your priorities is about learning how to hone your focus. This is less about determining what to say yes to, and more about understanding when you should be saying no.

We suggest selecting no more than three large, structural projects per quarter. Depending on the size of the project, some projects should be scheduled across more than one quarter. Quarterly projects could include:

- Develop a content marketing engine (one quarter)
- Build and optimize an end-to-end marketing funnel (one quarter)
- Enhance the operational rigor of the sales function (one quarter)
- Build out the sales team (two quarters)
- Automate and delegate product delivery (two quarters)
- Implement and optimize a CRM across the company (one quarter)
- Develop an accurate and meaningful financial forecast (one quarter)
- Write a culture handbook that explains our vision, mission, and values (one quarter)

USING YOUR GROWTH ROADMAP

The best way to develop your growth roadmap is to download it and start using it. You can find your free copy at www.the-entourage.com/elevate, and we suggest you go ahead and do so while it's fresh in your mind. Not only will it help you clarify the direction of your company—and your role within it—it will also provide you with a valuable reference point as you read through the next part of this book.

That said, we understand you may be feeling a little overwhelmed right now. If so, that's absolutely normal. We've covered a lot of concepts in the first part of this book, and it can take some time for them to fully permeate your consciousness. Probably what you've read over the past five chapters has helped you see your previous blind spots, and your head is still spinning as you figure out how to implement everything you've learned. In the next part of the book, we'll dive deeply into each one of the Six Elements, providing you with specific tools you can apply in each area of your business. If you'd like some support, however, the best way to develop your growth roadmap is with a business coach who has been there and done that.

Guiding business owners through this roadmap is the very first thing we do with all our Elevate members, and it's an immensely helpful tool for taking founders from that depressing stuck state to a feeling of empowerment. To speed up your transition, we'd love to offer you a complimentary Elevate Business Growth session, where you can work with one of our entrepreneur development managers to apply the Growth Roadmap to you and your business, to give you confidence and clarity in your next move.

This session will help you take the strategies that have resonated with you from this book and begin applying them in your life and business. We will audit your business through the Growth Roadmap tool, identifying where the business is today, the potential it has for the future, and the core initiatives that will enable you to get there.

Right now, you are carrying challenges in your business that are keeping you stuck, and opportunities for growth that you aren't in a position to fully realize. That's inevitable, and it's why you picked up this book. As we said at the outset of this book, we are here not just to teach you, but to help you *implement*. The right strategic guidance will take your roadblocks and turn them into roadmaps, outlining exactly how to get unstuck and to capitalize on the inevitable opportunities for expansion.

To take a profound journey into the Six Elements of your business, keep reading. If you'd like to go ahead and book your complimentary, one-on-one Elevate Business Growth Session, head to www.the-entourage .com/elevate-session.

CASE STUDY: JOHN CAN COUNT ONE MILLION REASONS TO DEVELOP STRATEGY

John's business is as unique as they come; his vision is to transform the way people experience remote Australia. He enables travelers to land in the heart of outback Australia through his suite of private aircraft, giving them a unique luxury experience. The business was founded in 1977 by John's father, Rod, and when John took over the reins, he wanted to accelerate the growth of the business and build out the team so it wasn't reliant on the family to run it. When John started his Elevate journey, however, his business was doing reasonably well, but not growing at the rate he wanted. He didn't know what to do to drive the next stage of growth.

As a family business, John's company had never had a defined strategy. Operationally speaking, this meant processes remained manual and underdeveloped. John and his team made decisions by gut feel, which slowed down the decision-making process. John knew that addressing this challenge would start with gaining clarity over the company's strategy. "Before we joined The Entourage, we were ticking along okay, but we were making decisions slowly and growing slowly," John explained. "We weren't very strategic, and blissfully ignorant of a lot of the deficiencies within our business."

Like most business owners, John didn't understand the Six Elements or the Four Hats. Like his father before him, he unknowingly spent most of his time wearing the hats of technician and manager, focused on product delivery. As a result, the other elements of the business were stagnating. "I was very product focused," he told us, "but in terms of sales and marketing, we were Australia's best kept secret. Our digital marketing strategies were deficient, and we were surviving on repeat business and word of mouth, which is not sustainable. Although we knew sales inside out, we didn't have a sales process."

For John, like all our Elevate members, using his Growth Roadmap to develop his strategy was as much about asking the right questions and gaining clarity as it was about creating an end product he could share with his team. After defining the north stars that lit the path he wanted to travel, auditing each of the Six Elements, examining what hats he wanted to wear, and defining the core projects he wished to address each quarter, John went from feeling like he was flying blind, to feeling like he was finally in control.

"From a personal point of view I was on autopilot and The Entourage flicked the switch for me. It let me know that in my life, I'm in the driver's seat. Now I've got both the tools and the confidence to create the life I'm looking for."

This feeling of clarity has empowered John to grow into the business leader he always wanted to be, making an immediate impact on the company's performance.

"Since joining Elevate we've increased our revenue by over a million dollars. We've doubled the size of our team and all our people have bought into our vision of transforming the way people experience remote Australia. In practical terms, we've also built an eight-step sales system that's functioning really well."

Perhaps the most important benefit for John was that leveraging the clarity that came from getting clear on his strategy, he could develop each element of the business in a scalable way. No longer does he carry forward the family-business legacy of doing everything manually. Instead, the business is built strategically with a clear structure in mind.

"It's given us confidence and clarity. We've learned how to bottle and replicate our magic, and that's what makes us scalable."

JACK AND TIM DISCOVER THE IMPORTANCE OF A ROADMAP

At The Entourage, we created this tool out of necessity. Even after we developed a three-year strategy, operational plans, objectives, key results, and scoreboards, members of our team still expressed confusion about what was and wasn't important. The problem wasn't an absence of strategy and planning. The problem was that our plans were *so comprehensive* that no team member could digest them all.

Strategy and planning are useful only to the degree that they help teams to make better decisions, aligned with the company's unified direction. Our planning hasn't achieved that yet. We needed a method of getting everyone on the same page. We needed to consolidate our plans so we could communicate them succinctly, in a way people could remember in their day-to-day. We realized too much detail was causing people to get lost. The best plans need to capture the fundamental concepts with the flexibility to cascade into more detailed plans for different departments where required.

Once we developed, adopted, and refined the Growth Roadmap, we noticed a distinct shift in our team's understanding of where we were going. More importantly, we witnessed a lot more *buy-in*. When people understood the plans, they oriented their behavior toward executing on those plans. Perhaps the most important lesson we've gleaned from decades of strategizing at a small- to medium-sized business level is: *people cannot buy in to that which they do not understand.*

After experiencing the power of brevity firsthand, we took this tool and made it the starting point for every new member as they began their Elevate journey. When we coach members through this process, they are forced to ask the questions and have the conversations that bring them clarity and align them to a unified direction. Our members love this process because the insights it captures are brief enough to fit on one page, but the information it contains is still broad enough to ensure they are thinking about their business across all Six Elements.

Keep your plans concise. Capture the most important concepts. And then allow the detail to cascade out from there as needed. This approach gets teams on the same page.

NEXT UP...

In Part I of this book, we've covered the fundamental paradigms that capture the approach of the world's most successful entrepreneurs: transitioning from a reactive startup to a scalable company, elevating from technician to entrepreneur, building a company that functions across each of the Six Elements, understanding your zone of genius and how to build a synergistic team, and capturing your direction in a clear and compelling way that enables you to truly *lead*.

In Part II, we outline in depth how to drive the growth of your business through building a marketing engine, developing a replicable sales process, and delighting your customers. After reading the case studies in Part I, we anticipate that you're inspired to accelerate growth in a way that enables you to make more money while working less. Part II covers exactly that.

PART II

THE DRIVE GROWTH CYCLE

E verything in the next three chapters of the book is about activities that will allow you to drive the growth of your business. These are the activities that bring in new clients and serve those clients with products that light up their lives.

Every company that scales does so by driving growth, and the three elements in this section—marketing, sales, and product—feed each other, creating a self-reinforcing cycle. The reason we codified this relationship into what we call the Drive Growth Cycle is because we wanted to illustrate the connections between these areas of the business, and the way that elevating all of them has a compounding impact.

When you execute every element of the Drive Growth Cycle well, you will create an upward spiral of growth in your organization, as your marketing feeds your sales, which feeds your product, which once again feeds your marketing.

Depending on your natural inclination, you may resonate immediately with the concepts in this section or find them a little more challenging. If you're a drive-growth-focused entrepreneur, you'll quickly be at ease in this realm and eat up the strategies you'll find here. If you're an enable-growth-focused entrepreneur, you'll probably need to make a conscious effort to lean into these elements—or find support from drive-growth-focused team members—to turbocharge the growth of your business.

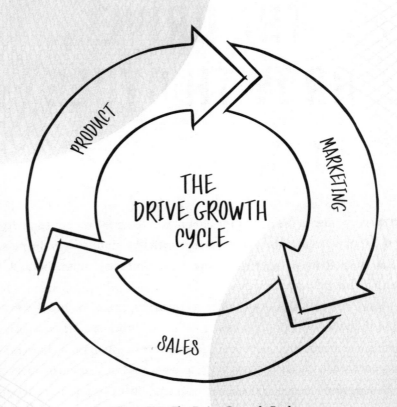

Figure D.1: The Drive Growth Cycle

6

MARKETING

Construct a Marketing Engine to Generate Leads

Without marketing, the growth of your business is seriously limited. Your marketing is the tool that generates the leads you will convert to sales, building your customer base.

And yet, many business owners significantly undervalue marketing. Most businesses market reactively, on an ad-hoc basis, or—even worse—not at all. If you lack a unifying strategy to systematically win more customers, it's likely that you scramble to work on your marketing only when you desperately need more leads. After these short spikes of effective but unpredictable marketing activity, you settle back into product delivery mode. Most of the time, marketing sits on a shelf gathering dust until you need it again. This often results in a plateau that translates into extended periods of low or no growth.

Like many other aspects of your business, your unstructured approach to marketing is likely the legacy of habits developed during the startup stage. When your business was smaller, you needed fewer customers to get by. Those early customers often discovered you through word of mouth. Marketing was a tactical play, not a strategic one. Whenever you ran out of customers, you relied on your grit and determination to bring new prospects through the door. You probably thought of marketing as a necessary expense, a pill you had to swallow when customer numbers were running low.

If so, you're not alone. Too many business owners think of marketing as an activity that *takes* time and money, rather than one that *gives* time and money. This is a damaging myth that keeps startup-stage businesses from graduating into the scaleup phase, and is only true when your marketing is poorly planned and executed. If you lack strategy and employ inconsistent, sporadic marketing activities, they will not generate the quality and quantity of leads you need. Even if a disjointed marketing campaign accidentally performs well, it will be hard to measure and fully quantify the return on investment (ROI).

This haphazard approach with fragmented bursts of activity and unreliable ROI, leads many founders to throw the marketing baby out with the bathwater. They see the poor performance of their marketing campaigns and perceive marketing as an expense, failing to realize that executed effectively, it could become their company's most important profit center.

WHY MARKETING MATTERS SO MUCH

All growth is sales and marketing-led. If your growth has plateaued, or even if it has just been slower than you would like, it is a signal that you have not placed enough importance on your marketing function. Amateur marketers think in terms of tactics. Professional marketers think in terms of campaigns. As an entrepreneur, you need to think of your marketing not in terms of a tactic you turn to when revenues are dwindling, but in terms of developing an engine that can consistently achieve targets without your operational involvement.

In this chapter, we'll share the core strategies you need to put in place to create a marketing function that systematically builds your brand, grows your audience, and generates the right quantity and quality of leads to drive the growth of your business. When you approach marketing strategically, you can test, measure, and optimize each stage of the process, until it's ROI positive. We'll discuss the three stages of marketing that make this possible: **attract**, **convert**, and **nurture**.

We'll also outline how to construct a marketing engine in a way that puts these stages together, and explain how to integrate the key operational components—strategy, team, metrics, and tech—into your business.

The ultimate goal is to build an engine that brings you a consistent ROI on your marketing efforts. Once you know that every dollar you spend on marketing returns three to four dollars to the business, you will have created a *self-liquidating marketing funnel* that pays for itself. When you can triple or quadruple your return on every marketing dollar spent, your marketing budget essentially becomes infinite. This is how you become an industry leader.

No longer will you need to view marketing as an expense. Instead it will become a proven profit center. That's what this chapter will unlock for you.

THE THREE STAGES OF MARKETING

First, let's discuss the three stages of any marketing campaign: **attract**, **convert**, and **nurture**. Together, these three stages form the strategic foundation you'll use later in this chapter to implement a comprehensive marketing engine, which runs smoothly without you.

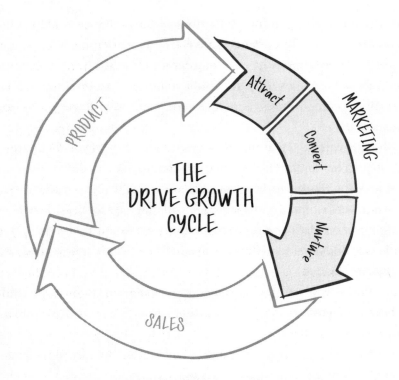

Figure 6.1: Marketing Components of the Drive Growth Cycle

Stage One: Attract

The first stage of marketing is to attract your audience. In the age of the internet, this is essential. In an online world, the scales have tipped. Marketing power no longer resides with those who have the most money. Instead, it rests with those who can add the most value to their market-place and therefore build an audience they own.

The era of *interruption marketing*, which often sounded like, "Stop! Listen to me! Buy from me!" has given way to *relationship-based marketing*, which is value-led and *nurtures* people into making thoughtful buying decisions. We stopped talking *at* the audience and started talking *with* the audience.

A few decades ago, there were four primary ways to get a marketing message in front of people: TV, print, radio, and outdoor media such as billboards. Large media companies owned the audience, and business owners rented people's attention for short bursts of time, at exorbitant cost, by paying for that real estate. In terms of budget, most small business owners couldn't hope to compete with large corporations. On the battleground of consumer attention, whoever dropped the most advertising dollars would win. This meant regardless of a product's quality, companies with bigger budgets grew and dominated the market, creating an uneven playing field.

When the internet came along and changed the business world, small business owners could suddenly speak to people at scale, without intermediaries or centralized owners claiming a monopoly on eyeballs. With businesses finally able to speak directly to their audience, the game shifted. Marketing was no longer about who had the most money, but about who could add the most value. Companies became more visible and accessible. If a brand shared something that resonated with their market, prospective customers could like posts, comment, share content with their network, and subscribe to channels, meaning that connecting directly with consumers was more important than ever. Instead of renting an audience, businesses were freed to build their own, engaged audience, made up of people who had expressed genuine interest in their brand. As a result, the entire marketing and communication landscape changed dramatically.

Today, the challenge and the opportunity for marketers and business owners is to build a relationship with their audience at scale. As an entrepreneur, the number one asset you own is the relationship you've built with an audience that recognizes, values, and trusts you and your business. In the internet age, relationships, more than money, crown industry leaders.

And there is such a large audience to build. Research by Global WebIndex indicates as of January 2022, 4.26 billion people, or 58.4 percent of the world's population, use social media.[1] Exclude kids under thirteen

---

[1] Dave Chaffey, "Global social media statistics research summary 2022," *Smart Insights*, Aug 22, 2022, https://www.smartinsights.com/social-media-marketing/social-media-strategy/new-global-social-media-research/.

and that represents 75 percent of the populace. Average daily usage clocks in at 2 hours and 27 minutes, a significant chunk of our waking hours. And the numbers continue to grow. In 2021, 424 million new users came online. Today, people spend more time on social media than any other media, including television. As an entrepreneur, this is good news for you. The internet, particularly social media, has evened the playing field by allowing you to connect directly and regularly with your audience.

How can you leverage this vast potential audience? The fundamental principle of building a relationship with your audience at scale is *recency and frequency*. When a consumer is ready to make a buying decision, the company that has added value to them most *recently*, and most *frequently*, tends to be top of mind. This same concept highlights your key to becoming an industry leader; add more value to your market than anyone else. Make your free stuff better than your competitors' paid stuff, and you'll become the most trusted go-to brand in your space.

Building a relationship with your audience not only expands your brand and magnifies your impact, but it also makes financial sense. Marketing to an audience of people who recognize your brand significantly increases your conversion rates and average dollar spent per sale. In simple terms, when you're visible and recognizable, more people buy from you, and when they do, they spend more. When consumers follow a brand on social media, 89 percent say they will buy from that brand, 84 percent say they will choose that brand over a competitor, and 75 percent say they will increase their spending with that brand.[2] When searching for a product or service in Google, 82 percent of searchers choose a familiar brand for their first click.[3] To demonstrate this tendency, let's look at The Entourage. Our marketing converts at a rate seventeen times higher with our social media followers than with a cold audience who doesn't know us,

[2] "Sprout Social Index," *Sprout Social*, accessed Nov 28, 2022, https://media.sproutsocial.com /uploads/2020-Sprout-Social-Index-Above-and-Beyond.pdf.

[3] Rebecca Sentance, "82 percent of searchers choose a familiar brand for the first click," *Econsultancy*, Oct 29, 2018, https://econsultancy.com/82-percent-searchers-choose -familiar-brand-search/.

which *significantly* reduces our cost per acquisition (CPA). In summary, by building an audience, we reach more people for less money.

You may wonder how to consistently add value to your market without being spammy, pushy, or sales-y. The answer lies in developing and distributing content that speaks directly to your customers' hearts and minds.

The Four Forces Model

Great brands stand for something. If you're drinking a Red Bull, you're an adrenaline junkie, but if you're walking down the street holding a Boost Juice, you're youthful. If you're riding a Harley Davidson, you're tough, but if you're behind the wheel of a Mercedes, you're successful. Great brands hold a place in our hearts and minds that transcends the products and services they offer: they *stand* for something, and they say something about *who we are* when we use them.

One of the most common mistakes we see businesses make with their marketing and content strategy is engaging in a rational, one-dimensional conversation that is overly product focused. The fastest way to be dismissed as a commodity is to speak mostly about your product, its features, and why you believe customers should want it. You don't want to be a commodity—commodities get discarded; you want to be a consumer champion.

At The Entourage, we use the Four Forces Model to coach our members on how to tap into the hearts and minds of their audience. And when we recommend speaking to the hearts and minds of your audience, we're not being poetic. We're being literal. You *must* go beyond talking about your product to talking about your prospect. Once you understand the four forces that shape and drive all consumer behavior, you can create compelling content, powerful messaging, and marketing that truly moves people.

Everything we do as human beings is motivated by these four forces:

1. **Away from Motivators:** Humans avoid pain—physical, mental, or emotional pain or discomfort, now or in the future.

2. **Toward Motivators:** Humans move toward pleasure—physical, mental, or emotional pleasure, now or in the future.

3. **Emotional Drivers (Heart):** Humans make decisions based primarily on emotion—how something makes us feel.

4. **Rational Drivers (Head):** Humans justify these decisions afterward—based on reason and logic.

Everything in your life, macro or micro, is a result of these four forces, from what time you set your alarm this morning (or if you chose not to set an alarm), to what you had for breakfast, and the clothes you're wearing right now. Your reasons for reading this book or building your business, where you live, and how you spend your time, and who you've chosen as your life partner (or if you've chosen to remain single) can all be traced back to these fundamental four forces.

The crucial insight here is that the same is true for your customer.

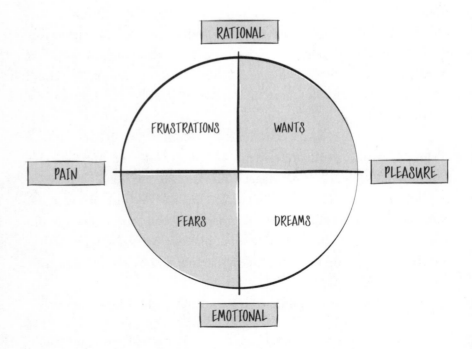

Figure 6.2: The Four Forces Model

When you realize this, you have the key to speaking to your audience. What are their frustrations, fears, wants, and dreams? How does your brand help alleviate or fulfill those drivers? How the four forces impact your customers, and how your brand can help them, should inform your messaging throughout your marketing and sales journey. Your business is not here to sell products. Your purpose is to help your customers go from their undesired current state to their desired future state. It is not about your product; it's about your prospect.

If this feels overwhelming, it needn't be. Since 2010, we have helped tens of thousands of brands produce world-class content that truly reaches and moves their audience. Over a decade of experience, we've refined our content creation methodology into one central framework called the Content Blueprint.

The Content Blueprint

The Content Blueprint enables you to become the most visible brand in your industry. Content is just a different word for digital communication, so in effect the Content Blueprint is a framework for communicating digitally. This formula enables you to communicate with your market in a highly effective and efficient way. Your communication is the foundation for building your relationship with your market.

A key feature of the Content Blueprint is the deployment of a multi-channel approach. When prospects see your content and marketing messages on numerous channels, it creates a multiplier effect, building greater top-of-mind awareness, brand recognition, and ultimately lead generation.

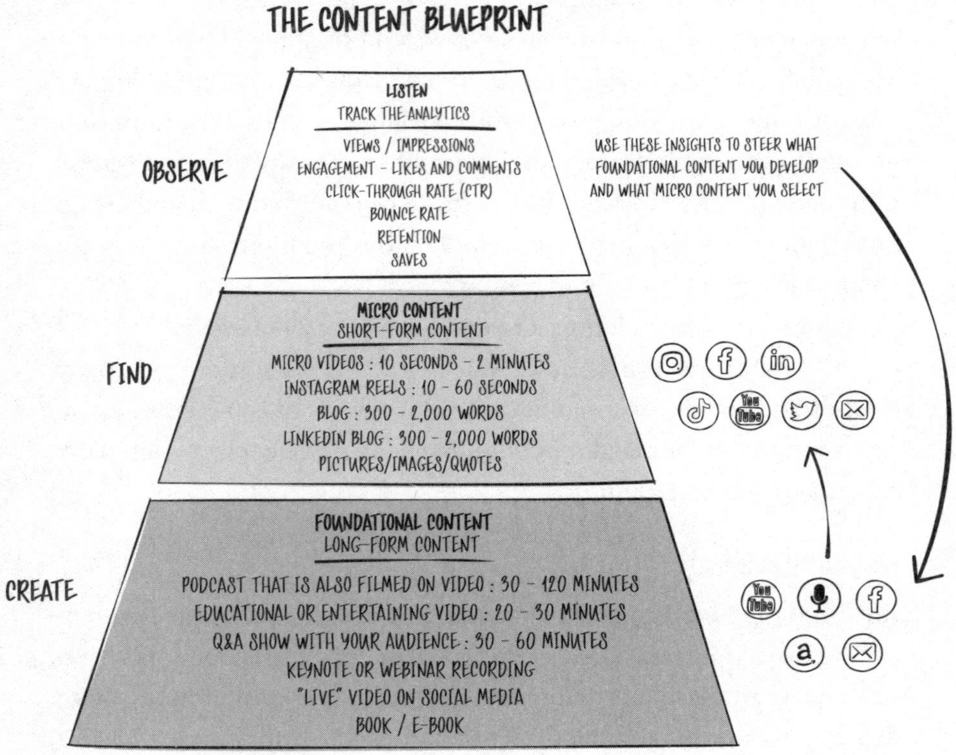

THE CONTENT BLUEPRINT

OBSERVE

LISTEN
TRACK THE ANALYTICS

VIEWS / IMPRESSIONS
ENGAGEMENT - LIKES AND COMMENTS
CLICK-THROUGH RATE (CTR)
BOUNCE RATE
RETENTION
SAVES

USE THESE INSIGHTS TO STEER WHAT
FOUNDATIONAL CONTENT YOU DEVELOP
AND WHAT MICRO CONTENT YOU SELECT

FIND

MICRO CONTENT
SHORT-FORM CONTENT

MICRO VIDEOS : 10 SECONDS - 2 MINUTES
INSTAGRAM REELS : 10 - 60 SECONDS
BLOG : 300 - 2,000 WORDS
LINKEDIN BLOG : 300 - 2,000 WORDS
PICTURES/IMAGES/QUOTES

CREATE

FOUNDATIONAL CONTENT
LONG-FORM CONTENT

PODCAST THAT IS ALSO FILMED ON VIDEO : 30 - 120 MINUTES
EDUCATIONAL OR ENTERTAINING VIDEO : 20 - 30 MINUTES
Q&A SHOW WITH YOUR AUDIENCE : 30 - 60 MINUTES
KEYNOTE OR WEBINAR RECORDING
"LIVE" VIDEO ON SOCIAL MEDIA
BOOK / E-BOOK

Figure 6.3: The Content Blueprint

The Content Blueprint gives you tremendous leverage. Once you've built out your marketing team, you'll reach the point where you can allocate one day every two weeks to shoot three pieces of foundational content. As we'll break down shortly, each one of those pieces translates into 170 pieces of content, giving you 510 pieces of content every two weeks, or more than a thousand per month. At this point, you'll be adding more value to your market than anyone else, which puts you on a path to becoming the industry leader.

Initially, however, you may need to roll up your sleeves and do more of the content production yourself. Our members often ask: *When I'm producing content, am I wearing the hat of technician or entrepreneur?* If you're doing all the ancillary content tasks: filming, editing, identifying micro pieces, posting on different platforms, writing and sending content emails, and creating ads to reach more people, you're wearing the technician or manager hat. When you're in front of the camera, not behind it, *presenting* content, you're wearing the entrepreneur hat, because you're building the brand and increasing the value of your asset.

Although you may need to wear the hat of technician or manager when creating content at first, your ultimate objective is to wear the entrepreneur hat and deliver foundational content to your team, who will follow the Content Blueprint to take care of the rest. Foundational content is a long-form piece of content delivered by you, which your team turns into many different, smaller pieces of content to use across platforms. As we said, this gives you significant leverage, because recording just one sixty-minute podcast can generate 170 pieces of content. Here's an example to illustrate the power of the Content Blueprint.

Start with foundational content, such as a sixty-minute video of a podcast. Then, use the Content Blueprint to upcycle these sixty minutes into a wide variety of smaller pieces for different platforms. For example:

- **Ten Micro Videos.** Pick the ten best one-to-three-minute moments from the foundational piece. Post these videos on Youtube, LinkedIn, Instagram, Facebook, TikTok, and Twitter. **Sixty pieces of content.**
- **Ten Reels.** Pick the ten best sixty-second or less moments from the foundational piece. Add text, color, emojis, and music to make each reel more fun and engaging. Post the reels to Instagram and Youtube Shorts. **Twenty pieces of content.**
- **Five Blogs.** Pull out the foundational piece's five core paradigm shifts and turn each of them into a blog post. Post them to the blog on your website and LinkedIn. **Ten pieces of content.**
- **Twenty Tweets.** Take the twenty best quotes from the foundational piece and turn them into tweets. **Twenty pieces of content.**

- **Twenty Quote Tiles.** Take the same twenty quotes and turn them into designed quote tiles. If you don't have a designer, just screenshot your tweet. Post these tiles to Instagram and Facebook. **Forty pieces of content.**
- **Five Photos from the Podcast.** Get creative and have fun with this one. These pictures could include a hero picture of you shooting the podcast, a couple of images from behind-the-scenes or preparations, a photo of you with your guest or team, and an image of you having fun on set that humanizes you. Post the photos to Instagram, LinkedIn, Facebook, and Twitter. **Twenty pieces of content.**

When repurposing the same content for different platforms, amend the format, design, and copy to match the style of the environment. When posting to LinkedIn, for example, your copy and design should be professional. On Instagram, your content must be visually appealing and aesthetically pleasing. When posting to TikTok, you can be more playful and shouldn't take yourself too seriously. Creating native content means considering each platform's nuanced feel and audience, so your content will resonate deeply, spur engagement, and increase your reach and audience size.

Another strategy we have always used at The Entourage to attract an audience at scale and fuel our Content Blueprint, is public relations (PR)—aka getting noticed in the media. This is a potent addition to any marketing engine with benefits that multiply threefold. First, you get in front of a much wider and larger audience than if you focus solely on social media. Second, those who find you through the media will instantly accord you a prominent position in their hearts and minds. And third, being publicized in the media does wonders for your brand, instilling trust and confidence in prospects who may be considering whether to buy from you. Like all marketing activities, the value of PR is in how you leverage it. Each time you are featured in the media, share this with your audience, pushing the coverage through your Content Blueprint.

Once you're consistently building your audience at the top of your marketing funnel, the next step is to ensure you're converting this audience onto land that you own. Let's dive into stage two of our marketing process: *convert*.

Stage Two: Convert

Many business owners tell us, "We tried social media, but it didn't convert to sales." You must remember there is a huge chasm to cross before your social media followers will be ready to buy from you. Following you on social media will absolutely lower buyer resistance and increase buyer acceptance, but it's not sufficient on its own. Although social media followers are *more likely* to buy from you, you still need a solid process to move people from content consumers to paid customers. Therefore, the next step in the journey is not to sell to your audience, but to *convert* those followers who are most interested into hot leads.

Many business owners get impatient at this point and try to move people through the buyer's journey too quickly. They end up selling to prospects before there is a need. That's a mistake. Asking your prospect to get married on the first date is not attractive. Let them fall in love with you first. Right now, a large portion of your entire addressable market isn't ready to buy yet. If your marketing messages only cater to those ready to buy right now, you're cutting off the vast majority of your market.

There will be a few prospects eager to buy immediately—those who want to jump the queue and go straight from following you on Facebook to buying your product or booking a sales conversation, and you never want to discourage this. Later in this chapter, we'll talk about our express lane for accelerating these kinds of hot leads. For now, however, let's discuss how to move your audience from platforms you *don't* control onto land you own, and—in the process—turn them from followers into *leads*. Your job as a marketer is not to get prospects to buy. It's simply to get them to take the next step in the funnel. To do this, your marketing funnel must systematically move your prospects through a series of steps, each one moving them closer to making a final buying decision. At each stage of the journey, you must propose a compelling offer that makes it easy for them to take that next step.

Once someone is following you online and digesting your content, the best next step toward turning them into a lead is capturing their details through a free opt-in offer. By opting in, your prospect shares their information, most commonly their name and email address, but sometimes also a phone number and mailing address. By opting in to receive communication from you, a prospect extends a powerful privilege to you; *permission* to continue interacting with them through their direct channels. You can now achieve *recency and frequency* not only through social media, but also through email, text, mail, and phone calls.

When your prospects opt-in, you can strengthen your relationship further through personal, direct channels, on land you own. While social media is the most powerful platform in human history for building relationships and marketing to a large audience, it's wise to remember that you're on rented land. Facebook, Instagram, and Google can and do change their algorithms with little or no notice, which often moves the goalposts and alters the rules for succeeding on those platforms.

The best way to harness the unprecedented power of social media while reducing the risk of disruption from any changes is to develop audience relationships *both* on social media and land you own. Once you have an email, phone number, or mailing address, the relationship is in your hands, and your prospect is one step closer to becoming a paid customer. You can communicate with them directly without an intermediary. This is how you achieve the best of both worlds.

What should you do to persuade people to give you their direct contact details? One key to remember is, when designing opt-ins for your business, don't ask people to sign up for your newsletter. Nobody woke up this morning eager to subscribe to more newsletters. Most people are highly selective when sharing their contact details, so your offers at each stage of the marketing funnel must be both relevant and compelling for your avatar.

The best approach is to offer an attractive lead magnet—a free offer at the top of the marketing funnel, which you give the prospect in exchange for their details. A lead magnet solves a specific problem for a specific market, enticing prospects to opt in. This free content might be a webinar, event, e-book, style guide, video series, swipe files for download and use, checklist, cheat sheet, training program, or a fourteen-day free trial. In short, any piece of high-value content that you give away in exchange for nothing more than a name and email address is a lead magnet. This is how you turn members of your audience from followers into warm leads who have expressed interest in progressing through your funnel.

It's totally okay for a lead magnet to encourage your prospect to sign up to receive your emails, as long as you avoid the term newsletter and can name three tangible benefits for opting in. For example, your lead magnet copy could say, "Join the movement/community/club. Get instant savings, join a community of thousands of others just like you, and be the first to receive exclusive strategies on how to [insert desired results here]." Provided your offer is free and adds value, it's considered a lead magnet.

Most businesses should never try to sell something directly on social media, unless they are retargeting someone who has already become a lead in the past. Rather than selling on social media, you should simply publish content that adds value, occasionally offering a free lead magnet you know members of your audience are interested in. Once someone opts into a lead magnet, you have permission to progress the relationship. With this approach, you are constantly *giving* in public, and *selling* in private. This strategy will enable you to build an abundance of brand equity with your audience and achieve much higher conversions through your funnel.

Once your prospect claims their lead magnet, they are officially a lead. They are also part of your email subscription community, and you have permission to continue nurturing the relationship.

Stage Three: Nurture

Most businesses unknowingly sit on an untapped gold mine. They own a database of email addresses from people who have opted in, yet they are not consistently communicating with these prospects. Out of your entire addressable market, no one is closer to buying than those who have opted in. These prospects have recognized a need, expressed interest, and taken the first step toward building a relationship with you. Developing a way to systematically nurture these relationships by adding value is one of the most immediate levers you can pull to increase profit.

If you build an audience and offer lead magnets without setting up an ongoing nurture sequence, you're missing an opportunity. No matter how engaged your audience, and how strong those lead magnets, they will only translate into sales when you craft an ongoing nurture sequence to move them toward a buying decision.

At The Entourage, we teach five core principles for developing a highly effective nurture sequence. All five factors are essential pieces of a nurture sequence that increases conversions and drives sales: **automation**, **frequency**, **value**, **offers**, and **reach**.

First, automation. The north star objective of your nurture sequence is to create numerous touch points, simultaneously nurturing thousands of relationships across multiple channels. Thus, it's imperative you allow technology to do the heavy lifting. At The Entourage, we use HubSpot as our CRM, and for all our nurture sequences. Using tools like HubSpot allows you to write and load the content once for automatic, on-time delivery to each prospect, with each stage triggered according to where *they* are in *their journey* through your funnel, not by *your* needs.

Next, get the frequency right. People often ask how often they should contact their list. Your rate of communication should mirror your prospect's emotional peaks and valleys. When someone opts in, they're experiencing an emotional peak. They're engaged and excited, with your brand top of mind. Use this momentum by communicating with them more frequently early in the relationship, then gradually slowing down to a weekly cadence. The Market Leader Map later in this chapter highlights the exact frequency to follow.

Automation and frequency are of little value unless you are providing value to your audience. Value is key both to building and nurturing your audience. As we discussed in the Attract section of this chapter, when nurturing, you must continue to speak to your prospects' hearts and minds, directly addressing their challenges and giving them useful strategies. For your nurture sequence to be effective, your community must look forward to hearing from you, and open your communication in excited anticipation. Your nurture sequence should be a best-of compilation from your audience-building content, including blogs, podcasts, and videos. Pick the most popular content, with the highest levels of engagement, and repurpose it in your nurture sequence. Start with your best piece of content, proven to address your prospect's number one challenge. Your second communication should include your second best piece of content, and so on. Be sure to base your rankings on your prospects' responses and engagement, not your own preferences.

Having some entertaining pieces in your rotation can also be very effective. This content isn't educational or solution oriented, but surprises and delights your prospects by making them smile, laugh, and connect with the human side of your brand on a personal level.

In addition to adding value, strategically embed offers in your nurture sequence, giving your prospect an opportunity to move to the next stage of their buyer's journey. Every third or fourth piece of communication should include a call to action relevant to the topic and invite the prospect to take the next step.

At each stage of your marketing process, your offers must guide prospects through the journey in a way that maximizes conversions. If you sell a retail product that doesn't require a sales conversation, your offers will direct the prospect to a landing page for frictionless purchase. Let's suppose, however, that people buy your product through a consultative sales process. In that case, the offers in your nurture sequence will invite them to take the next step in your sales process, such as scheduling a discovery call or strategy session. We'll discuss this more in the "Develop" section of Chapter Seven: Sales.

Finally, using a PS at the bottom of an email is the perfect way to include a call to action relevant to the topic. It's an invitation for prospects who got value from the email to take the next step.

While email should form the base of your nurture sequence, research shows that connecting with your prospects via multiple channels substantially increases conversions and replies. SalesLoft's Data Science team researched over 200 million interactions and found that if your nurture sequence solely uses email, it will be 77 percent less effective than a multichannel sequence. Only using phone calls is a staggering 91 percent less effective than a multichannel approach.[4]

Your nurture sequence should primarily utilize email, with the addition of text, phone calls, voice messages, and direct social media messages. Because frequency is so important, the key is to be pleasantly persistent, so you remain top of mind without being intrusive. Use HubSpot or a similar tool to seamlessly deliver your communications across multiple channels.

Attracting, converting, and nurturing your audience are essential steps to becoming a leader in your industry. When your audience is ready to buy—and you've used the principles of recency and frequency to stay top of mind—your business will be the first place they go. Below you can see a map of the kind of marketing ecosystem you need to create to become the market leader in your field.

---

[4] "33 Tips for Optimizing B2B Sales Emails," *Salesloft*, Sep 23, 2019, https://salesloft.com /resources/guide/33-tips-b2b-sales-emails-ultimate-guide/.

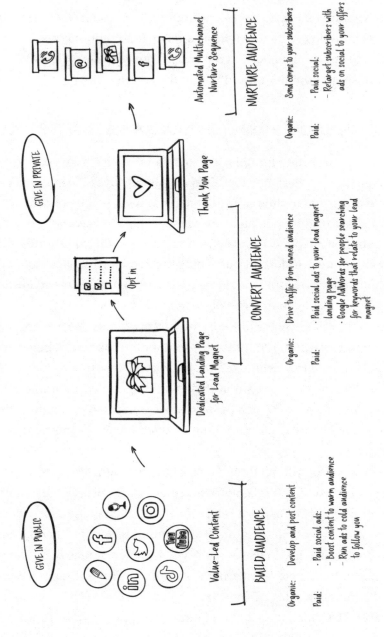

Figure 6.4: The Market Leader Map

Sounds simple, right? Well, when you have a framework to help you architect your strategy, in many ways, it is. Before we move on, however, there's another scenario we need to address. For certain types of business, it's essential to create an express lane, giving potential customers an option to buy immediately. In the next section, we'll explain why, which businesses this applies to, and how to do it right.

THE EXPRESS LANE: WINNING THE CUSTOMER WHO IS READY TO BUY NOW

Not every marketing funnel is created equal, so it's important to have different funnels designed for different types of buyers. In every industry —even those that traditionally use longer funnels—a percentage of prospects want to buy immediately. We call these people *high-intent prospects*. They know what they want, they are actively searching for it, and within a very short time window they are going to make a buying decision. *Every* business wants to ensure they are getting in front of high-intent prospects because they convert into paying customers, fast.

If your business sells a low-cost product or service, chances are you're in an industry where your prospects frequently make quick buying decisions. If you sell fast fashion online, for example, most of your prospects will be looking for a dress that they intend to buy either today or this week. Therefore, having an *express lane*—a funnel that enables them to buy quickly—in your marketing mix is critical to winning them as a customer.

Alternatively, you might be in an industry where longer funnels are more common. If you're a high-end consultancy business for example, your prospect requires nurturing, numerous touch points, and a consultative sales process to trust that your solution is right for them. Even in an industry like this, however, there will be a percentage of high-intent prospects. These people will want to shortcut the marketing process and rapidly initiate a sales conversation, so they can get started as soon as possible. Therefore, they don't require a lead magnet or need to be nurtured. They want to have an immediate buying conversation about how you can tailor your service to their needs, a conversation you certainly don't want to discourage. To facilitate this conversation, you'll want to give these prospects a route to rapidly making a decision.

In the context of the three marketing stages (**attract**, **convert**, and **nurture)**, the express lane allows you to **attract** a high-intent prospect, skip the **convert** and **nurture** stages, and usher them straight to the point of purchase. As a fast fashion business, you'll send them to a product landing page where they can click "buy now." Alternatively, as a high-end consultancy, you'll initiate your sales process, scheduling the necessary conversations to tailor your offer to their needs.

The golden rule of funnel length is that the more nurturing your prospects require, the longer your funnel should be. Conversely, the higher their buying intent, the more important it is to give them a way to act on that intent, right away!

The Express Lane in Practice

Think about this principle in your own life. When you want to buy something and don't have a company in mind, where do you go to search for potential solutions? The same place we all go: Google. There's a high probability that right now, high-intent prospects in your market are turning to Google to find what they need. The best way to get in front of these people is to ensure that when they search, your company appears at the top of the page with a compelling offer.

In this scenario, there are two ways to be at the top of the page: Google Ads and search engine optimization (SEO). Both are extremely useful for attracting customers actively searching for specific products and services. These customers have a high level of intent and are close to making a decision. Therefore, adding Google Ads and SEO to your **attract** strategy enables you to get in front of high-intent prospects with an offer that aligns closely with their needs, often fast-tracking a website sale or buying conversation.

Let's look at an example as to how the express lane works in conjunction with the **attract**, **convert**, and **nurture** strategy. In 2010,

Jane Lu started Showpo, an Australian online fashion retailer primarily aimed at young women. Showpo's vision is "to be her go-to place to shop."

When Jane started with The Entourage in 2012, Showpo had grown to $120,000 in annual revenue. In the following years, Jane scaled her social media audience, converted them to email subscribers, and nurtured her email community with regular emails. Her communications were fun, sometimes silly, but always on-brand. Because of this, Jane created an online ecosystem that her audience *loved* being a part of.

In addition to building and nurturing her own audience, Jane also got serious about offering high-intent prospects both an express lane to buy quickly and an easy route to joining the Showpo community. These were prospects who discovered Showpo via Google, loved the ethos and products, and made a purchase. Once someone clicked on an ad and bought a dress from the company's landing page, they became part of an ecosystem that nurtured them as part of the Showpo community. Next time this consumer wanted a dress, their engagement in the community attracted them back to the brand they knew and loved. Google offered Showpo a channel to initially attract high-intent prospects. Once they bought from the brand, however, they became part of a community that continued to nurture the relationship, driving extremely high rates of repeat business.

During the three years Jane was with The Entourage, she experienced rapid growth, becoming an industry leader in the Australian market and launching in international markets. Today Showpo continues that trajectory, recording annual revenues in excess of $85 million.

Are Google Ads and SEO Right for Your Company?

Google Ads and SEO both provide a similar experience to people who are close to making a buying decision, serving the most relevant search results first. To determine whether these strategies are valuable for your business, you'll need to do a little research. Use Google search to find the Google Keyword Planner. Select the geographic location you serve and enter some search terms you think potential customers would use to find your services. The planner will show you the search volume for these keywords.

Your research will tell you how frequently potential customers are likely to discover your services using Google search. If you have a model that works on higher volumes, and there are thousands of searches or more for your keywords per month, then Google Ads and SEO will most likely be viable strategies to capture customers who are ready to buy now. This applies in the fast fashion world, of which Showpo is a part, for example.

If you're a boutique consultancy business like the one we described above, however, then you don't need huge search volumes. You likely only want a few clients at any given time, so low search volumes need not deter you from employing this strategy.

Implementing an SEO strategy takes longer than running Google Ads, because you need to convince Google that your content is relevant to your target audience. This process includes writing compelling content and growing trust indicators, such as backlinks from high-quality websites. While this can take several months, implementing the Content Blueprint we shared earlier will ensure that you are best-in-class and that the end result is worth it. Once you've earned a top spot in Google's organic search results, you can expect a consistent flow of very high-quality leads, without paying for each one. Whether your leads come from Google Ads or SEO, high-intent prospects will convert higher, faster, and easier than anyone else in your funnel.

The best marketers use a combination of strategies. They **attract** an audience at scale, **convert** that audience to land that they own, and continue to **nurture** those relationships through email and social media marketing. They also use ads and SEO to capture high-intent prospects, offering an express lane for those who are ready to buy now. Weaving these strategies together, so that each reinforces the others, will enable you to create an ecosystem that both builds your brand and drives sales.

BUILD YOUR MARKETING ENGINE: BRING YOUR STRATEGY TO LIFE

In every element of your business, there are two distinct components. First, you consider *what to do* (strategy), and second, you figure out *how to do it* (practice). At The Entourage, we look at each element through the lens of dynamics and mechanics. The dynamics are the principles and strategies that guide what we do, and the mechanics are how we embed those strategies and make them happen. We've covered the "what do do" aspects of marketing (attract, convert, nurture). Now it's time to dive into *how* to do it. To achieve everything we've described previously, you'll need to develop a structure and team beneath you to ensure the work happens consistently, without your operational involvement. This is what we call "building your marketing engine," and it includes four key components: your **marketing strategy**, **marketing team**, **marketing metrics**, and **marketing technology**.

Your Marketing Strategy

The first step toward bringing your marketing engine to life is determining how you can best apply the principles of attract, convert, and nurture to *your* marketing process. Where will you start building your audience? What platforms do your prospects use, and where will you have the best chance of reaching them? What content do you need to produce to speak to their hearts and minds, thereby initiating the relationship? Once you've started a conversation, what lead magnets could move your followers from rented land to becoming part of your owned audience? When a prospect joins your owned audience, how will you nurture the relationship, make compelling offers, and encourage them to take the next step?

We often work with founders who have developed an understanding in their head of how their marketing fits together, but who haven't captured it or communicated it in a way that can be transferred to their team. When you're building your marketing engine, everyone involved needs to understand the underlying strategy guiding how you will build and nurture your relationship with your audience. Otherwise, everyone will pull in different directions, your prospects will find your marketing journey fragmented, and conversions will decrease significantly.

Therefore, once you define your marketing strategy, it's critical to capture it clearly in a strategy document. This document doesn't need to be fancy or complicated, but it should be accessible and actionable. Imagine a wordy, convoluted corporate strategy document...then do the opposite of that. Yours must communicate the core principles and practices for building your audience and generating leads, and assign each component to the person responsible for execution.

Our members use our Marketing Strategy Template to build out a tailored strategy. Hundreds of members have used this template to generate billions of dollars in revenue. You can download it for free at www.the-entourage.com/elevate.

Clarifying your strategy is the first step toward building an effective marketing engine. The second is recruiting your marketing team.

Your Marketing Team

As we described in the beginning of this chapter, during startup, marketing is often an orphan that no one really owns. The founder drives it when they remember, often drawing in junior members of the administrative team to assist with ad-hoc activities like design, posting on social media, and sending the occasional email. As such, the business often lacks a defined marketing strategy, which makes it an ineffective expense rather than what it should be: a profitable investment.

As we've said many times in this book, what got you to where you are is not going to get you to where you want to be. In the marketing element of your business, building a marketing team commensurate with your stage of business is critical to your continued growth.

As a business grows, every founder reaches the point where they feel like they have hit a glass ceiling. For a while, startups can grow despite a lack of concerted marketing effort or a dedicated team, so the founder often doesn't realize that its lack of marketing firepower that's preventing further growth. When we look at the organizational charts of our seven- and eight-figure members at the outset of their Elevate journey, we often find that other areas of the business are far more advanced. There may be fully developed teams in product development and delivery, some people conducting the necessary administrative tasks in operations, and either the founder or members of the product team handling sales. A dedicated marketing team however, is nowhere to be found.

Take a look at your organizational chart, and you will quickly be able to tell whether you have been undervaluing marketing. If your organizational chart looks similar to Figure 6.5, there is a huge opportunity for you to start building your marketing team.

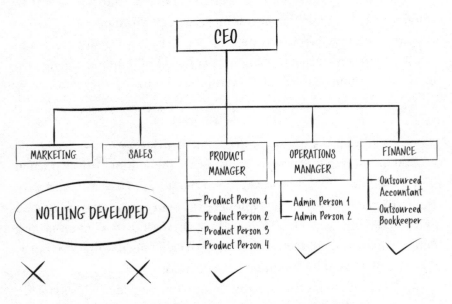

Figure 6.5: Organizational Chart with No Marketing

When developing your marketing team, there are always two sides of the coin: your content team who builds your audience, and your paid team who converts your audience into leads. Whether you are developing your marketing team from scratch or enhancing your existing team, it's important you are advancing both of these synergistic capabilities. This chart reveals the distinctions.

	Content Team	Paid Team
Context	Brand and following	Ads and optimization
Disposition	Creative	Analytical
Key Outcome	Audience growth	Return on Investment (ROI)
Key Focus Areas	High focus on audience growth and nurturing: podcast, social media, website content, blogs, and SEO	High focus on lead generation and conversion-rate optimization: paid ads, paid search, retargeting
Approach	Implementing The Market Leader Map and continually optimizing according to audience response	ABT: Always Be Testing new channels, new ads, new creative, new audiences
Social Proof To Use	Success story videos: one to four minutes highlighting successful customer journeys	Testimonial videos: under one minute, highlighting tangible customer results
Achieving Recency and Frequency	Email marketing and nurture sequences to add value and convert to leads	Retargeting is absolutely key for acquisition: invest here

The development of your marketing team will follow four major phases. You can adapt each of them to your current stage of business and your unique set of challenges and objectives. We'll discuss a high-level summary of each phase below.

Phase One

You bring on your first marketing team member. If you need support creating content, this may be a content manager. If you've already built an audience but need help creating compelling offers and generating leads, you may choose a digital marketing manager as your first hire. Here, you're essentially deciding whether you want your first full-time marketing team member to be on the content side or the paid side.

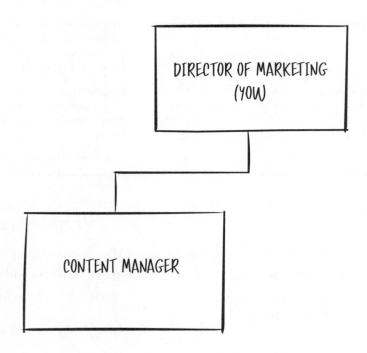

Figure 6.6 Marketing Headcount: 2.
Approximate revenue bracket: $300k–$1m

Phase Two

Phase Two should see you start to build out both sides of your team: content and paid advertising. At this stage, each person is still a generalist with a wide range of responsibilities. As the team develops and the roles become more specific in scope, you will hire fewer generalists and more specialists. Often, this phase is also the right time to find an outsourced graphic designer and videographer to produce relevant content and advertising.

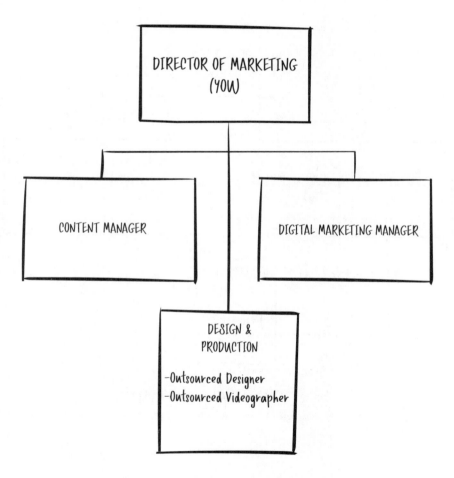

Figure 6.7: Marketing Headcount: 3.
Approximate revenue bracket: $1m–$2m

Phase Three

Once your marketing function demonstrates a positive ROI, you may want to expand the team to further scale your audience and generate a higher quantity and quality of leads. At this stage, you may consider hiring an internal graphic designer and a videographer, part time or full time. This ensures your team's output isn't constrained, increasing your capacity to develop both content and high-converting ads.

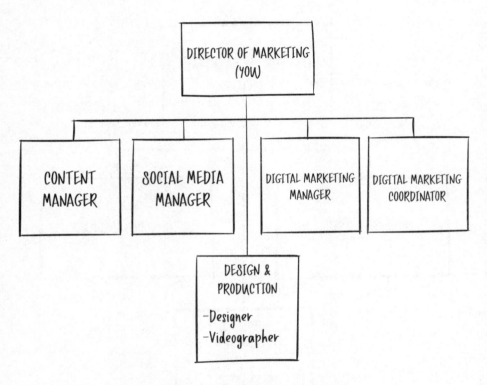

Figure 6.8: Marketing Headcount: 6 or 7.
Approximate revenue bracket: $2m–$5m

Phase Four

This graphic illustrates an example of what a fully functional marketing engine looks like. It's important to note that it may take years to build to this point, because you want to grow the team in direct proportion to the revenue they help generate. *Costs should follow revenue*, meaning that as a function contributes more to the business, you have license to invest more money into it.

By the time you implement phase four, you will have a team developing world-class content that attracts an audience at scale. You'll be nurturing this audience to ensure that you are front of mind, and you will be able to generate as many high-quality leads as you want each month, fully fueling the growth of your business. All this will be driven by an experienced executive, your director of marketing. At this point, your company will be extremely high growth, leaving your competition wondering how you're doing what you're doing.

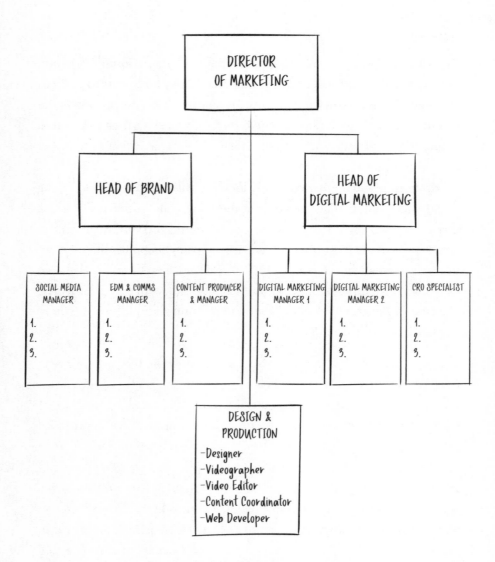

Figure 6.9: Marketing Headcount: 9–14.

Approximate revenue bracket: $5m+

For fully developed position descriptions that explain the roles and responsibilities in these diagrams, head to www.the-entourage.com /elevate.

Your Marketing Metrics

American retail magnate John Wanamaker famously said, "Half the money I spend on advertising is wasted; the trouble is, I don't know which half." Fortunately, that's no longer the case. The attribution model has finally solved one of marketing's most enduring and fundamental problems. In this section, we'll explain both the rationale and the practicalities of creating an attribution model that's right for your business.

As you expand your marketing budgets, it becomes increasingly important to measure which activities and tactics are performing the best. As we described in the introduction to this chapter, marketing done right is an investment, not an expense. When you understand your core marketing metrics, you can begin to measure the ROI of every piece of content and advertising. These metrics enable you to scale your marketing and turn it into a profit center.

With the rise of content marketing, personal branding, and social media, too many companies fall prey to vanity metrics. Vanity metrics may look good, but they offer little in the way of genuine insight. Your attribution model, on the other hand, tells you exactly which pieces of content and ads outperform the rest and contribute the most to sales and which fall short. This level of visibility allows you to cut spending on underperforming campaigns and channels while allocating more of your marketing budget to high-performing campaigns and platforms. Scale the marketing that works. Scrap the rest.

Let's look at the most fundamental metrics critical for your success in building a profitable marketing engine. Understanding and measuring these metrics will allow you to develop your attribution model—the holy grail of marketing. When you have a solid attribution model, you will be able to track all the marketing touch points a customer encounters on their path to purchase. The power of the attribution model is that it gives you complete visibility into which touch points have the most significant impact on *sales*.

When discussing marketing ROI and metrics, our members often ask, "How much should I be spending?" The answer is, "as much as is profitable." Building an attribution model to track what is and isn't effective allows you to optimize constantly. When a funnel, campaign, or even a single ad proves profitable, scale your investment until the ROI starts to plateau.

In most industries, a good benchmark is spending 8–12 percent of your forecasted revenue each year on marketing and advertising, over and above what you spend maintaining your marketing headcount. If you want to achieve a revenue of $5 million over the coming year, your goal should be to establish a marketing engine that can *profitably spend* between $400,000 and $600,000. We hope it goes without saying that this is not to suggest you simply spend $600,000 in the next twelve months—you may need to work up to this level incrementally, as you build up conversions and demonstrate positive ROI.

Provided both your marketing *and* sales conversions are sound, the closer you are to the high end of the range, the faster your business will grow. Some of our members spend significantly more than this, in percentage terms, because every dollar they invest into marketing is profitable. Think back to the Verge Girl case study in Chapter Three: The Six Elements: each dollar they spend on marketing has a positive ROI, meaning they can continue to scale their budget with confidence. Others spend less because they're happy with lower growth rates. As long as your marketing is bringing you an effective ROI, you can customize it to your unique business goals, circumstances and, of course, personal preference.

	Stage of Funnel	Metric	Acronym	Description
Attract Audience	Impressions	Total Impressions		How many times your content has been displayed
	Follower Growth	Net Follower Movement		How many people follow you after seeing your content
	Engagement	Engagement %		How many people like, comment, and share your content
Convert Audience	Clicks	Cost per Click	CPC	How many people click on an offer for your lead magnet, taking them to the landing page
	Landing Page Conversion for Lead Magnet	Conversion %		The percentage of traffic that visits the landing page and ultimately signs up for your lead magnet

Nurture Audience	Open rates	Open rate %		The percentage of your audience who open your communication
	Conversion rates to become a sales-qualified lead	Cost per Lead	CPL	The percentage of your audience who take your offer to go to the next step of the buyer's journey
	Conversion from lead to customer	Lead to Sale %		The percentage of leads who become paid customers
	How many advertising dollars it costs to acquire each customer	Cost per Acquisition	CPA	Your total spend on a particular campaign divided by the number of customers won
	How much each customer spends	Ave $ per sale	AVE$	The average dollar amount your customers spend when buying with you
	The lifetime value of the customer	Lifetime Value	LTV	This is a critical metric. You must understand how much each customer spends with you, not just in the beginning but over their lifetime. Knowing this metric will help you gauge how much you should be willing to invest to win each customer.
	How much revenue you generate from new sales	Return on Advertising Spend	ROAS	How much you earn from each campaign divided by how much you spent on that campaign
	How much revenue you make back from the money you have spent on marketing	Return on Investment	ROI	How much you earn from each campaign, minus the amount you spent, divided by the amount spent, times 100 percent

Your Marketing Tech

As we've discussed, the core ingredient in going from startup to scaleup is *leverage*; increasing the ratio of inputs to outputs in any given element of the business. In many small-to-medium-sized businesses, technology is still a highly underutilized tool—used well, it allows organizations to get significantly more done, expending a lot less effort. How do you know whether you need to update your tech stack? If you find yourself tracking prospects and previous conversations manually, using spreadsheets to collect information, or simply not having the data you need to reach insights around what is and isn't working, adopting some simple technologies will make your life easier, and the business operations *a lot* smoother.

Technology is a core ingredient in turning your marketing strategy into practice. Whether it's automatically communicating with your prospects to ensure they are all getting the right message at the right time, enabling your marketing team to be more productive and move faster, or tracking the data that is going to give you the insights to build a profitable marketing machine, technology will do the heavy lifting.

Fortunately, developing a streamlined and cost-effective technology stack for your marketing activities and overall customer journey has never been easier. These are the core pieces you need:

- **CRM (Customer Relationship Management):** How do you track the progress of every prospect in your marketing and sales process? How do you ensure you're communicating with all your prospects in a way that is relevant to where *they* are in their journey? And when someone buys, how do you ensure accurate and full information is shared with your product team, so that the business delivers on its promises every single time? A CRM is a centralized database that keeps track of your prospects and customers, storing all the necessary information to enable you to deliver to them in a way that is tailored to their needs. While most founder-led companies *have* a CRM, most are not using it to its full capacity. Used properly, a good CRM makes your marketing more efficient by organizing and automating your buyer's journey.

- **Email Marketing:** Email marketing tools help you connect with your audience to promote your brand and increase sales. Coupled with your CRM (and increasingly a core component of modern CRMs like HubSpot), they allow you to develop elegant nurture sequences that provide value to your audience and move prospects through your funnel. Segmenting your CRM according to the different stages of your buyer's journey, coupled with utilizing an email marketing tool, enables you to tailor your communication to each phase of that journey.

- **Google Analytics:** Google Analytics provides insight into the identity of site visitors and their activity on your website. Use Google Analytics to understand the performance of marketing campaigns and how your website's user experience impacts conversion, retention, and attribution.

- **SEO Tools:** SEO Tools like Google Search Console and SEMrush are essential for keyword research and online ranking data. They will give you access to metrics including search volume, current search rankings, and cost per click for your brand, products, and services. This enables you to understand what consumers are searching for, and then build funnels that you know are going to attract high levels of traffic.

MARKETING IS YOUR MESSAGE TO THE WORLD

Whether you're building your marketing engine from scratch or optimizing your existing marketing setup, it's not uncommon to feel intimidated. In startup, marketing is often approached reactively, in silos, and without an underlying strategy, with the result that it requires the founder's personal involvement. When you implement the strategies and tools contained in this chapter, you will transition from reactive marketing to the creation of a finely tuned marketing engine that can run without your operational involvement. In many cases, this will be a multiyear journey; nonetheless, handling this element of your business is the key to turbo-charging your growth.

Even if you're selling an industry-leading product that is significantly better than what's offered by your competitors, the growth of your business is dependent on how many people know about it. Too many founders are still the world's best-kept secret. They *know* they have a superior product, yet they're being out-marketed by companies with inferior products. Implement the tools and templates in this chapter, such as the Content Blueprint and the Market Leader Map with your content and paid marketing teams. You'll add value to your audience while gaining trust and catapulting your company into an industry leadership position.

It's time we changed the entire conversation around marketing and turned outdated ways of operating on their head. When building a scalable and sustainable company, marketing is a critical element to master. Taken together, the key components shared in this chapter provide the actionable steps to create your own marketing engine.

CASE STUDY: SHIRAN FAAST MOVES HER ENTIRE BUSINESS ONLINE IN A MONTH

Shiran Faast, one of our Elevate members, had to implement massive marketing changes while facing the total loss of her business during COVID lockdowns. When COVID restrictions hit Australia in 2020, the retail sector was one of the hardest hit. Immediate lockdowns forced retailers to shut their doors, cutting off 100 percent of their foot traffic. For many businesses, shuttering physical locations meant losing 100 percent of their revenue. At the time, Shiran ran a brick-and-mortar gardening store, empowering people to master their health by making gardening accessible, sustainable, and successful.

When Shiran learned that she would have to close the doors to her shop in 2020, she thought her business was doomed. Like so many retailers, Shiran understandably couldn't see how she would survive after losing

100 percent of her revenue overnight. At this low point, she reached out to her Elevate coach for guidance on managing the seemingly unmanageable.

Together, we quickly developed a plan to digitize her entire store, enabling her customers to buy online. "We executed a massive digital pivot, shifting to 100 percent online and to click and collect," Shiran reflected a year later.

Although the strategy we adopted with Shiran was multifaceted, it was laser focused on one primary goal: rapidly increasing her online sales. We immediately installed the Market Leader Map into Shiran's business. We developed lead magnets about DIY gardening, ran digital ads on key platforms Shiran's prospects frequented and activated her existing database. Shiran invited prospects who'd previously opted into her email community to try gardening during lockdowns. She retargeted her existing customers to lean into gardening as a productive and calming activity during stressful COVID restrictions. Within days we implemented a fundamental business model pivot from a retail store reliant on foot traffic to a digital gardening shop using the **attract**, **convert**, and **nurture** framework.

This strategy significantly increased traffic to Shiran's website. As demand increased, Shiran converted her shop into a warehouse to hold and deliver more stock to her online buyers. This ability to buy and hold stock at higher volumes increased her profit margin significantly. Optimizing each stage of the funnel led to higher conversions in her online store than she had previously achieved in her retail store.

When lockdowns hit, Shiran was doing $150,000 per month in sales. During the subsequent thirty days, a time when she briefly believed her business could not survive, she tripled her monthly revenue to $450,000. With the visibility her attribution model provided, Shiran was able to continue scaling her marketing activities, safe in the knowledge that they were profitable. Further, thanks to the efficiency of the new online model, she significantly increased her overall net profit margins.

"The shifts we've made will change how we do business, forever," Shiran wrote to us in a thank-you letter. While COVID restrictions were initially scary for Shiran, they ended up becoming a catalyst for her to develop her marketing like never before, strengthening her business in ways she could never have imagined.

THE ENTOURAGE GOES THROUGH UPS AND DOWNS

At The Entourage, we have always been an audience-first brand. Today, we serve a vast community of 1,200,000 business owners worldwide with a globally respected brand, but it wasn't always this way. To attract and nurture an audience from scratch took strategy and resourcefulness.

When Jack started The Entourage, he wanted to interview the best entrepreneurs in the world to create compelling content. The strategy was to provide people with real-world insights on entrepreneurship from names they recognized, and in doing so build an engaged audience of business owners. Initially, however, like every person who starts out creating content, Jack was caught in a catch-22. He wanted to interview entrepreneurs to help build an audience for The Entourage, but—lacking an audience *and* a brand—he had nothing to offer the entrepreneurs he wished to interview! Jack knew there was a play to make it happen—he just had to figure it out.

Then Jack came up with a plan. At the time, Janine Allis was perhaps the most popular entrepreneur in Australia, having built Boost Juice into a much-loved industry-leading brand. Jack approached a personal and business development publication, *ThinkBig Magazine*, which had a distribution of 180,000 subscribers. He asked, "If I interview Janine Allis, the founder of Boost Juice and write an article on her, will you run it?" The editor of *ThinkBig* responded, "If you can interview Janine Allis, we'll give you the front cover." Jack reached out to Janine and said, "I represent *ThinkBig Magazine*. We have an audience of 180,000 business owners, and we'd like to put you on the cover." Janine replied that she'd love to be involved.

Jack engineered his first break in the media by getting resourceful before he had the resources. Following Janine, every time Jack wanted to interview another entrepreneur, all he needed to do was mention his previous interviewees, which would usually win their agreement. As

Jack interviewed the world's best entrepreneurs, distributed the content through different media publications, and built his own profile and owned audience, The Entourage became a recognized brand among business owners in Australia.

As our audience grew rapidly, so did our momentum. We ran events all over Australia. Our cornerstone event, The Entrepreneurs' Unconvention, continues to attract thousands of people in each city, and has been named one of the Top 3 Events for Entrepreneurs worldwide by *Forbes*. Building our audience turned into a growing movement that galvanized our brand in the eyes of consumers. That is, of course, until everything came to a screeching halt.

When the regulation changes of 2016 sent The Entourage into a tailspin, we triaged every single business function. Anything that didn't contribute to our immediate survival over the forthcoming thirty days was off the table. Gone. For many years, we didn't have the luxury of gradually developing an excellent marketing strategy. Rather than building a new audience or even nurturing our existing subscribers, our marketing revolved around sending out offers that would result in immediate revenue. We were forced into playing the short game.

We were so focused on putting out fires and stopping the bleeding, desperately trying to survive another month, that we begrudgingly veered from our own principles. Instead of adding value and nurturing our audience, we kept selling to them. Predictably, open rates and engagement declined. As people unsubscribed, our audience shrunk. It was a painful way to rediscover the importance of nurturing and loving our audience.

Two years later, in 2018, we finally got our heads above water. By then, the marketing and social media landscape had evolved, requiring much more sophistication than we had previously developed. To bring our approach up to date, we focused on building an end-to-end marketing engine to attract an audience, convert them to an owned audience, and nurture them through a transformational journey that grew their businesses and improved their lives. These early beginnings led to the inception of the Market Leader Map.

Ever since 2010, when Jack interviewed Janine Allis for *ThinkBig Magazine*, our preferred marketing approach has always been an audience and value-led method. We build an attraction model that attracts the right people to the brand, delivers value in a way that improves their life and business, and ultimately—when the time is right for them—helps them apply for the appropriate coaching program. We're selective about who we let into our inner circle programs, because our members build a great camaraderie, learning from and supporting each other. To protect this dynamic, it's essential that we choose carefully who to admit.

Today, our marketing engine follows the exact blueprint we have shared with you in this chapter. The same blueprint is the foundation for installing supercharged marketing engines into our Elevate members' businesses across 150 different industries. In other words, we build, test, and optimize ourselves, so that the formula is proven before we share any strategies with the world.

Our foundational content, comprising podcasts and keynotes, is our main route to attracting our audience. Jack's podcast, *Elevate with Jack Delosa*, interviews the world's top performers from different fields to reverse engineer what makes them great. When Jack launched his podcast, it quickly became the #1 business podcast in Australia on iTunes. The Entourage's podcast, *The Make It Happen Show*, hosted by Tim, goes deep into the practical strategies and tactics that CEOs and entrepreneurs employ to achieve high growth. Upon release, this podcast also shot to the top of the Australian business iTunes charts.

After we record each episode, we turn it into micro-content distributed across our social channels and through our email database. Following the Content Blueprint, our team tracks each piece's response rates and engagement, and uses this feedback to inform our continued micro-content creation strategy. This process also highlights which content resonates most strongly with our audience, so we can make more of it.

Our lead magnets, which we use to convert our public audience to our owned audience, range from large-scale events like the Unconventions mentioned previously and our online Make it Happen Summit, to webinars, e-books, and yes—you guessed it—the book you are reading right now.

We use a detailed multichannel nurture sequence, communicating with our audience across multiple channels with messages aligned to where they are in their journey with us. Across every channel, with every piece of content, we make it a point to nurture our audience with a high degree of care. We want even our free stuff to be the best content in the world for business owners, better than any MBA. We're committed to helping our audience experience personal and commercial results with our free content, *before* they apply for a paid program. This creates a relationship of trust—a necessary foundation when working together to unlock their growth and potential. Once someone is a part of our community and starts digesting our content, they can't help but improve their business.

So far, this value-led approach has reached over 350 million people, built a community of 1,200,000 world-class business owners, and has ultimately resulted in our members generating billions of dollars in additional revenue. After the disaster of 2016, we started from nothing (again) to reestablish ourselves as a market leader, while earning a special place in the hearts and minds of our audience.

NEXT UP...

Now that you understand how to architect your marketing engine, we'll turn our focus to converting those leads into paying customers. When you combine your marketing engine with your sales process, this culminates in your overall buyer's journey. The vast majority of businesses do not have a unified and well-developed buyer's journey that moves prospects all the way from not knowing who they are, to begging to buy. Building this end-to-end process is the key to achieving scalable growth.

In the next chapter, we'll outline exactly how to craft your unique sales process in a way that lines up perfectly with your marketing. We'll share exactly how we built our sales function at The Entourage, along with the secret sauce that bridges the gap between your marketing and sales teams for extraordinary results.

7

SALES

Drive Growth and Profitability

Do you believe you're better at selling than anyone else in your organization? You're probably right, and you're in good company. Most founders are gifted salespeople, bolstered by the conviction that comes from their belief in the company they created. Unfortunately, this often tempts them into making a significant business error—treating sales as a unique skill that can't be systematized or taught.

This doesn't work. You may have single-handedly made the sales to launch a successful startup, but once you reach the scaleup stage, this approach will reach a ceiling. No matter how brilliant you are at selling, there is only one of you. If the entire sales function relies solely on you, you're putting a handbrake on how many customers your business can generate. As you'll remember from the previous chapter, all growth is marketing and sales led. Sales is where we take your marketing strategies and turn them into paid customers. So, if you're doing all the selling, *by definition* you're capping the growth of your business far below what it could potentially achieve.

Sales is one area that founders really struggle to scale. In most businesses you, the founder, are the main revenue driver. To test whether this is true for you, just ask yourself this simple question: If I stepped away from my business for six months, would the sales in my company drop? The answer is probably yes, of course, in which case you're not alone. This is a near-universal truth among business owners. The question is, how can you overcome this challenge? How can you create a sales function that drives growth without your operational involvement?

Many founders think the problem is that their team can't muster the same level of belief, competence, and enthusiasm as they do, but that's rarely the case. Most of the time, the problem is they don't have a structure or process that serves as a roadmap, giving them the confidence, skill, and certainty that come naturally to you as the founder.

The idea that selling is not an intuitive talent, but something you can bottle and replicate, may be new to you right now. But we've coached thousands of founders to make the transition from doing all the selling to putting in place a dedicated and highly effective sales team. The magic that you instinctively conjure, and that motivates your customers to buy, can be captured, codified, and replicated into a process. If you're like many founders, this is one of the most impactful changes you can implement to drive growth and profitability while freeing you up to spend more time doing what you love.

DEVELOP, BUY, ASCEND

In this chapter we're going to outline the sales component of the Drive-Growth Cycle. This component consists of three elements: **develop**, **buy**, and **ascend**. As you **develop** prospects, you identify and progress those who are your highest-intent leads. Once someone is ready to have a buying conversation, how do you help your prospects to **buy** more from you, more often, faster? We'll cover the core principles to crafting your own unique sales process that maximizes conversions and reduces time to sale. When you deliver on your promises, your customers will be open to moving through a product suite that continues fulfilling their needs and deepening the relationship. To help them **ascend**, we will outline how to systematically put the right offer in front of the right person at the right time, to increase the lifetime value (LTV) of every customer you win.

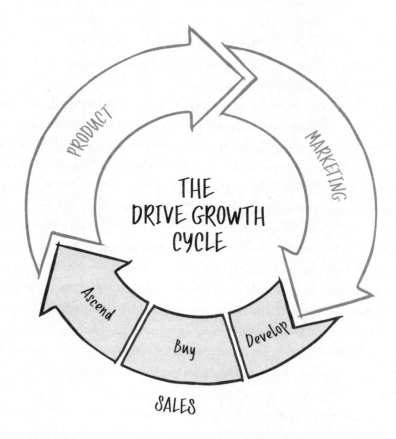

Figure 7.1: Sales Components of the Drive Growth Cycle

As we did in the previous chapter, we'll also talk about the people and mechanics you need to put in place to build an engine around your sales process, one that can drive profitability and cash flow without your involvement at the level of technician or even manager.

A NEW SALES MINDSET

First, we need to address the way most businesses think about sales. Most businesses view sales completely backwards. Back in the '80s and '90s, sales were all about pushing products *at* people. What mattered was pitching and closing. Thankfully, the world has moved on since those days, but unfortunately the way most businesses think about sales still hasn't progressed, and it is killing their growth.

The world has changed. Consumers have changed. If your organization has not kept up, you will find that there is a disconnect between you and your consumers during the sales process. We live in a world where people love to *buy* but hate being *sold to*. We want to *buy* a car, we want to *own* a car, but we don't want to be *sold* a car. We want to buy a home, we want to own a home, but we don't want to be sold a home.

Forget pitching people and closing the sale—those tactics can stay in the eighties. Instead, think of yourself as a facilitator who advises your customer on their purchasing decisions. The customer must have complete ownership over every decision. You don't convince them. You confidently lead them, asking them the right questions and matching them with the right solution, so that the customer convinces themselves. Herein lies the fundamental psychological shift you'll need to make to revolutionize your sales function: stop creating a *selling* mindset in yourself and your team, and start creating a *buying* mindset in your customers.

The companies that grow faster than any others are the ones that have achieved these two things:

1. They've developed an offer that connects with the hearts and minds of their consumers.
2. They have turned that connection into a sales process that can be bottled, trained, managed, and scaled.

While these two factors will drive significant growth, what happens if you don't do this? Companies without a defined sales process can expect to experience the following three problems:

- **A drop in conversions**: In a world full of uncertainty, people crave certainty. Sales is nothing more than a transference of certainty. When we haven't developed the ability to elegantly and confidently lead our consumers, we second-guess ourselves. If this is you, guess who picks up on this? That's right. Your customer. When you don't have a sales process, you and your team lack the certainty and confidence required to get people to take action. In contrast, what happens when you give your customer greater certainty, faster? Your conversion rates and average dollar per sale increase, meaning you make more money without working harder.

- **Time to sale increases:** When you fail to lead your prospect, sales becomes a game of phone tag at best, and cat and mouse at worst. Objections such as, "I need to think about it," and "we're not ready" are all symptoms of not leading your prospect effectively. A highly effective sales process gives you the foresight to know where you are leading your prospect. In turn, this gives them comfort that they are in good hands and the psychological safety to make a decision. Sales is leadership and your prospects are begging to be led.

- **You can't scale your sales function:** Most founders sell intuitively. As they start to build their sales team, this translates into *everyone* selling intuitively, according to their own personal preferences. A sales function composed of multiple different people, selling in numerous different ways, based only on their personal intuition and preferences, is completely unmanageable. When someone is performing exceptionally well, you have little choice but to attribute it to their unique gifts, as opposed to reverse engineering specifically what they are doing differently to everyone else. On the other hand, when someone is not performing, you cannot pinpoint what's not working and how they can improve. Without a defined process, you cannot benchmark best practice and you certainly can't manage performance.

Yes, it is critical that everyone on your team sells in a way that is authentic to them, and the process should complement that, not conflict with it. A defined sales process will enable you to capture and train best practices within an architecture that allows people to bring their own authenticity into the process. Your company needs an "our company way of selling," a methodology that bottles how you and your business systematically and elegantly move someone from "I'm interested" to "How do I buy?" Once you define this methodology, you can delegate it, measure performance against it, manage it, and optimize it. This is the unlock to creating a truly scalable sales function.

DEVELOP: IDENTIFY AND IGNITE THOSE WHO ARE READY FOR A BUYING CONVERSATION

Most businesses don't even realize that the Develop component of the Drive-Growth Cycle exists. Therefore, they don't act on it. If you lack a systemized method of developing your prospects to become buy-ready, you succumb to two fatal errors: first, you try to sell to people who aren't ready to buy, which can backfire, reducing their buying intent; second, you spend a lot of quality time with not-so-quality prospects, which significantly reduces your sales conversions and wastes everybody's time in the process.

This is where sales development comes in. Think of sales development as the middle ground where marketing and sales meet: the process of sifting through leads, qualifying those who are ready to have a buying conversation, and passing them to the sales team. Building a bridge between these two functions allows both to perform at their peak level. No longer will you need to play referee, adjudicating between your marketing team as they complain that the sales team isn't following up on leads, and your sales team griping about how marketing is jamming their pipeline with low-quality prospects. No longer will you wonder why on earth you're spending all that money on lead generation, when no one on your team is happy and sales results are dismal.

It may seem counterintuitive, but in fact generating new business can be much simpler during the startup stage. Your marketing and sales teams may consist of one person—you—perhaps with the support of a couple of additional team members. In this scenario, most of the responsibility for building interest and generating leads falls on your shoulders, as does converting those leads into buying customers. You may do all the work and carry all the responsibility, but you also have near-perfect insight into the entire experience from start to finish, and a high level of control over both process and outcome.

As you grow, however, implementing the strategies from the previous chapter, you'll see an influx of leads greater than you can handle alone, meaning you need to grow your marketing and sales teams. This higher volume of leads will consist of both high-quality and low-quality prospects, requiring you to allot precious human resources toward working the high-quality leads, while cost-effectively qualifying and developing the leads that are going to take longer to buy.

The most effective way to do this is to employ sales development representatives (SDRs), who act as a bridge between your marketing team and your sales team. SDRs are almost always less expensive than salespeople, allowing you to direct your less-expensive resources toward the heavy lifting, and simultaneously freeing up your more expensive resources to focus on the highest quality prospects.

What exactly should your SDRs focus on? Different businesses generate different types of leads. Depending on your business model, you may skew toward inbound or outbound leads. Inbound leads are people who were searching for your solution and came across your company. Think back to the express lane we outlined in the previous chapter: these high-intent prospects are *inbound* leads. Outbound leads are people who you actively contacted, who weren't necessarily searching for your solution, but who are now interested. With inbound leads you are tapping into *existing* demand, whereas with outbound leads you are *generating* demand. Because inbound leads are already searching for a solution, they will usually have a much higher buyer's intent than an outbound lead, and as such can be fast-tracked through your sales process.

You can use SDRs for both outbound and inbound leads. For outbound leads, SDRs play a very effective role in helping identify and develop the prospects along the sales process. If you have an inbound model however, then you will generally use SDRs to follow up with those who have simply dropped out of your funnel. For a visual representation of how this works, see Figure 7.3: E-commerce Sales Process, later in this chapter.

You'll also want to distinguish clearly between high- and low-quality leads. Your sales team should be spending most of their time and effort on high-quality leads. This is the most efficient way to drive growth. As the volume of leads increases, however, that gets harder to achieve. If your sales team is overwhelmed, they will waste precious time and resources on low-value prospects. This is where your SDR team will really demonstrate their value. By sorting leads for your salespeople and warming up the lower-quality leads before passing them on to a salesperson, they allow you to meet every prospect where they're at. The ultimate objective is for your sales team to spend only high-quality time with high-quality prospects.

If your marketing strategies generate inbound leads, for example through Google Ads or an SEO-based strategy, it's likely your leads are actively searching for a solution to their problem. You need to act fast and make their path to purchase as short as possible. The fewer steps to talk to a salesperson, the better. In these interactions, your task is to eliminate friction and make a transaction as easy as possible. If a salesperson isn't needed and prospects can buy straight from your website, even better! In that case, you should obsess over making that transaction as frictionless as possible.

If your marketing strategy focuses on generating rather than tapping into existing demand, the resulting leads will likely have a lower level of intent. When you're developing a high volume of leads through opt-in strategies, webinars, and e-books, engaging an SDR team to consciously and proactively warm them up will ensure that they are ready for a buying conversation before they get to the sales team.

Why Can't I Just Teach My Marketing Team to Generate Highly Qualified Leads?

You may be wondering why hiring a team of SDRs is necessary. Can't the marketing team simply process and sort leads as they come in? The answer is that no matter how well you educate and guide your marketing team, you can't make all your leads behave exactly how you want them to. That's not how humans work. Even with an excellent marketing team, The Entourage is living proof of this principle. A marketing-qualified lead for our Accelerate program is a business owner whose company is currently doing between $100k and $500k in annual revenue; for our Elevate program, we work with companies doing more than $500k in annual revenue, but in many cases seven or eight figures. The reason we've designed our programs this way is that those who are doing under $500k simply need to accelerate their growth: they need help to drive revenue and profitability. Accelerate helps them get to a point where they are ready to elevate. At $500k+, business owners need to continue to scale while also elevating from technician to entrepreneur, to ensure that their growth is sustainable. This is why our Elevate program is so effective for businesses in this revenue bracket.

These aren't arbitrary numbers. The revenue figures previously mentioned represent a proven, historically consistent data point, allowing us to direct potential customers to the program that meets their needs most effectively. In our lead magnets, landing pages, and event-registration promos, we constantly discuss these figures. We do this because we want to help people who are not business owners, or who haven't hit the relevant revenue thresholds, to self-select *out* of our acquisition process. But, even though we couldn't be any more explicit about the qualifying threshold, we *still* find that somewhere between 52–55 percent of the leads we generate each month don't qualify for either program.

The remaining 45 percent of leads, those that do qualify from a business and revenue point of view, are still a long way from becoming Entourage members. Together, we need to determine their core challenges and most important objectives, tailor a plan that will bring them the results they need, and ensure that they are the right fit for our program. For each marketing campaign we run, we might generate between 500 and 2,500 leads. That's a lot of people who have reached out for help, and who are eager to have a preliminary conversation as soon as possible. That's the gap between our marketing and sales teams, where our SDR team slots in neatly, increasing our overall efficiency.

What Are the Benefits of a Functional Sales Development Team?

We've helped many of our members establish their own SDR functions, modeled on the approach we use at The Entourage. In doing this, we've shown them how to map out their sales process, implement the technology needed to manage leads and deals, and hire and train SDR teams. As a result, they've seen the same benefits we see in our own business: increased responsiveness and lead contacts, higher conversion rates, and improved campaign flexibility.

Faster Response Times

An immediate benefit our members have experienced once we've helped them embed their SDR function is reduced response time. This significantly increases the number of prospects reaching the later stages of their sales process and ultimately buying. Time lags kill deals, especially when a warm lead comes in. Numerous studies show that the faster you contact leads, the more likely you are to make the sale. In fact, speed to lead is so important that businesses which respond within an hour are almost seven times more likely to have meaningful conversations than those that don't. Companies that get their response time down to one minute can improve lead conversions by a massive 391 percent, and the first vendor to speak with a lead wins up to 78 percent of sales.[5] If your prospect is shopping around, and you're the first company to get in touch with them, you're

---

[5] "9 Lead Response Time Statistics," *ServiceBell*, Oct 8, 2022, https://www.servicebell.com/post/lead-response.

massively more likely to gain their trust and, ultimately, their business. When it comes to sales, speed matters.

More Leads Contacted

When you implement the Market Leader Map we covered in the last chapter, you will reach a point where your problem is no longer, "We don't have enough leads," but rather, "How do we keep up with the leads that we're generating?" This is a much better problem to have. Combining faster response times with a dedicated SDR function increases the total volume of leads you actually get to contact. It can take up to twelve attempts to successfully contact a lead, especially if you miss that first golden window.[6] If you want to speak with a larger number of your leads, it's essential to have a team devoted to repeatedly attempting to contact them. SDRs can also work back through your database to reengage leads who have stalled in the sales process. Combining these two activities achieves a much higher contact ratio than relying solely on your sales team.

Better Conversion Rates

Using a well-trained SDR team to qualify leads will result in higher conversion rates at every stage of the sales process. When the lead first comes in, SDRs' faster response times will produce a better lead-to-booking conversion rate. After your SDR team qualifies these leads, they'll be more likely to convert from an initial conversation with a member of your sales team to a sales meeting. For the sales team, this is a huge advantage: they can focus their time and attention on speaking with high-quality leads, so they'll convert more prospects into paying customers.

More Campaign Flexibility

A well-resourced SDR team gives you the flexibility to execute a wide range of marketing and sales campaigns efficiently. Whether you're running a

---

[6] "Average Follow-up Attempts," *Geckoboard*, accessed Nov 17, 2022, https://www.geckoboard .com/best-practice/kpi-examples/average-follow-up-attempts/.

special promotion to generate a high volume of leads, or a reengagement campaign to reignite leads that have cooled off, your SDRs will ensure a productive campaign by passing only vetted leads to your sales team. This means you're not bogging down your more skilled sales team in high-volume activity; instead, you're freeing them to spend high-quality time with high-quality prospects. Trained SDRs offer a rapid approach to addressing large volumes of leads efficiently, preventing bottlenecks and friction between the marketing and sales teams.

BUILDING AN SDR TEAM AT THE ENTOURAGE

The power of SDRs is not commonly understood in the business world. We therefore see many businesses that would benefit from an SDR function, but are yet to put one in place. To give you an example of how integrating an SDR team into your business might progress, we'll share some of our own experience. As you'll see, we're intimately familiar with the power and perils of building a highly competent and functional SDR team.

When we turned up our marketing engine in 2018, as we described in the previous chapter, the leads started flowing in. While we were happy about the increase in volume, we quickly realized that too many leads were getting stuck at the top of the funnel, not making their way to our sales team efficiently. First we attempted to get our sales team to increase their call volume to top-of-funnel leads, but we quickly learned that this approach created new problems. Time spent following up with these low-quality leads distracted our sales team from the conversations we needed them to have with high-quality leads further along in our sales process. On top of this, the sheer volume of leads we were receiving meant that even with our sales team working at full capacity, we weren't adequately addressing the large volume of leads we had.

Clearly, we needed exactly what we've been recommending to you: a team of dedicated, trained SDRs to qualify the mountain of leads we had accrued and keep them flowing through our lead pipeline. The problem we ran into immediately was cost. Our sales team was located in Sydney,

Australia, one of the world's most expensive cities. Employing professional salespeople at the volume required to process all the high-volume leads was simply cost prohibitive.

Fortunately for us, a member of our advisory board had spent the past few years building an outbound sales development team in Manila, the capital city of the Philippines. They offered to help us set up a team with the intention of unblocking the top of our funnel and keeping prospects moving through our sales process. This was a more affordable solution, which promised higher volumes than our Sydney-based team at a fraction of the cost.

In October 2018, we started with three, Manila-based SDRs, at roughly the cost of one junior salesperson in Sydney. We began to see results almost immediately, most notably tripling our lead-to-discovery-call conversion rate. By July 2019, we had added another three SDRs and an SDR manager. Since February 2020, our Manila-based team comprises eight SDRs, one SDR manager, and one sales operations manager, all playing vital roles in most of our sales funnels.

Today, most of our high-volume lead generation activities pass through this SDR team for qualification and booking into discovery calls with our sales team. When we run our large public events, such as The Entrepreneurs' Unconvention, we attract between five and ten thousand registrations each time. Our SDR team springs into action even before these events begin, helping to increase attendance rates with "can't wait to see you" calls. Afterwards, they follow up with attendees to determine whether they'd like to have a conversation with us about how to grow their business and those who do are introduced to our team of professionals in Sydney.

BUY: CORE PRINCIPLES AND PROCESSES TO HELP YOUR PROSPECTS BUY MORE FROM YOU, MORE OFTEN, FASTER

Now that we've outlined the value of a structured SDR team, let's talk about how to lead your prospects through the next stage of their buyer's journey. To develop your unique sales process that helps people buy more from you, more often and faster, you first need to understand what drives decision-making. Not from the perspective of your business or yourself, but from the perspective of your customer. This fundamental understanding underpins every component of your messaging throughout your entire buyer's journey, from your marketing right through to helping someone buy. Let's take a look at how the human brain works and how your customers *actually* make decisions.

In the previous chapter, we outlined the Four Forces Model and discussed how everything we do as human beings comes down to two forces: *away from* motivation and *toward* motivation. Away from motivation is when we are motivated to move away from pain or anticipated pain. Toward motivation is when we are motivated to move toward pleasure or anticipated pleasure. It's important that you understand both your customer's away-from motivators and their toward motivators, so that you can speak to both throughout your marketing and sales journey. Away-from motivators are great for helping people get started and take action, whereas toward motivators are great for sustaining motivation and keeping people moving.

To move your prospects to take action, you must understand, elicit, and speak to their buying motivators; their away from and towards motivators. For example, let's imagine an interior design business that helps families improve the look and feel of their home. The table below brings together the likely away-from motivators, and corresponding toward motivators, of prospects.

Away-from Motivators	Toward Motivators
I don't want our home to feel cold and impersonal	I want our home to feel like a sanctuary
The thought of designing or styling our home feels really overwhelming. I don't even know where I'd start	Having someone who knows what they're doing to hold our hand through the process and help us make the right decisions would be so empowering

I don't want to spend days and days sorting through catalogs and spending money on things that I'm not even sure are going to be right	I'd love to have someone who really listens to what we love and can turn our vision into reality, making it easy and fun
I don't want to be embarrassed when my friends and family visit	I want to be proud when touring people through our home, and when we entertain for family and friends
I don't want our house to be like everyone else's	I want our home to be a beautiful representation of who we are as a family
My biggest fear is that our family feels disconnected from each other	My deepest hope is that our family feels connected to each other, and we have a beautiful home where we can create magical moments together

Notice that these motivators are not a list of product features, but a summary of what's going on in the heart and mind of the *prospect*. The away-from and toward-buying motivators of your consumer underpin everything in your marketing and sales process, from your content to your lead magnets, from your nurture communications to the questions you ask during your sales process, right through to how you present your product. For this reason, it's incredibly important you and your team understand the buying motivators of *your* consumer.

To download your free Entourage Selling Essentials Playbook and fill out your own buying motivators table for your customer, head to www.the-entourage.com/elevate. This table will become the bedrock of your marketing and sales messaging.

RED BRAIN AND GREEN BRAIN

Next, let's discuss the vital importance of your prospect's emotional state. You're probably familiar with the concepts of left-brain and right-brain thinking. The left brain is known for logic and analytical thinking (to remember this, think "L" for left and "L" for logic), whereas the right side of the brain is known for emotion and creativity. At The Entourage, we label the left side of the brain "red brain" and the right side "green brain." What do you do when you come to a red light? Stop! What color is a stop sign? Red! What are you looking for when you get to a stop sign? Danger. Warning signs. Reasons *not to go*. When your prospect is anchored in the left side of their brain, their red brain, they will stop, wait, and look for danger. They will be thinking "what if." "What if I make the wrong decision? What if it's too expensive? What if there's a risk I don't know about? What if there's something else better out there?" Red brain increases procrastination, causing your prospect to pause, stop, and go back.

On the other hand, what do you do when you get to a green light? You go! There have probably been times where you've driven through a green light, reached the other side, and thought to yourself, "Was that light green?" You felt so safe to proceed that you did so unconsciously, without fully registering the color of the light. Maybe there have been times when you approached a green light, a pedestrian or bike rider started to encroach onto the road, and you were startled. Why were you startled? Because you weren't looking for danger. When a human being is operating from the right side of the brain, they make decisions faster, without worrying excessively about negative consequences. They put the pedal to the metal, and *go*. We call this state of mind "green brain." Green brain is the psychological key to helping your prospects make quicker, more confident decisions.

All over the world, the biggest and most common problem of salespeople is that they are forever having red-brain conversations. A red-brain conversation is any conversation about your product, the features of the product, deliverables, terms, contracts, or price. We love speaking to these things because they are familiar; we know them and they're what we're comfortable with. Unfortunately, for most business owners and sales people, red-brain conversations become their comfort zone. They end up locking their prospects into the left side of the brain, and "red brain" themselves out of making sales.

When you orient marketing messages and sales conversations toward the product or service, you are having a red-brain conversation that will drive your conversions down. In contrast, when you help your prospect feel into or articulate their current lived experiences and challenges, their frustrations, fears, wants, and dreams, you activate their green brain. Green-brain thinking is about moving past your product and into the motivations of the customer. It is about going beyond the rational, so that your prospect can connect to their heart, and to the emotion that conveys *why* they are seeking a solution. The *why* makes them buy.

For someone to make a decision, you need both hemispheres of the brain activated. The most critical sales principle, which underpins every sale you will ever make, is this: people make decisions emotionally and justify those decisions logically. There is a place for red-brain conversations in sales—at some point we need to handle the logistics. The key, however, is to understand that it's a *much smaller* place than most people's current sales conversations. When a prospect is engaged because their green brain is activated, they will happily take care of the red-brain stuff. If you put them into their red brain as soon as you start talking to them, you'll be met with objections, delays, and the words every salesperson dreads hearing: "I want to think about it."

Every marketing message, every email header, every social media post, every piece of copy, every sales conversation, every question you ask, every single touch point, from the language you use right through to how you tour your product or service, puts your prospect in either a red brain or a green brain state of mind. To maximize your conversions, therefore, you must know when to activate the red brain, when to activate the green brain, and how to use them together.

Red-Brain and Green-Brain Language

Throughout your buyer's journey, the language you use will be the number one determinant of whether your prospect is rooted in their red brain or their green brain. When you use logical language, ask logical questions, and give logical answers, your prospects are going to be locked in their red brain. This will give rise to objections, procrastination, and ultimately a lack of decisiveness. If your marketing and sales conversations are completely red-brain-based, you'll struggle to increase your sales.

Let's use the following table to tease out some of the most common examples of red-brain language, and explain how you can convert it to language that helps the prospect stay in green brain.

Red-Brain Language	What's Wrong with It	Green-Brain Language	The Benefit
Pay "How are you going to pay for that?"	While everyone knows they need to pay for a product or service, it's the part of the process that's the least enjoyable. Sometimes it may make people anxious, or even sting a little.	"How would you like to *look after* that?" "How would you like to *take care* of that?" "Easy, now all we need to do is *fix it up...*"	People love looking after, taking care of, fixing up. It takes the sting out of the payment and enables the prospect to stay in their green brain.
Appointment "Let's set up an appointment."	Appointments are boring and often painful. You make an appointment to go to the dentist. Please, don't force your prospects to make an appointment.	"Make a time to *get together...*" "Chat further to *make a plan...*" "Have a chat and *build a roadmap together...*"	People cancel appointments, they don't cancel on people. Green braining this step ensures you get a higher show rate and that people are excited to be there.
Direct Debit "We do a monthly direct debit."	No one loves having a monthly direct debit; it feels heavy and burdensome.	"It's just a *monthly rollover* that *makes it easier* on your cash flow. Or you can take care of it *upfront and get a saving*. Do you want the easy option or the saving?"	It explains the benefit of each option in green-brain language. Here, we are making every decision easy to make.

Contract "I'll need to send you a contract."	Contracts are intimidating and cause people to think about worst-case legal scenarios playing out. This is very red brain. In some industries, you will need a contract, but conversationally you can make it less intimidating.	"Once we make a plan we'll be able to *sign off on it* and get you started." "All we need to do now is take care of *a little bit of paperwork...*"	The green brain language here softens this step, making it less scary and more inviting. You can still use a contract if and when you need to, but you can frame it conversationally in a way that makes it less intimidating in the psychology of your prospect.
Proposal "Once we have that appointment, I'll send you a proposal."	A proposal suggests you're proposing something, just like every other company the prospect is talking to. You don't want to propose something; you want to present the plan.	*Tailor* the name of your document to your avatar and their *outcomes*: Business coach or accountant: "A Growth and Expansion Strategy" Interior designer: "A Beautiful Home Blueprint" Personal Trainer: "Your Rapid Weight Loss Program."	Never present a proposal. Always label it and language it according to the *outcome* the prospect is going for. Further, do not ever send your plan to the prospect. You must *present* your plan to the prospect either face-to-face, digitally, over the phone, or in person.
"Submit" button on a website	We've been trained that the submit button is the final stage to committing. We need to make it less sterile and more enjoyable.	"I want it!" "Send it to me!" "Give it to me!" "Let's do it"	Green braining your buttons personalizes your prospect's journey and makes it fun, keeping them in green brain so they enjoy the process.

As you can see, small changes to the language you use throughout your sales process has a huge impact on how that process *feels* for the prospect. You're still addressing the red-brain points and logistics, but you're employing a language palette that is easily digestible. A main thread that you'll pick up on throughout this chapter is that a fundamental factor in drastically improving your communication is moving beyond *your* product, *your* wants, *your* outcome, and speaking from the perspective of the consumer. Let's take a look at a framework that enables you to weave green-brain language throughout every component of your sales process in a way that is easy and conversational.

Utilizing Green-Brain Language to Present Your Solution: SSOFA

Right now, are you one of the many business owners who *knows* they have a great offer for their customer, but you just don't know how to communicate it in the most compelling way? One way we help our Elevate members to embed green-brain communication throughout their sales process is using the SSOFA—Scenario, Solution, Outcome, Feeling, Agreement—model. SSOFA can help you to present any product, service, feature, or solution in a way that helps your prospect make good decisions, faster. It's a process that mirrors how the human brain likes to make buying decisions. When you use this model, you will increase conversions, shorten and accelerate your sales cycle, and increase the average dollar spend per sale.

Most businesses have a one-step sales process. Whether the conversation is happening through the landing page of an e-commerce business, or via a one-on-one consultative sales process, they simply talk through the product and its features. This approach is one-dimensional, red-brain-dominant, and comes across as salesy, because the salesperson or copywriter sounds as though they are focused on selling a product, rather than approaching the interaction from the perspective of the prospect. The SSOFA approach, by contrast, is empathetic and encouraging. When you integrate this model into your sales process, your prospects will thank you for it, because you will be one of the few businesses that actively demonstrates an interest and understanding for what's going on for *them*, rather than just trying to sell *at* them. Counterintuitively, the more skillful you become in sales, the less salesy you will become, and the more confidence you will feel.

Regardless of how you market and sell, you should apply the SSOFA model to every step of your marketing and sales process. When you're talking one to many, through copy on a landing page, an email to your subscribers, a social media post, or a stage presentation to a live audience, use the SSOFA model to present your solution. Similarly, if your sales process involves one-on-one conversations with your prospects, utilize the SSOFA model to tailor each step of the conversation to the prospect sitting in front of you.

S: Scenario

As we discussed, the product is the comfort zone for most business owners and salespeople. They can talk about their product and the features of it all day long. The problem with this is that they often present the product itself prematurely, before establishing a need. You need to understand that *in and of itself* your product has no value. Solutions derive their value *only* from the problems they solve. Therefore, you should never speak about your product before uncovering and addressing the need that it solves for your prospect.

This is what the **scenario** step of SSOFA does. It gives you a framework for speaking to where your prospect is now, their experiences and emotions, and their core challenges. This step is about uncovering the problem state, the pain that they are looking to move away from. Scenario is where we establish their buying motivators. If you're utilizing SSOFA in a one-to-many forum, such as a landing page, email, social media post, or presenting to an audience, then you hit the scenario mark by explicitly stating where the audience is now; their current problem state, that they have come to you to move away from.

If you're fortunate enough to be in a one-on-one sales conversation with your prospect, you elicit their scenario by asking them the right questions. When it comes to asking the right questions, the model our members find most helpful is what we call 4Ws and H. Yes, in practice, it's 3Ws, an H, and then another W, but we're sure you get the idea!

The reason why questions are the most powerful tool in a one-to-one environment is that they elicit a response from your prospect. This is much better than you simply making statements about why you believe the product or service is right for them. If you say it, they can question it. If they say it, *it's true*. Asking the right questions, in the right way, helps lead your customer while still giving them ownership over both the conversation and the ultimate solution.

Even when you're communicating in a one-to-many environment, you can think through these questions before you get on stage, or before writing a landing page, to develop a clear idea of how you're going to speak to the scenario your prospects are facing.

1. **What: "What's your number one priority, that if achieved would make the biggest difference for you?"**

    You ask this question to help the prospect identify and articulate their desired outcome, and communicate how important it is to them. This number one priority is their *toward motivation* and will be the key to them ultimately buying at the end of the process.

    Once they have answered this question you can help them go deeper by asking one or two follow-up questions, such as:

    - That makes sense; why is that one most important to you?
    - That's great, what is it that stands out for you right now?
    - I thought you were going to say that! Tell me why that resonates.
    - Why do you say that?
    - In what way?
    - That's super interesting, elaborate on that for me.
    - How specifically?
    - And what's been standing in your way of achieving it?
    - And what do you feel is your second priority right now?

2. **Where: "Where do you feel not having [first priority] the way you want it is impacting you the most, both personally and professionally?"**

This question helps both you and your prospect understand their current problem state; it encapsulates their *away-from* motivation. This question also helps your prospect to excavate what's going on below the surface so that both of you understand *why* the problem state is a problem for them.

Listen for their response, and then follow up with:

"I get it. And where do you think not having [second priority] the way you want it is impacting you the most?"

3. **Why Now: "Why is this important to you now? Why is this a now-conversation for you?"**

This question helps you establish urgency. One of the most common objections salespeople face is, "Thanks, that was great, let me go away and think about it." When, early in the conversation, you ask the prospect to articulate why this is a "now-conversation" for them, you prevent this objection from arising further down the track, because you have already agreed that this is not a decision the prospect wants to delay.

If the prospect doesn't express any urgency, we suggest politely wrapping the conversation by pointing them in the direction of something that will help them in the meantime. This is where the automated nurture sequence we discussed in Chapter Six: Marketing, comes into play. By placing them on an automated nurture sequence you can help them progress their thinking and ensure you stay front of mind for when they are ready to pick up the conversation again.

4. **How: "How long have you been feeling this way?"**

This question also helps prevent the "I want to think about it" objection from arising later in the process. Once your prospect acknowledges that they have been thinking about this solution for some time, and resolving it is at the forefront of their mind, they will not want to delay the decision any further.

Alternative ways to frame this question include:

- "How long has this concern been building up for?"
- "How long has this been going on for?"
- "When did you first notice this?"

5. **When: "When do you need to see this changed/done/ completed by?"**

This question creates a deadline by which your prospect wants to reach a solution. It draws a line in the sand and helps to provide impetus for them to act. It also gives you an understanding of their future timeline, and in doing so enables you to tailor your presentation of the solution accordingly.

S: Solution

Once you have elicited and spoken to someone's current scenario, you have *permission* to introduce your product as the **solution** to their *known* problem. As mentioned, we never present a product or a feature until it is a solution to a known problem.

This is the part of the sequence where you introduce your product, a particular feature, or a particular part of your solution that will functionally solve their challenges. This part of the process can be more red-brain-dominant, and gives them a logical understanding of what your product is and how it fits into their scenario.

We then move back into green brain territory by speaking to their desired *outcome*.

O: Outcome

This step is where we help the consumer start to associate with their desired state. If you present your product as a solution and stop there, you leave it up to your prospect to work out how it will benefit them, tacitly assuming that they'll figure it out for themselves. While the outcomes of your solution may be obvious to *you*, they're not yet obvious to your prospect.

We mentioned earlier that sales is leadership, and you need to lead your prospect to an understanding of exactly what outcomes your solution will help them to achieve. What is the *result* of the solution you just introduced? What **outcome**—directly connected to their desired state—will this product or feature take them toward?

Show them what's possible and paint a picture of the future. And don't stop there. Why? Because people don't buy products. They don't even buy outcomes. Products and outcomes are all just steps on the ladder to what people really buy...*feelings.*

F: Feeling

As we've discussed, everything we do as human beings is driven by two forces: the need to move away from pain and the need to move toward pleasure. By systematically ingraining feelings into your sales process, you ensure that every time you or your team speak to a potential customer, they are emotionally connected to how the solution will improve their lives.

When you touch on feelings, do so by addressing both the away from and the toward motivators. Bringing back the example of the interior design business, this may sound like: "So you can stop feeling *overwhelmed* by the huge task of making your home beautiful (negative emotion), and instead feel *empowered* knowing that you have someone who will support you through the process and ensure you're making the right decisions (positive emotion)."

This is so important that it's worth repeating: your customer is not buying your product. They're not even buying the outcome of the product. They're buying the **feeling** that the outcome gives them. Therefore, it's critical that you embed this step into your sales process.

Once the prospect is connected to these feelings, you can move on to the last step.

A: Agreement

You need to ensure that in each sales conversation, whether it's one-to-one or one-to-many, you are pacing the conversation. Too many people rush through their sales communications, and in doing so they lose their audience. Throughout each sales conversation, presentation, or landing page, you need to ensure that you are gaining micro-agreements along the way. This ensures that your audience (even if it's an audience of one) is enrolled and happy to be on the journey with you.

An easy and useful way to gain micro agreements throughout a sales presentation is by using tag questions. These are questions that end with a clause that elicits a yes response in your prospect, inviting agreement. That makes sense, doesn't it? You can see what we're doing here, can't you? We just made you say yes, didn't we? We've done four of them now, haven't we? Well that's because they're easy, aren't they? You've just got to practice them, don't you? We've done seven of them now, haven't we? But if you do too many of them they're annoying, aren't they?

You get the point. We suggest only ever using one or two at a time. These micro agreements enroll your prospect into the conversation and keep the conversation progressing in a common direction.

When you're seeking a deeper agreement and want the prospect to articulate something, you do this by using open questions. Open questions are questions that can't be answered with a simple yes or no. Instead, they elicit an opinion. In a sales context, the key to asking open questions is to ensure the question frames a positive response and gains **agreement**. For example:

- "From what we've discussed, what's sticking out as the most important part for you?"
- "How do you think that would help you achieve your outcome?"
- "How would you feel knowing that the end result is exactly what you have in your mind?"

Whenever you have a lack of rapport in any sales environment it is due to poor pacing: usually proceeding too fast. Instead, pace the conversation at the rate at which you can maintain agreement. When you take the time to gain agreements throughout your conversation, you help your prospect to feel comfortable and ensure they are *taking ownership* of the solution.

SSOFA: Tying It All Together

Let's revisit the interior designer example again and imagine a hypothetical presentation, to illustrate both how most salespeople screw up conversations by triggering the red brain, and how the five elements of SSOFA should come together, comfortably and conversationally, to rev the green brain into action.

A standard red-brain presentation might go something like this:

"OK great, we've got three options, the Gold, Silver, and Bronze Options. The Gold is $10,000 because that includes everything: we develop a style guide with you, buy everything for you, and then help you install and style it in your home. The Silver is $8,000. With the Silver we develop the style guide and help you buy the items and you place them in your home as you see fit. And the Bronze Option is $5,000, where we develop the style guide and offer some support, but the rest of the process is really over to you."

Not good. We feel awkward just writing that. We hope you felt awkward reading it. It's no wonder most people hate sales. When done in this kind of style, it feels weird. As you can see, this type of conversation is centered entirely around what? The products and the price. In other words, it's based on the agenda of the person selling and *not* the consumer. The salesperson is literally just presenting options; even worse, they are doing so in a way that triggers the red brain over and over again. If you're a consumer hearing this, all you're thinking about is price, whether you want to install the items yourself to save $5,000, whether you can find a similar service cheaper somewhere else, or perhaps whether you just do it yourself.

Selling this way locks prospects into their red brain, causing them to resist and avoid buying. Their internal dialogue will sound something like: "Oh I think she wants me to make a decision soon; this feels really awkward. What excuse can I make to buy myself more time?" To put off saying no, prospects may say something like, "Okay great, let me discuss it with my family and come back to you." Or, even worse, "Are we able to get the Gold Package for $8,000?" Whenever you get into bartering, discounting, or talking about features, you know the consumer is deeply entrenched in their red brain.

Now let's take a look at how a similar presentation may sound using the SSOFA model. Usually, SSOFA would be handled in a very conversational way. For the purpose of this example, however, we'll assume you've elicited responses to each of the steps in a one-on-one forum, and are reflecting them back to the prospect. This should feel natural, even fun. Remember what we discussed earlier; the more skilled you become in sales, the more you will be able to lead people without coming across as remotely salesy.

> *"[Scenario] So just to recap, you feel like you've fallen out of love with your current house, because it's not functional nor does it feel like a home, which is very important to you. This prevents you and the family from wanting to spend more time at home. Indirectly, this is leading to some disconnect and isolation from each other, which is, as you say, our number one priority for the project. We get it, the vast majority of our clients end up arriving at the same conclusion, that styling their home is less about look and more about connection, so we've been here before.*
>
> *[Solution] That's exactly why we created the Bespoke Home Beauty Program, to support families like yours through a journey of transforming their house into a home they love. Together, we navigate the journey of designing your beautiful home, bringing everything into the space, and making it really sing once it's here.*
>
> *[Outcome] So that one day soon you'll walk into this very space with it feeling like a beautiful and connected home where you can start creating magic moments together.*
>
> *[Feeling] That way you can stop feeling like you're living in a house that really isn't you, and instead feel nestled in a sanctuary that the family won't want to leave.*
>
> *[Agreement, Open Question] How does that feel?"*

Present the offer like this, and you'll likely hear a response along the lines of:

> *"Thank you! That is exactly what we've been looking for."*

To which you respond:

"Perfect, tell me why you think it's ideal for you right now."

Gauge the prospect's response, and only *then*, once you *know* that this is the solution they want to go ahead with, do you present the price.

First you want to tell the prospect what happens once they get started. This takes away the sense of the unknown about what happens next, on the other side of them making a decision. It also anchors them in something they should want to do, making the decision an easy one to cruise through. This will sound something like:

"Great, well let's get you started, so we can schedule in the first envisaging session, which is where the real fun begins."

Once they know what happens after they get started, present two different pricing options in a green brain way. Note that you're not presenting two different product options here. By now, as the leader of the conversation, you should know enough about them, their challenges, and their objectives, to be able to prescribe the right path for them. While it may be necessary in some businesses to present several product options, wherever possible we strongly suggest confidently leading your prospect in *one* direction.

"There's two really simple ways to do that: we can get you moving on the Easy Start, which is just $2,990 per month over four months, or if you want a saving we can use the Quick Start package, which comes to just $9,990. Which are you leaning toward more, the Easy Start or the Quick Start with the saving?"

As you read through the red brain and green brain examples above, can you feel the difference in how the prospect experiences the two approaches? It's vital to understand that *sales is service*. The purpose of a sales conversation is not to get someone to buy; it's to encourage someone to decide. If, once you've elicited their needs and overlaid your solution to those needs, it's not right for them, that's a successful outcome. You've helped them clarify what they do and don't want. Alternatively when you go through a process like this with someone, you will often come to the conclusion of the conversation and—rather than it being awkward and uncomfortable—they will feel heard, seen, and excited to get started. This is also a successful outcome.

Sales doesn't need to be weird. If you're coming from a place of, "How do I sell my product?" then you've already lost. If you're coming from a place that says, "I want to help this person get really clear on what they want and need, and give them the best opportunity to solve their problem, whether it's with us or in another way," then you're truly coming from a place of service, and your words and actions will resonate differently with your prospects.

We need to move beyond thinking about ourselves and our agenda, put ourselves firmly in the hearts and minds of our audience and, from there, *lead*.

ASCEND: GUIDE YOUR CUSTOMERS THROUGH A PRODUCT SUITE

When businesses seek to drive revenue and profitability, they tend to spend all their time and energy focusing on winning new customers. While you absolutely must focus both your attention and the attention of your company on winning business, you must also complement it with continuing to make offers to your existing customers.

Why does this matter? You already have a relationship with your existing customers, so it is significantly quicker, easier, and cheaper to invite an existing customer to buy again than it is to acquire a new customer. According to *Forbes*, it costs five times more to acquire a new customer than it does to encourage an existing customer to buy again.[7] Your existing customers know, like, and trust you, and therefore are significantly more likely to buy from you than to seek out new options from a competitor, which will be more time consuming and costly for them. Once you have established a relationship with a customer, they will naturally prefer to continue engaging you to solve their problems, as opposed to looking for someone else. The question is: how are you serving your customers with more offers?

---

[7] Jia Wertz, "Don't Spend 5 Times More Attracting New Customers, Nurture the Existing Ones," *Forbes Magazine*, Sep 12, 2018, https://www.forbes.com/sites/jiawertz/2018/09/12/dont-spend-5-times-more-attracting-new-customers-nurture-the-existing-ones/?sh=12cd0a325a8e.

To determine how you can help your existing customers buy more from you, ask yourself, "What problems does my solution create?" Once someone purchases their initial product from you, what other needs, wants, or challenges will arise for them as they use it? The answer to this question contains your opportunity to add more value to your customers and ultimately see them buy repeatedly from you.

When making new offers to existing customers, the main thing business owners get wrong is timing. We must ensure that we are making the right offers, at the right time for each customer. In the next chapter we will discuss why and how to develop a Customer Journey Map—an outline of how to address the needs of your customer and speak to their emotions at each stage of their journey with you. For now, however, let's lay some of the groundwork for understanding this concept.

Once your customer buys from you, there will be times when you're right at the front of their mind, and they're highly engaged. At this point, they are at a peak of emotion. There'll be other times when they have other things going on, and they're not so focused on your brand. During these periods, their levels of emotion—related to your business—are lower. In every business, there are three key moments in your customer's journey where they are at a peak of emotion, and therefore these are prime opportunities to make the next offer and invite them to buy more.

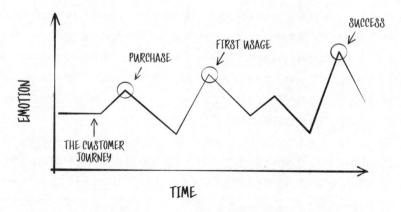

Figure 7.2: Mapping Your Customer's Emotional Peaks

These three key peaks of emotion are:

1. **The point of purchase.** As your customer makes a purchase from you, they feel a heightened sense of optimism. They are excited to receive a solution to their problem and have their needs met. This is an ideal moment to cross-sell another product that will benefit them even further, or upsell to a premium offering that will do even more for them.

2. **The point of first usage.** The second peak occurs when your customer first receives and/or uses your product. At this point, you can speak to their current experience, what challenges may arise from here, or further wants and needs, to offer them something that will complement the core product.

3. **The point of success.** The third peak of emotion happens when your customer experiences their first point of success using your product or service. At this point, they are experiencing firsthand the benefit they have been seeking. They now have proof that you and your company deliver on your promises, and that your solutions truly work for them. If you can link your next offer to their renewed wants and needs at this exact moment, they will be willing to spend more with you.

Let's look at some examples of how this works in practice. First we'll apply the model to a familiar product-based business, and then we'll take a look at how it might work in a service-based business.

When customers purchase a new iPhone, they are usually excited and full of anticipation about how it will enhance their lives. At this **point of purchase**, they may be keen to upgrade to a more premium model or add AirPods to their basket.

Soon, they get the phone home, or—if it has been preordered or ordered online—receive it. Apple are experts at making customers feel something, so this **point of first usage** is designed to feel like a personal mini-product-reveal. The white box slides open with just the right amount of suction to generate suspense. The phone switches on and is quick and intuitive to set up. Customers feel a sense of satisfaction and curiosity about what they can do with their phone. This creates an opportunity for Apple to demonstrate how other products, such as AirPods, an iPad, and a MacBook, sync naturally and easily with the phone.

Within twenty-four hours, customers have customized their new phone with their choice of apps, used it to connect with people via call and text, and perhaps added personal touches, such as a unique home screen or ringtone. At this **point of success**, they are feeling comfortable with the phone and intrigued by its capabilities; another opportunity to demonstrate how beautifully other Apple products sync with it and improve the experience further.

For a service-based business such as a personal trainer, the principles are similar but the process is slightly different. Let's say a potential new client meets with a personal trainer to discuss their challenges and goals and decides to enroll in a program. At this **point of purchase**, they have harnessed their sense of commitment, and their enthusiasm for getting in great shape; the perfect time to upgrade to include a nutritional plan or to lengthen their course from six to twelve weeks.

Following the first session, the client feels strong, energized, and refreshed. They have just begun to experience the benefits of the program. During this **point of first usage**, the trainer mentions some of the basic principles behind the personalized nutrition plan, piquing the client's curiosity and encouraging them to add it to their program.

As the six-week course comes to an end, the client has attained the goals they set at the outset of the training. They feel confident, disciplined, and self-assured, ready to build further on their achievements. This **point of success** is the perfect opportunity for the trainer to invite the client to sign up for an additional six or twelve weeks.

While the specifics of each business will vary, these examples demonstrate the importance of systematically introducing cross-sells and upsells at the right points in the customer journey. It's especially important that the offer matches the customer's level of emotion. When you strategically embed cross-sells and upsells at peaks of emotion throughout your customer's journey, you rapidly and significantly increase your profitability by further serving your customers.

THE MECHANICS AND MANAGEMENT OF BUILDING A SALES TEAM

In sales, the key to elevating from startup to scaleup is to establish the structure, process, and team that lay the foundation for achieving your sales targets with progressively less hands-on involvement from you. We guide our members through four steps to customize and operationalize their sales strategy:

- mapping out your sales process to fit how your customer wants to buy
- identifying who in your team is in charge at each juncture
- codifying the company's communication and sales formula
- calculating how to hit targets

Bringing together these four aspects will enable you to build a sales function that captures best practice, and can ultimately be trained, delegated, and scaled.

1. Map Out Your Sales Process

First, identify the exact sequence of steps a prospect needs to take to convert from a lead to a paying customer. Too many businesses don't have a codified sales process, and as a result they cannot *lead*. In the absence of leadership, the prospect ends up controlling what happens and when, which they don't want to do! Remember, when you define your sales process, which you can communicate to the prospect upfront and lead them through with confidence, this significantly reduces their buyer's resistance and increases their buyer's acceptance, because they can foresee the decision points throughout the process. Knowing when they will be expected to make certain decisions alleviates anxiety around the unknown and lets them know they are in experienced hands.

Further to this, lacking a defined sales process is unmanageable and unscalable for the business internally. You need an agreed pathway, optimized at every step, which you can delegate to your current or future sales team. This is the "our company way of selling" we described earlier. Each business is unique, so the exact steps will vary slightly, but you must map each step to give your sales process structure.

For examples of two different sales processes, for two different business models, see Figure 7.3 and Figure 7.4, in the following section.

2. Pinpoint Ownership of Each Interaction

Once you have identified which steps in your sales process require personal interaction, you must determine who takes ownership of each one. Generally speaking, the more high-volume conversations should be handled by SDRs, and the more high-quality conversations handled by professional sales people.

In some cases, such as an e-commerce business where customers can perform most of the steps online, they may not need to interact with someone at every turn. On the other hand, we're currently seeing that the best online businesses increasingly enhance their sales process and customer experience using online sales agents. These agents may guide the customer through the process and even facilitate the sale through mediums such as chat.

Let's take a look at two examples of different sales processes; one for a consultative sales process and one for an e-commerce business. These diagrams outline the step-by-step sequence, who should be taking ownership of each step, and one important key that most businesses miss: what to do with a prospect who *doesn't* continue onto the next stage.

E-COMMERCE SALES PROCESS

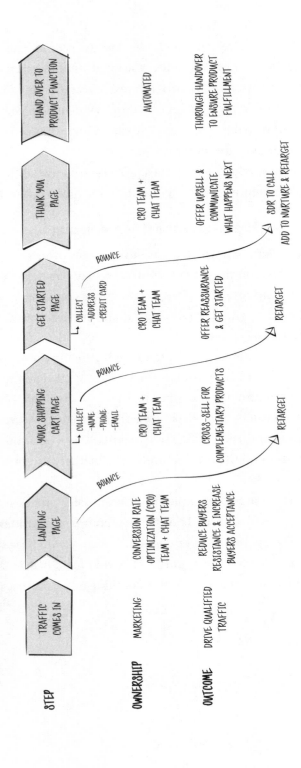

Figure 7.3: E-commerce Sales Process

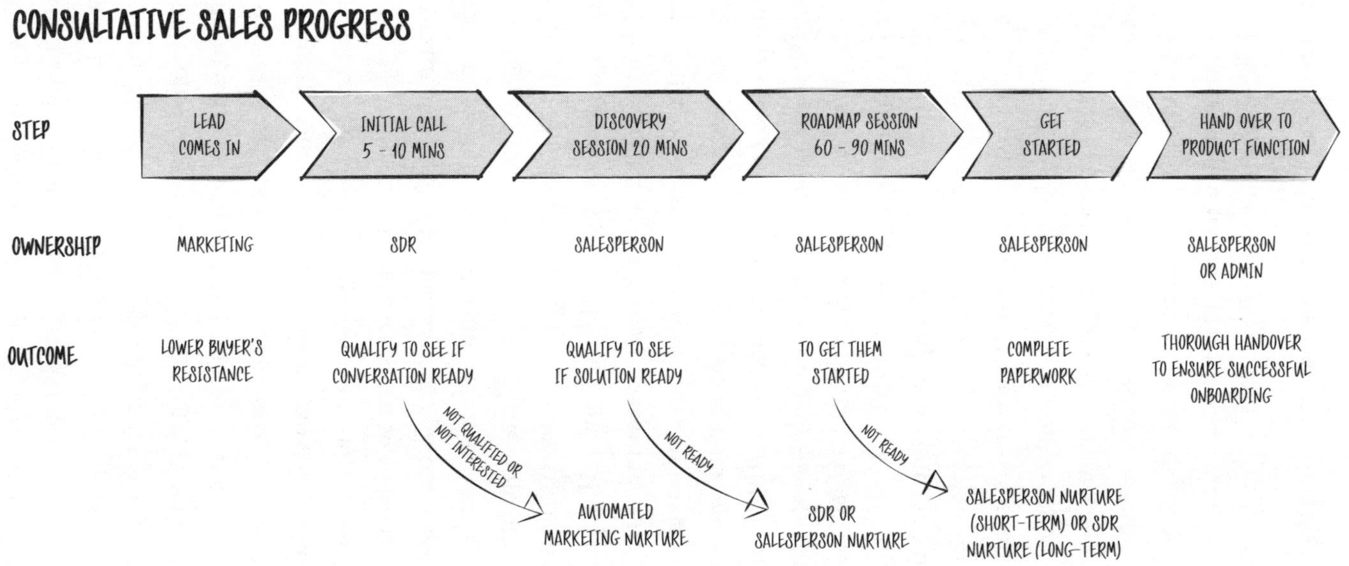

CONSULTATIVE SALES PROGRESS

STEP	LEAD COMES IN	INITIAL CALL 5 - 10 MINS	DISCOVERY SESSION 20 MINS	ROADMAP SESSION 60 - 90 MINS	GET STARTED	HAND OVER TO PRODUCT FUNCTION
OWNERSHIP	MARKETING	SDR	SALESPERSON	SALESPERSON	SALESPERSON	SALESPERSON OR ADMIN
OUTCOME	LOWER BUYER'S RESISTANCE	QUALIFY TO SEE IF CONVERSATION READY	QUALIFY TO SEE IF SOLUTION READY	TO GET THEM STARTED	COMPLETE PAPERWORK	THOROUGH HANDOVER TO ENSURE SUCCESSFUL ONBOARDING

NOT QUALIFIED OR NOT INTERESTED → AUTOMATED MARKETING NURTURE

NOT READY → SDR OR SALESPERSON NURTURE

NOT READY → SALESPERSON NURTURE (SHORT-TERM) OR SDR NURTURE (LONG-TERM)

Figure 7.4: Consultative Sales Process

3. Bottle the Communication Models of Your Sales Process

As we discussed at the beginning of the chapter, most businesses never capture the communication models that will most effectively help their prospects to buy. The reason for this is that the majority of founders still live with the old-school belief that sales and communication are a form of intuitive black magic. Like the gift of the gab, you either have it, or you don't. This belief couldn't be further from the truth. The most effective communicators are *trained* communicators with models that underpin almost everything they say, and scripts they can turn to when responding to common questions and objections.

In startup, you probably did most of the selling yourself, and your intuitive approach worked. This may have created the misconception that you don't have any communication models, when the truth is that you do, they are just in your head. How do we know? If we observed you walking ten different prospects through your sales process, we guarantee that we would see *patterns*. Patterns in how you introduce each conversation, what questions you ask and why, what you extrapolate from their responses, how you tailor and present your solutions, what aspects of their situation you do and don't focus on, how you prevent and overcome objections, and ultimately how you get someone started when they decide to buy. These are your communication models, and the scripts that operate within these models. But you haven't taken the time to capture them in a format that can be transferred to your team.

Models and scripts are essential for creating consistency throughout your sales process. What's a communication model? Simply, a structure you can follow to deliver each piece of your sales process in a way that is effective for your prospect. You just learned two of them: The 4 Ws and H, and SSOFA. When you get your sales wisdom out of our head and onto the page, creating models for each stage of the sales process, you ensure that everyone sells the same way to every prospect, every time. This is like handing out the recipe so everyone on your team can replicate your secret sauce. Without doing this, you're leaving the dynamics of your sales discussions to chance and the individual skill of each salesperson.

Further, when you have defined communication models, you can use them as a baseline from which to optimize each time you discover an improvement. For example, you or someone on your team might develop a better way of asking a question, leading the prospect, or touring the solution. Each time someone finds a better way of doing something, it gets integrated into the model. This ensures best practice becomes standard practice.

The difference between a model and script is that a model provides the architecture, whereas a script provides exact language. You can use models to communicate almost anything, but scripts should be used mainly for training and preparation. One important caveat about using scripts is that you and your team shouldn't become too attached to them. Although we develop scripts to capture and train best practice, we should never *rely* on the script when speaking with a prospect. The script is mostly a training tool. The reason we encourage you not to become attached to a script is because you can never fully predict what the prospect is going to say. You say A and the prospect says B. So far, so good. Then you say C, and the prospect says X. If you are attached to a script, you will be thrown off balance whenever the conversation veers away from your expected lines. When operating to a *model*, however, you can naturally and easily bring the conversation back on track. Once you get in front of a prospect, you should have some language prepared, but this should not replace real human interaction and connection. You and your sales team should train using both scripts and improvised role play, but with prospects you will want to embody the communication *models*, so that you can use them elegantly and conversationally.

To ensure that salespeople use the correct models and connect with customers consistently, we run entire workshops on advanced communication and sales skills for each stage of the sales process. We've made our Selling Essentials workbook full of the most fundamental communication models for selling, available in the resources section of our website for

you to grab and tailor to your business. Just head to www.the-entourage
.com/elevate to download yours.

4. Define Your Lead Measures and Lag Measures
to Consistently Hit Targets

When you start turning your sales function into a predictable engine, a
fundamental starting point for your planning is to forecast how many sales
you expect the company to make each month for the next twelve months.
Not only does this set the tone for everything that you want to achieve in
marketing and sales, it also helps you forecast overall company revenue,
which enables you to plan right across the Six Elements of the business.

How many customers will you have? How much do you need to
develop your operations? How much can you invest in recruitment and
building your team? What profit will the company deliver? All this starts
with being able to forecast how many sales you plan to make. In Chapter
Ten: Finance, we cover how to translate your growth plans into actionable
financial projections, and why your revenue model is an important first
step in generating accurate forecasts. Once you've defined your sales
targets, you then reverse engineer, calculating how many people you
need at each stage of your marketing and sales funnel to hit your targets.

Let's take the consultative sales process from Figure 7.4 and assume
that your team target is twenty sales per month. Knowing that this is
your desired outcome, how many people need to do a roadmap session?
Let's assume that your conversion from roadmap to making a sale is 50
percent. In this case, the team needs to do forty roadmap sessions across
the month. Your next step is to ask, "How many discovery sessions do we
need to do to hit forty roadmap sessions for the month?" Work out your
conversion rate from discovery to roadmap, and use this information to
define the exact number.

Continue applying this process right back to the beginning of your
marketing funnel, and determine how many leads you need to generate to schedule the right number of initial SDR calls, discovery sessions,
roadmap sessions, and ultimately sales.

You can apply exactly the same formula to the e-commerce sales process. Start with your sales target for the month, and then work out how much traffic you need and what conversions you require at each stage of your funnel to ensure that you consistently hit your targets.

Most businesses go wrong by calculating roughly how many sales they want to make, but failing to reverse engineer the numbers at each stage of the funnel, so they don't know what it will take to get there. The problem with this approach is that the number of sales is what we call a lag measure. It's an output. By the time you reach the end of the month and realize that you haven't made as many sales as you wanted, it's too late. By assessing the number of people you need to pass through each stage of the funnel, however, you switch your focus to what we call lead measures. These are inputs you can control and manage throughout the month, to ensure that you achieve your lag measure.

One fundamental tool our Elevate members love using to establish and track their lead and lag measures in their sales function is our Sales Activity Summary Sheet (SASS). We've captured an editable version of this in your resources section, here: www.the-entourage.com/elevate.

SCALING SALES COMES DOWN TO PROCESS

We understand why sales feels like magic. The moment when a prospect you're keen to work with and know you can help, agrees that your solution is a perfect fit for their business is indeed a magical one. It's the spark on which every successful business is built. As a founder, it's incredibly tempting to believe that you're the only person who can unleash this magic. It may be stressful to think that no one else can sell as well as you can, but it also makes you feel special, as though you wield a unique power others don't understand.

Because sales deals with human psychology and communication, most people view it as something that can't be bottled or captured. As we've shown in this chapter, however, this is not the case. Effective communication, just like any other skill, can be defined, formulated into models, optimized, and scaled. You just need the frameworks to get you started. Once you start turning your previously intuitive sales approach into a replicable process, knowing something you thought couldn't be harnessed has now been bottled, you will be struck with an overwhelming feeling of empowerment.

To move from startup to scaleup, however, you'll need to recognize that your abilities become even *more* powerful when you share them with your team. That's how you multiply them, enabling every member of your sales team to sell at a world-class level. A systematized sales process is a non-negotiable part of growing your business, and it drives every other function, because the number of sales you make defines the budget you can allocate to every other element of your business. Transitioning away from being the main revenue driver in your business, and no longer needing to wear the hat of technician in your sales function, is usually accompanied by a triumphant feeling of seeing your monthly sales numbers grow, without a need for your direct involvement.

Combined, the mechanisms in this chapter represent a step-by-step guide to building a sustainable sales team that can take the heavy lifting off your hands and give you the breathing room to elevate your contribution to the business. There's a lot to absorb here, so pick the parts that are most relevant to your business at this moment. Maybe that's hiring a single part-time salesperson; maybe it's taking the time to document your own sales process and sharing it with your existing team; or maybe it's looking into recruiting a full-scale SDR team to handle a higher volume of leads and enable your sales team to focus on high-quality conversations.

CASE STUDY: BEN TRANSFORMS HIS SALES FUNCTION FROM STAGNATING TO SUPERPOWERED

Ben founded his marketing agency in 1999 and had been running it for twenty years when he initially reached out to us. Although he had always loved what he did, he had hit a plateau just under the $1 million revenue mark. He was feeling despondent and wondering whether he'd ever break through. "I was working really hard," he told us. "I was overworked, stressed, frustrated, and definitely burned out. That was what really got me to reach out to The Entourage."

Ben's first challenge was that he was spending the vast majority of his time delivering work for clients. Just like Frances from Chapter One, Ben was constantly wearing the hat of technician and was buried in product development and delivery. In our first strategy session, Ben started to understand that to drive the growth of his business beyond the $1 million mark, he would need to empower his team to deliver client projects without him, so that he could focus on sales.

Ben's roadmap started with structuring and systemizing his product delivery capacity. He had always delivered projects to a world-class standard; the next step was developing his team to a point where they could not only match his standards, but ultimately exceed them. When business owners backfill themselves, this is one of their key outcomes. While not every individual can be as capable as the business owner, organizing a team, training them to operate within a specific structure, and assigning them to spend 100 percent of their time on a specific function, leads to an overall higher quality of work, even as the founder does less. This phenomenon enabled Ben to gradually dilute his presence in the product delivery department, freeing up the time to focus on improving his sales capability, and on developing a sales process that others would also eventually be able to take over.

Ben's sales journey started like so many others: first, he identified and connected with the real value that he and his team offered clients. So often, business owners trapped in the day-to-day lose sight of the real value they deliver. Therefore, they end up underestimating their own worth, which is reflected in how they present their product throughout their marketing and sales process. When Ben got clear on the real benefits of his services, we were able to build a replicable sales process that communicated these benefits in the most impactful way. A vital key here was integrating the SSOFA method throughout the sales process which greatly improved the quality of the communication with prospects. This allowed Ben to stop using proposals altogether, which significantly shortened his sales cycle.

These changes brought Ben a range of benefits. First, he increased conversions and achieved a faster sales cycle. Second, because he was communicating the value of his work more clearly, it became possible for him to dramatically increase his prices. "We used to do projects that were $20,000," he explained to us, and now "the projects we consistently do are $60,000 to $70,000. During COVID, we signed our biggest project ever, which was $220,000, and we did that without a proposal. At this point, that's consistent, so I don't see it as a surprise anymore."

When Ben placed his focus on sales and developing his sales process, he achieved significant revenue growth, profit growth, and ultimately built out his team to a point where he is supported right across the business. As he explained it, "For eighteen years, we were typically doing $60,000 months; now we're consistently doing $130,000 months, with our higher months reaching $200,000. Previously, I wouldn't have thought that was possible, but now it's the norm. Sales used to be all on my shoulders, and I thought it was something I would have to do forever. I couldn't see a way out. Now, the process is defined, so I can scale my sales department. It's completely transformed my approach to selling."

Shifting his focus to sales necessitated that Ben successfully built a product delivery function that now works completely without him. He says, "Another great outcome has been that I'm no longer operationally involved in the delivery of our products and services. What that means is that when a project comes in, my team is already empowered to be really great at what they do, and now I'm not a bottleneck within that process. They're actually delivering projects better, without me."

Ben's story is a reminder that even if you've been operating via old habits for twenty years, you can transition from technician to leader, you can improve the service your customers receive, you can transform your approach to sales, and you can do all the above while significantly increasing your profitability.

JACK LEARNS TO SYSTEMATIZE SALES

As we've mentioned, most business owners sell intuitively. This is especially true when sales is your core skillset. Early on, this was certainly the case for Jack. With a naturally deep empathy for people, and having studied psychology and communication since he was a kid, Jack was a highly effective salesperson. At the beginning of his business career, this meant that sales was always a core strength of his businesses. As the businesses that he founded and invested in scaled into larger companies, however, it became apparent that the sales functions depended on Jack's involvement. When he was involved, the businesses achieved their targets. If he was out of the loop for too long, however, performance would decline. He hadn't yet developed the ability to create a scalable and replicable sales process that could be transferred to others.

This became most evident in 2008, when he started to speak to large audiences from the stage. Jack noticed that when he was talking to a bigger audience, as opposed to a small group or another person, the sensory feedback he usually relied on to lead a conversation wasn't forthcoming. After studying his presentations, trying to locate the disconnect, he realized that when presenting to larger audiences, he became very rational and one-dimensional. He was cutting off his greatest gift: his ability to *connect* with his audience. While he hadn't yet developed the language for it, he was having what he would now call a red-brain conversation with his audience.

These core challenges forced Jack to acknowledge that if he was going to truly lead his teams to success, in a way that removed their reliance on him, he needed to approach sales from the positions of leader and entrepreneur, instead of technician. At the time, many experts still thought of sales as "the gift of the gab," a skill that people either had or they didn't. Nonetheless, Jack was certain he could reverse engineer the principles of his communication and collate them into frameworks and models that others could follow. Jack got busy developing models and frameworks, a process that would culminate in the creation of an overall sales process that could be trained, delegated, and managed. He was determined to take the invisible and make it tangible.

As he started to train his teams using a sales *process*, they became more capable and competent and consistently performed at a high level. This led to the core realization that when people believe they lack confidence in sales, it's not actually confidence they lack. It's *structure*. Members of a sales team with a process to follow and models to guide them each step of the way develop into people who confidently lead both their prospects *and* other members of the team. With lived experience of how their communication can influence others to transform for the better, their confidence grows in an upward spiral.

In 2012, to keep up with the demand and level of enquiry that was coming into The Entourage, Jack brought in a sales executive to whom he could delegate the management, leadership, and continued development of the sales team. This shift points to another key pattern that is true in every business: it doesn't matter how strong you personally are in sales, when you bring in a senior person who can dedicate 100 percent of their time to scaling your sales function, this will always be a key inflection point in the trajectory of your business.

As the years clicked by, we took a great sales process and turned it into a sales engine, making our sales function a lot more sophisticated. We achieved this by first bringing on a sales executive to lead the function, then hiring more senior and more experienced sales people and training them extensively in our sales process and models. Next, we implemented a best-in-class CRM to manage, track, report on, and refine the effectiveness of our entire sales process. Finally, we focused on enhancing the depth of our sales team, bringing on SDRs, operational and administrative support to further turbo-charge the productivity of our existing sales capability.

Today, Jack has stepped away from operational involvement in the marketing and sales functions. Instead, he is focused on building the brand globally, while helping guide our marketing and sales functions from a strategic level, activities that give him and the business far more leverage. In the brand building component of his role, he is the figurehead and spokesperson of the business, driving meaningful PR through the media and presenting to large audiences at Entourage events around the world. When working strategically to help shape our sales function, Jack is always developing new sales architecture, processes, and models that further enhance our connection points with consumers.

With a world-class director of sales in place, and a highly trained team of professionals, Jack is free to build the brand and enhance our overall buyer's journey, safe in the knowledge that the team is having hundreds of conversations every week with people who have reached out to learn more about how The Entourage can support them in transforming their business.

NEXT UP...

When you start to build your marketing and sales engine, you create another problem: looking after your growing base of customers. Great brands are consumer-first brands, meaning they care deeply about the people they serve, what the consumer wants, and how as a business they can deliver on their promise. In the next chapter we will look at how to build out your product development and delivery function in a way that not only wows your customer, but—yes, you guessed it—doesn't rely on you being operationally involved.

8

PRODUCT

Develop and Deliver Products That Delight Your Customer

During the startup stage, you probably spent the majority of your time at the coal face, delivering your product or service to customers. This may actually have been the reason why you started your business in the first place. You felt a deep affinity with your customers' needs, and—knowing that you could serve those needs better than anyone else—you proceeded to turn your passion and insight into a business. This is how almost all businesses start: someone attempts to solve a problem, either a problem of their own or one they see customers experience every single day.

It's one thing to solve this problem for a few people; it's a completely different playing field to solve this problem at scale. As an entrepreneur, you should be striving not to solve the problem for just one or two people, but for as many people as you can possibly reach. If you're currently spending most of your time delivering your product, you don't have a business; you have a job. Unless you break out of this mode of thinking and doing, you'll be destined to stay in the startup phase forever.

One of the challenges we see in businesses that still operate like a startup, is that they're hampered by inconsistent product and service delivery. Their offerings are often undefined, untested, unwieldy, and unmanageable. They may have figured out how to get customers through the door—often by promising anything and everything that the customer wants, but when their delivery doesn't match their promises, things fall apart, and they end up losing as many customers as they are gaining.

To break through the Seven-Figure Ceiling, you first need to create consistency in your customer journey. Once you're delivering on foundational customer expectations, you then have permission to go above and beyond to delight your customers. To reliably achieve these goals, you need to build a product development and delivery function that includes the necessary frameworks, processes, and people to consistently deliver on your brand promise, all without your direct intervention.

Over the long term, your job as an entrepreneur is not to deliver a product or a service to a customer. It's not even to market and sell that product or service. Your job is to build a business that can market, sell, and deliver a product, and do so again and again, with ever-reducing demands on your own personal time.

KEY PRODUCT GOALS

In the previous two chapters, we covered the marketing and sales elements of the Drive Growth Cycle. In this chapter, we take a look at the third section: product. To become a consumer champion in your space, you must consistently deliver what customers want, when they want it, how they want it.

We'll explore the two sides of product delivery. The first is mechanics: the logistics and moving parts that enable you to fulfill your promises. The second is dynamics. This addresses what the customer is feeling and experiencing at each stage of their journey, how well you speak to their emotional wants and needs, and how effectively you align your offerings to those wants and needs.

By putting in place the structure to consistently deliver on the mechanics, you achieve consistency in your delivery and therefore build foundational trust with your consumer. When you overlay this with a process that enlivens the *dynamics* of their journey, you become more than just a business providing a commodity—you become a brand providing a memorable experience. As we discussed in Chapter Six: Marketing, *great brands stand for something,* and they transcend the products they deliver to occupy a space in the heart of their consumer. *This* is how you become an industry leader and experience an upward spiral of growth.

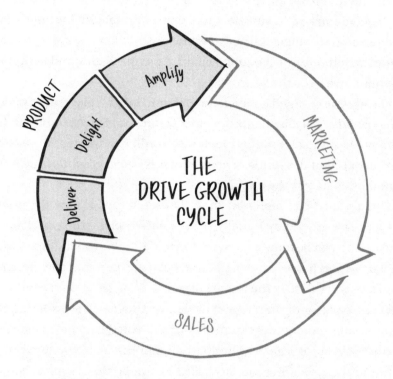

Figure 8.1 Product Components of the Drive Growth Cycle

The product section of the Drive Growth Cycle, and the main lessons in this chapter, consist of three components: **deliver**, **delight**, and **amplify**.

These three components are sequential. First, ask yourself how you're going to deliver on the promises you made in the sales process. When you're getting the fundamentals right, you have permission to speak to the hearts of your customers, delighting them in unexpected ways. Once you are doing this on a consistent basis, you will have a growing base of happy customers. At this point, you will want to capture the positive experiences of your successful customers and pass them through to marketing. Marketing can then amplify these experiences through testimonials, case studies, and success stories that let your audience know that as a brand, you are the real deal.

This final step will give the next cycle of new prospects the confidence they need to make a buying decision, while also reinforcing your value for returning customers, so they continue trusting you to serve them. This creates an infinite, self-reinforcing loop, thus completing and perpetuating your Drive Growth Cycle.

Once we've outlined how you can **deliver**, **delight**, and **amplify**, we'll bring *everything* in this chapter together in one simple tool: the Customer Journey Map. The reason this tool is so incredibly important to you and your team is that delivering great products is usually significantly more complex than meets the eye.

If you're an e-commerce business for example, you know all too well that a process that may initially seem easy (receive order, pack order, send order), can become a lot more convoluted when operating at scale. What if the warehouse is out of stock? What if the customer changes their mind? What if you're in the middle of a once-in-a-generation pandemic and *everyone* is ordering online, while every logistics provider on the planet strains under the pressure of unprecedented demand? Managing product delivery at scale requires both simplification and systemization.

Similarly, if you're a service-based business, the situation can be equally complex, especially as you build out your delivery team and strive to ensure that your service is always delivered to the high standards you require.

These challenges cut to the heart of our reasons for developing the Customer Journey Map; to bring together every element of world-class delivery into one simple, highly effective tool. Whether your business is product based or service based, the key is to map out the entire delivery process in a way that marries the mechanics and the dynamics, documenting each and every step, and to identify what's truly important for the customer at each stage. You can use this tool to bring together your entire customer journey, in a way that enables you to get on top of *it*, rather than it being on top of *you*.

The key performance metrics this chapter will help you to increase are customer retention, renewal and repeat business, public-facing customer satisfaction ratings, word-of-mouth referrals, and ultimately the lifetime value (LTV) of each and every customer. When you push these performance levers, you will add to the momentum you've gained through marketing and sales. Rather than filling a leaky bucket, you'll achieve an immediate uplift in profitability and an upward spiral of growth.

For now, let's start, by ensuring you're delivering on your fundamental promise.

DELIVER: INCREASING YOUR PRODUCT-MARKET FIT AND KEEPING YOUR PROMISES

A key part of moving from startup to scaleup is scaling the delivery of your product in a way that creates consistently world-class customer experience. This means ensuring that your newly acquired customer transitions seamlessly from buying your product to consuming your product.

To put yourself in the right mindset to achieve this, try reframing product delivery as the stage of the customer journey where you deliver on your *promises*. Throughout the marketing and sales process, you will have made numerous guarantees to your customer about what they can expect from your business. Now is when you deliver—and deliver you must, because whether or not you do will determine the entire rest of your relationship with the customer, and everyone they speak to.

Deliver on your promises, and chances are good they come back for more. Fail to deliver, and they probably won't. Worse still, there's a chance they'll tell others to avoid you as well. In today's world of social media, word of mouth has a megaphone—one that can easily be borrowed by any customer who feels like you have failed to deliver what you promised them.

This step is so vital that it might require you to consider tapering growth temporarily. If ever you take on so many new customers that important deliverables start to fall through the cracks, and customers aren't receiving what you promised them, it's time to pull back on growth and instead focus on ensuring you have the resources to nail your product delivery.

Product delivery starts with maximizing your product-market fit. What is product-market fit? Fundamentally, it's the degree to which your product satisfies a strong demand in the market. Product-market fit underpins the success of all six elements of your business. From the efficiency of your marketing, to the conversion rate of your sales process, from the morale of your team, to the overall growth and profitability of the business, *every* element of your business relies on the extent to which you have achieved product-market fit. As a strong-willed entrepreneur, when you don't have product-market fit, you can still push forward, but the rest of your business journey will be an uphill battle. A lack of product-market fit will act like an anchor, dragging behind you and slowing down your entire business.

In the early stages of your business it's often easier to achieve product-market fit as a service-based business than a product-based business. This is because you can start with an idea and easily tweak it in response to customer feedback. You can market your initial product, then finesse it as you go, which can be hugely beneficial in finding product-market fit. As you begin to scale up, however, things get trickier; at some point, you need to stop iterating and package up the services you offer. At this point, you will need to phase out the "go-anywhere, do-anything" approach and focus on defining your core product pillars in a way that enables you to deliver consistently.

Counterintuitively, putting structure around your service offering improves the experience for your customer. The Entourage is an example of a service-based business that continues to scale while offering best-in-class services. We've created an ecosystem with defined pillars—business coaching, training, and community—that give our offering consistency and reliability. Within those pillars we are able to individualize the journey for every member according to their unique set of challenges and objectives. In addition to this, each member benefits from the scale at which we operate, because we are able to attract the best talent from all around the world to deliver to different members according to their needs. Productizing what we do and creating an ecosystem means we're able to offer tailored experiences at scale. In this way, the more the ecosystem grows, the more value there is for each individual member.

Product-led businesses need to stage things differently. They need to make quality progress on their product *before* they can add marketing and sales to fuel the fire. Often, the best product businesses spend countless hours perfecting their product before proceeding to marketing and sales.

As an example, let's look at Four Pillars Gin, a gin brand out of Australia that has won countless international awards, and makes arguably the world's best gin. Four Pillars went through *years* of product development before ever launching their first gin, even going on a world tour to sample different gins and ordering the best still (gin-making equipment) in the world—an order that took a year to fulfill. They used all that time to rigorously test their product (it's a tough job, but someone has to do it) and hone their product-market fit. While they may continue to innovate, the product core of their business was relatively settled before they ever sold a bottle of gin. By the time they launched, they had created a product that they knew met the needs of the market.

Whatever your business model, product-market fit will continue to evolve. It is not a state that you magically obtain and then never have to worry about again. It's a temporary alignment of your product with market demand. When you have a strong product-market fit, everything flows. When your product-market fit wanes, it becomes much harder to sustain growth and profitability.

The market can shift in unexpected ways. Customer expectations may change, new competitors may emerge onto the scene, new technology or methods may evolve. A previous offering, which may have had strong product-market fit, can very quickly lose that distinction. As your business moves from startup to scaleup, it's vital to constantly check and confirm that you have product-market fit. For this reason it's critical that you're regularly measuring and quantifying customer happiness. As soon as you start to see indicators that customer happiness is waning, it's time to dive into consumer feedback, market trends, and begin to innovate on your product to stay ahead of consumer needs.

KEEPING YOUR FINGER ON THE PULSE: MEASURING AND MANAGING YOUR DELIVERY

The extent to which you have achieved product-market fit is determined by your customer, and your customer alone. When assessing how well they are delivering to their existing customers, the most common mistake businesses make is using their own assumptions as a benchmark. While your gut feel should guide you, and may often be right, it is simply not rigorous enough to assess the happiness of your customers at scale. At any given moment, it is imperative that you have your finger on the pulse. In other words, you should always know how satisfied your existing customers are.

The more you build a business that works without you, the more important this type of quantifiable data becomes. During startup, when most of the product delivery is done by you, you have a visceral understanding of every nuance of your customer. Once you build out your business, however, and elevate into wearing the hat of leader and entrepreneur, you'll spend less time at the coal face. In this context, it is critical that you have a reliable method of regularly measuring customer happiness, and soliciting feedback directly from those who matter most: your customers. In the absence of this type of data, the quality of your product delivery could slip for months before it comes to your attention. Your first indication of the problem might only come when it begins to impact customer retention, renewal, and ultimately P&L performance. Should the corrosion spread this far, reversing the trend will take a lot more time and effort than it would have done had you identified the problem sooner.

The first thing to understand about consumer insight is that *everything* that happens in your business is consumer insight. The content people engage with, the ads they respond to, which landing pages convert best, the sales models and communication that resonates, which parts of your product they utilize and which parts they don't, what they buy more of, what they complain about, what they tell their friends about...*all* of this is consumer insight!

How do you make the most of the information your customers are giving you all the time? In addition to you and your team keeping your eyes open for indicators of customer satisfaction, there are two fundamental ways to gain direct customer feedback:

1. **Survey your customers at different stages of their customer journey.** Construct your surveys to suit your business model and consumer. They can be as concise or as comprehensive as they need to be. Some of the best retailers and restaurants have a touch screen at the counter where people pay. The screen displays a simple graphic: a smiley face, a neutral face, and a sad face. Customers press one of the faces to rate the service they have received. If your product or service necessitates a more comprehensive feedback system than this, you might email your customers at key points throughout their customer journey with a link and an incentive to fill out a survey. These surveys should ask for scores that give you quantifiable data, while also giving people room to add comments if they wish to, providing you with qualitative insight.

2. **Assess the net promoter score (NPS) of your customers.** A very telling—and unforgiving—method of gauging customer happiness is through a metric called the net promoter score. The NPS asks your customer just one question: "On a scale of zero to ten, how likely are you to recommend us to a friend or colleague?" Anyone who provides you with a score of zero to six is classed as a detractor; those who rate you at a seven or an eight are counted as passives; and those who score you a nine or ten are counted as promoters.

To calculate your NPS, you then take the proportion of respondents who are promoters, subtract the proportion of respondents who are detractors, and end up with a score anywhere between -100 to +100. There are apps and websites that will save you the headache and do the math for you. Given that the NPS isn't simply a score out of 100, but instead includes those who feel negatively about your business, anything above +30 is considered quite a good result. Google has an NPS of +7, Apple is +47, and these days Facebook has an NPS of -21. It's an unflinching and incredibly valuable measure of how well you're delivering to and delighting your customers, and an exceptionally useful tool for gauging satisfaction throughout your customer journey.

Once you've got a barometer of how your customers are feeling about your product, you then send them down one of three follow-up paths. If you've used the NPS method that we've just outlined, these paths might look something like this:

First, anyone classified as a detractor should be directed to a feedback form that asks about their experience and what you could have done better. It is these responses that are actually the most valuable to you because they are your greatest source of learning. Every business makes mistakes; however, too many founders feel so much shame around these types of scenarios that they retreat from these cases rather than leaning into them. In addition to providing invaluable insight, counterintuitively your detractors are also a huge opportunity to create advocates; turn their experience around, and they will be fans forever.

Second, those who rated you a seven or an eight fall into the passive category and therefore receive a different question: ask them to tell you the one thing you can do to increase their score to a nine or ten. These responses are also invaluable as they will give you insight into the small, quick improvements that you can make to move a portion of your customers from relatively happy to raving fans.

Finally, for anyone who qualifies as a promoter by rating you a nine or ten, you want to swing into action and amplify their story. Too often product review sites simply act as a complaints board for companies that for the most part are doing a great job. To counterbalance this, you want to send your promoters to Google Reviews or other product review sites. This will ensure that those who have had a great experience with you are prompted to share their experience. This is an effective strategy for significantly boosting your online presence for any prospects that may be researching your brand and considering making a purchase.

DELIGHT CUSTOMERS BY CONNECTING EMOTIONALLY

As you'll see, this section and the next are considerably shorter than the previous one. This is a reflection of the relative importance of each one. It's only once you're consistently delivering on your foundational promise to the customer that you have *permission* to go above and beyond and delight them. A lot of business owners skip straight to trying to delight their customers without first ensuring there is consistent and reliable delivery of the fundamentals. Counterintuitively, *the* most impressive thing you can do for your customer is to deliver on your fundamental promise. Only once you're doing that at scale, should you move to delighting them.

The key to doing this is moving beyond the mechanics of product delivery and honing in on the dynamics of your customers' emotions. This will take you far beyond simply building a business and into the realm of building a brand. Your brand is not your marketing, nor your product. Your brand is the *feeling* that your customers associate with you and your business, and there's no part of the journey where you get to influence how your customer feels more than when you are delivering your product or service to them.

Fail to deliver, and customers will tell everyone they've had a poor experience, in a way that damages your brand. Fail to delight, and they just won't say anything at all. If you can delight your customer to the point where they feel a deep and genuine connection with your brand, however, they will become your biggest fans, shouting about you from the rooftops and promoting you to others. The key to achieving this connection is to speak to your customer's emotions at every stage of their journey.

For example, let's say a customer has just purchased a service from you. If you're focused on simply delivering that service, you'll most likely send them a confirmation email, any booking details, and a receipt. Those are the essentials, but to step it up a notch and speak to their emotions, consider sending them another email that reads something like this:

Hey Sam,

Experience tells us that right now you're feeling super excited, but maybe also a little bit unsure how to immerse yourself in the experience. We thought we'd let you know, through the lens of our existing customers, exactly how they moved past trepidation and ultimately maximized the journey that you are now on.

1. When you find yourself feeling [emotion], [insert recommended action here].
2. You'll inevitably get to the point where you find yourself thinking, [insert customer thought here]. This is completely normal, in fact all of our customers go through this stage. When you get there, the absolute best thing to do is simply [insert recommended action here].
3. If you find that you reach a point where you really want to talk to someone, we get it. That's what we're here for. The best way to get a hold of us is simply [insert best contact point here].

We've been doing this a long time and there isn't much we haven't seen, so wherever you are right now, just know that you're definitely not alone. We are cheering you on.

Lots of love,

Jack

On the one hand, this is a functional email that shows the customer how to get the most out of the service. But it frames the instructions they need through the prism of their current emotional state. The real clincher here is the phrase, "Experience tells us that right now you're feeling." When you connect your customers with how most others are feeling at this point in their journey, you help them feel supported, recognize that they're not alone, and accept that how they are feeling is completely normal. As you can see from the email, the next step is to continue that thread by linking their emotions with a solution that leads them away from any uncertainty they may feel and toward loving the service.

An amusing example of going above and beyond to delight customers is Dialpad's conference call software. Dialpad delivers by creating a seamless conference room. However, when one person joins the meeting and waits on hold for other attendees, Dialpad goes a step further. They've thought through how the person waiting must be feeling: probably a bit frustrated and put out, and possibly wondering when the other person will turn up.

Based on these emotions, Dialpad wrote and recorded an amusing song poking fun at the idea of being stuck on hold, with lines like, "well I've been sitting here all day, I've been sitting in this waiting room," and, "I wonder where they are, yes I wonder where my friends have gone," which makes the process much more enjoyable for the customer. They've delighted their customers by going beyond the basic needs of their service and connecting with their customer's emotional state.

In addition to speaking to your customer's emotions at each stage of their journey, here are some more ways you can elevate your customers' experience and delight them frequently and consistently:

1. **Provide fast customer support.** One of the best ways to show your customers that you care is to address their questions or concerns as rapidly as possible. Even if the issue a customer raises can't be solved immediately, a fast, empathetic, informative response goes a long way. Prioritize this approach, and you stand a good chance of turning even customers who were originally dissatisfied into the raving fans we described in the previous section. A few strategies you can employ to respond to

customers more quickly include: using chatbots (that escalate to a human when required); employing autoresponder emails to let customers know when someone will be in touch, and ensuring that members of your team have the frameworks they need to make important decisions, and the resources they need to provide helpful information to customers.

2. **Empower your team to go above and beyond.** Going a step further, you can delight your customers by encouraging your team to proactively identify and leverage opportunities to impress. Zappos is a great example of a company that does this, first by setting a goal of ensuring that every customer interaction includes a moment of wow, and second by giving their customer service team enough time to achieve that goal, through purposefully overstaffing their call centers. Zappos call centers run at 60–70 percent agent occupancy—the proportion of their time agents spend on calls during a shift—which compares with an industry norm of over 80 percent.[8] Another example comes from the Ritz-Carlton Hotel Group, which gives every employee the authority to spend up to $2,000 to quickly resolve a guest issue, or to make an experience beautiful and memorable.

3. **Provide each customer with a personalized experience.** Another way to delight customers is to provide them with personalized experiences throughout their customer journey. The great news here is that only 14 percent of consumers expect personalized service (coincidentally, the same percentage that expect to be wowed by a company).[9]

---

[8]   Micah Solomon, "How Zappos Delivers Wow Customer Service on Each and Every Call," *Forbes.com*, Sep 15, 2018, https://www.forbes.com/sites/micahsolomon/2018/09/15/the-secret-of-wow-customer-service-is-breathing-space-just-ask-zappos/?sh=a0f8e741b2cf.

[9]   "An Opportunity to Delight: Just 14 percent of Global Consumers Expect to Be Wowed by a Company," *Freshworks*, Aug 18, 2021, https://www.prnewswire.com/news-releases/an-opportunity-to-delight-just-14-of-global-consumers-expect-to-be-wowed-by-a-company-301357258.html.

This means there is a huge opportunity to differentiate your business in the eyes of your consumer. Strategies you can use to provide a personalized experience to your customers include tailoring communications to them and their situation, connecting with them on special occasions, such as birthdays and anniversaries (this has even more impact if you send a handwritten note), and recommending additional products or services based on their previous purchases.

4. **Give preferential treatment to your best customers.** Loyal customers are the lifeblood of every business, so do everything you can to make your best customers feel special. You can give them free upgrades, early access to new products, reduced rates the longer they stay with your business, and even fully-fledged loyalty programs. Another strategy we use at The Entourage is profiling and promoting our best customers within our community, recognizing (and reinforcing) their achievements, and in the process giving them the feeling of significance they deserve. Your best customers should benefit from your best treatment, so ask yourself: what can we do to look after our most loyal consumers?

Fundamentally, people come to you because they value the service you provide or the product you produce. This is the bread-and-butter of your business. If your customers genuinely *like*—or better yet, *love*—your business, however, this will be a powerful magnet, drawing them back again and again. We're all human, and we prefer to buy from people who share our values, empathize with our emotions, and make a sincere effort to give us great experiences.

Now, let's discuss how to amplify customer delight, so that it resonates loud and clear with anyone who interacts with your business.

AMPLIFY CUSTOMER HAPPINESS

Through your marketing, you attracted the right prospects. In your sales process, you converted the right people into paying customers. Now, by delivering a world-class customer experience with your product, you have created raving fans. It's time to move to the final component of the Drive Growth Cycle: amplify. This is the step that the vast majority of businesses miss, and therefore never achieve an upward spiral of growth. The amplify step is where you take all the great work you've done up until now and feed the stories of your happy customers back to marketing to turn into testimonials, success stories, and case studies. *The* number one thing you can do to attract and convert more of the right prospects is to show them stories of customers who have walked the path before them, and got the results they are seeking, thus completing and perpetuating your Drive Growth Cycle.

The reason so many of us move from startup to scaleup without ever employing this strategy is that when we start out in business, we don't yet have any happy customers. From day one, we get in the habit of marketing and selling without utilizing the stories of happy customers or offering any reassurance to those who are about to buy. As the business grows, however, it inevitably builds a reservoir of happy customers.

Most business owners are unaware that they are sitting on a gold mine of happy customers, whose stories are not being told. The founder is sticking to their old, habitual marketing and sales messaging, missing the opportunity to offer prospects the one thing that would give them the confidence to buy more, faster. As we've highlighted time and time again in this book, a business owner's worst enemy are old habits that no longer serve them.

Throughout your marketing and sales cycle, the number one way to give your prospects more confidence is to show them success stories and case studies of customers who've come before them and loved the journey. Nothing reduces buyer's resistance and increases buyer's acceptance like seeing the human stories of people who were in their shoes and have gone on to achieve the results that they are looking for. When it comes to consumer psychology, social proof is fundamentally influential.

Are you guilty of keeping your happy customers a secret? The great news is, you probably don't need to look particularly hard for these advocates. If you've been in business for any period of time, you will have a goldmine of past and present customers to tap into. You wouldn't have reached six or seven figures if you didn't. Today, you've got hundreds, maybe thousands of happy customers, but you haven't yet captured that happiness and amplified it for your marketing.

As we discussed in the last chapter, sales is simply a transference of certainty. The same is true of your marketing. It's all there to do one thing: give your prospects greater certainty that your product will solve their problem. Do you want to give future customers more certainty? Show them people who've gone through the journey before them; help them understand how those customers were feeling at each stage, and how things worked out for them. You want to increase lead volumes? Use more testimonials. You want to increase conversion rates? Use more success stories and case studies.

There's a specific art to amplifying customer happiness and success, and when businesses start using success stories, they often do so in a way that doesn't shift their prospects' psychology. These look something like this: "I used [PR Agency] and they were very professional and a delight to work with." This tells us nothing. Being "professional and a delight to work with" is not the result your clients are coming to you to achieve. At best, this is an additional factor. Don't simply ask customers to say random nice things about the team at [Your Company]. Instead, take your potential customers on a journey and show them tangible *results*.

Let's look at three different formats you can use to capture these journeys and where they are best used:

1. **Testimonials.** Testimonials are super short and to the point. They need to be short and impactful, because they are used closer to the top of the funnel, for the prospect who doesn't

yet want to watch a four-minute video, read an entire landing page, or have a buying conversation; they simply just need to understand that what you do *works*. To achieve this, testimonials should quickly express the problem state the customer was experiencing, and the solution state they arrived at. We call this a "from/to," because it captures where your customer came from and went to. "Using [Your Company], I went from [old problem state] to [new desired state] in just three short months." Testimonials should be one paragraph, or even as short as two sentences. If the testimonial is in a video format, ideally it should be thirty seconds, but no more than sixty seconds.

2. **Success stories.** Success stories are slightly longer-form testimonials. If they are written, they should be three to four paragraphs. If they are in video format, they should fit within two minutes.

   Success stories follow a three-step story arc. They open with the old problem state and capture the challenges or pain that the customer once felt. This speaks to the *away-from* motivation driving people to buy your product. The middle section of the story arc speaks to what changed. What changed is that they bought your solution. They should describe the one or two most critical components of your product that helped them transition from the old problem state to the new desired state. The third arc of the story is—you guessed it—the new desired state in which they now find themselves. This part of the success story speaks to the *toward* motivation that inspires people to buy your product. If your product or service delivers tangible benefits, it's important that this third step in the story arc is specific, measurable, and explains how long it took for the customer to see the benefits.

   A success story that follows the three-step story arc would sound something like:

   [Before state/pain] "We spent years getting our marketing right, and while we were generating leads for our business, we felt like the world's best kept secret. If we didn't interrupt someone with an ad, they simply didn't know who we were. After being in business for ten years, we still didn't have a *brand*. Our marketing was expensive and always felt like an uphill battle."

[What changed] "That's when we got started with [PR Agency]. Immediately, they helped us define our brand strategy, which was worth its weight in gold and started reaching out to media and influencers to make us visible to our market."

[After state/pleasure] "In the last six months we've been featured in all key national publications, won our industry's most coveted award, and received invitations to speak on stages and podcasts that have got us in front of thousands of people in our target market. This has generated as many qualified leads as our paid advertising and resulted in over $250,000 of new business."

That's a success story. And you have customers right now who would be happy to say the equivalent about your business.

3. **Case studies.** Case studies follow the same arc as success stories, again in a slightly longer format. A case study will also go into more detail than a success story. Therefore, it will be five to six paragraphs in written format, or around four to six minutes in video form. Using the previous example of the happy client of the PR Agency, you would dive into a little bit more detail about the before state, quantifying the challenges. You'd expand on what it was about the service that really drove the change. And then you'd elaborate further on the end state, explaining all the knock-on effects of the improvement.

The reason these formats vary in length is that they are designed for different stages of your funnel. Generally speaking, testimonials are designed for the top of your funnel, to quickly communicate the integrity of your product. Success stories will be most useful from the middle of your funnel to the bottom of your funnel, throughout your nurture sequences and sales conversations. And you should generally keep case studies purely for the bottom of your funnel, to give a prospect who is about to buy the reassurance they need to do so with confidence. The exception to this rule is that you may also include case studies on your website (which is generally at the top of your funnel), for those who may not yet have engaged with your funnel, but who want to research the results you help your customers achieve more deeply.

While you and your team will often have a good understanding of which customers to select to capture testimonials and success stories, you can also approach the selection process systematically. As you'll recall, in the **deliver** section of this chapter, we discussed implementing a regular NPS survey for your customers, and sending the detractors to a feedback form, the neutrals to a different feedback form, and the promoters to Google Reviews or a product review site. An alternative is to send the promoters to a feedback form that asks them to share their story using the three-act story arc we previously discussed. It will look something like this:

- Where were you before you started working with us and what were your challenges?
- What did you find most useful about the product and your journey with us?
- What results have you since achieved?

From there, you can select the best response and request that you capture those journeys on camera and turn them into success stories. If they've had a great experience with your brand, and are truly grateful for what you have done for them, you will be surprised by how many people jump at the opportunity to share their experience.

When it comes to amplifying customer happiness, the key is to capture as many testimonials, success stories, and case studies as is practicable. Not only can they be used throughout your buyer's journey (marketing and sales), but they can also be integrated throughout your customer journey (product delivery). So often, when a business wins a customer, they stop reminding the customer of the value that they provide. When this happens, the *perceived value* of their product slowly wanes over time. One great way to remind your customers what you do for them, as well as educate them on how best to utilize your product, is to continue to amplify stories from happy customers.

THE CUSTOMER JOURNEY MAP

Now that we've covered **deliver**, **delight**, and **amplify**, how do we consolidate them all into one highly effective tool that you and your team can implement?

We use the Customer Journey Map. Your Customer Journey Map brings together all the steps a customer takes with you and how they're feeling at each stage. This map gives your product function the necessary structure to enable you to deliver, delight, and amplify, *at scale*.

CUSTOMER JOURNEY MAP

			STEP ONE	STEP TWO	STEP THREE	STEP FOUR	STEP FIVE
THE CUSTOMER'S WORLD	DOING	Customer Situation & Activities	What is going on in the customer's life at each step of the journey?				
	FEELING	Customer Emotions – & +	What feelings is the average customer experiencing at each step?				
FRONT STAGE	INTERACTING	Touch Points	What are the touch points and interactions they will have with you throughout the journey?				
	OBJECTIVE	What The Customer Wants	What is the core outcome the customer wants from each step?				
	BUSINESS GOAL	Any Business Objectives	What are your business objectives at each step of the journey?				
	ENGAGING	Who Is Responsible	Who is responsible for ensuring this step is successfully delivered?				
	DELIGHTING	Delight Opportunities	How can you speak to the customer's emotions and go above and beyond?				
	FEEDBACK	Feedback Opportunities	Where can you ask for feedback on how well you've doing and where you can improve?				
BACK STAGE	HAPPENING	What's Happening Internally	What's happening behind the scenes to make everything happen?				
	SYSTEM	Name The System	What is the process that captures and communicates in detail how each step gets done?				

Figure 8.2: Customer Journey Map

Your Customer Journey Map starts at the point of sale. Everything that happens prior to this point, through marketing and sales, is part of what we call the buyer's journey. Everything that happens *after* someone buys, falls under your product function, and is best referred to as the customer journey. While you should strive to create continuity between your buyer's journey and your customer journey, it is important to understand that they are two very distinct stages, each of which deserves its own strategy and structure.

Across the top of the Customer Journey Map, you'll see the steps that your customer will take with your business. For some businesses, the customer journey will consist of just a few steps, whereas others will have an infinite number of paths for the customer to take. To ensure that you and your team can view the process end-to-end, without it becoming too convoluted, you want to capture only the fundamental steps on your map—somewhere between four and ten steps is ideal. This tool should *consolidate and summarize* your customer's journey, making it easy for your team to usher each customer through a world-class experience.

We then break the map into three very important layers: **the customer's world**, **front stage**, and **backstage**. It is tempting to develop customer journeys through the lens of what the business wants or what's operationally easiest. Prioritizing the customer's world ensures that you start analyzing each step by thinking about what is going on in the life of the customer at that moment. Amateurs develop their customer journeys by first plotting touch points, whereas experienced entrepreneurs know that the best way to start is by assessing the current situation of the customer and what they are *feeling* and allowing the rest to arise from there. If we view the Customer Journey Map through the metaphor of a theater performance, this top layer speaks to what the audience is experiencing and feeling before they get to the auditorium.

The next layer of the map is **front stage**. This is everything the customer sees and experiences at each step of their interaction with your business. What channels are you using to deliver each touch point? Who are the actors, and what are they doing? This layer is everything the audience sees on stage that brings the experience to life for them.

The final layer is **backstage**. This is everything the customer doesn't see—what's going on inside the organization to make everything happen. It's what the team is doing behind the scenes. Using the theater metaphor, this refers to everything that's being controlled behind the curtains and outside the line of visibility: the staging, sets, lighting, and music. Everything that goes on backstage is very important to the play and the experience of the audience. What makes this metaphor so powerful is that it really reinforces for everybody on the team that whether they are front stage or backstage, *everyone's* role contributes enormously to the customer experience.

BE CONSISTENT, GO BEYOND, AMPLIFY THE POSITIVES

If you want to master the product element of your business, the essential baseline is being able to consistently **deliver** your product or service to a high standard. Then, to develop a relationship with your customers and transcend the product or service you offer, you'll need to go above and beyond the baseline and **delight** them. As we've discussed in this chapter, the way to do this is by speaking to the emotions of your customer and adding moments throughout their journey that make them say "wow."

Once you've achieved all the above, your next step is to **amplify** the results of your existing customers, through testimonials, success stories, and case studies. When you make your happy customers your loudest champions, you give your current prospects greater certainty, faster. This, in turn, will increase conversions, generating an upward spiral of growth and, once again kickstarting the Drive Growth Cycle.

As with so much else we cover in these pages, an essential element of this process is taking yourself out of the equation. For your business to scale, your product delivery capability must work without you, the founder. Very often, we see founders who are personally capable of delivering on their promises, delighting their customers, and amplifying that delight.

Unfortunately, they can't yet transmit the ability to do all of the above to the rest of their team.

You can't possibly delight every customer on your own: to scale your business, you need many team members who are all delivering extremely well. This is why frameworks such as the Customer Journey Map are so vital. They provide a route to getting everyone on the same page to deliver your product or service. They provide a way to codify what both your customer and your business are trying to achieve at each step of the journey. They provide an opportunity to document how the customer is feeling, how you connect with that emotion, and how you either amplify it—if it's positive—or address it—if it's negative.

In a product or service context, these are the keys to moving out of that scrambling startup mode and becoming a mature business, with a great track record, that people want to work with.

CASE STUDY: VICTORIA AND GEN CAPTURE AND MAGNIFY CUSTOMER SUCCESS

Victoria and Gen, the founders of SuperFastDiet, run an award-winning business and are part of The Entourage community. Victoria and Gen started the business with a mission to demystify the path to better health and happiness, a mission they fulfill through books, an online membership program, and one-on-one coaching that teaches women to easily incorporate intermittent fasting into their lifestyle. When clients follow their recommendations, they see a host of health and lifestyle benefits that help them grow into the happiest versions of themselves.

Prior to starting SuperFastDiet, both founders had experienced first-hand the ups and downs of their own health journey, losing forty-five kilos between them. Their driving motivation to start and scale the business was to empower other women by sharing the guidance and support they wished they had received themselves.

When Victoria and Gen started in Elevate, they were already experiencing considerable success but hadn't yet created a product function that could scale. They cared deeply about their customers and were committed to scaling in a way that would further improve the incredible results their members were already achieving. The problem they were facing, like so many of our members, was that they and their team were working ridiculous hours, with no immediate prospect of reducing those hours. Both Victoria and Gen knew the situation was unsustainable, and when they saw Jack speak at a large Entourage event, the strategies he outlined for getting out of startup and into scaleup resonated deeply with them.

In collaboration with their Elevate coach, Gen and Victoria worked on numerous elements of their business, with a particular focus on scaling their product offering and delivery. They wanted to build a product ecosystem that would help the SuperFastDiet community lead happier, healthier lives, and by doing so increase customer engagement, retention, and ultimately lifetime value (LTV). Like all meaningful product innovation journeys, their underlying question was, "How do we provide an even better experience for our customers in a more scalable way?"

Victoria and Gen were already delivering great results and delighting their customers, and they were ready to do this to an even greater degree. Utilizing the Customer Journey Map, they mapped out what was going on in the lives and hearts of their customers at different stages of their journey and tailored each and every touch point accordingly.

As most of us have experienced at one time or another, the journey to greater health isn't always an easy one, and sometimes negative emotions can take hold. Victoria and Gen particularly wanted to help their customers through these hard times. One way they offered a greater level of support to their community was through creating a weekly broadcast called Live at Five, which they shared with their Facebook community. Live at Five has become a fixture in their calendar; an opportunity to discuss challenges and celebrate achievements. Not only is it cathartic for their members, but it also provides real-time guidance, practical strategies, and a sense of camaraderie to those who would otherwise be on the journey by themselves. These events are also a great opportunity for Victoria and Gen to recognize those who contribute to the community each week, acknowledging those who are reinvesting back into the group and helping others. As a result, their community feels heard and supported at both the peaks and troughs of their emotional journey.

While Victoria and Gen's everyday interactions already kept them close to their community, they began to systematize surveying their customers, seeking both qualitative and quantitative feedback on their greatest challenges and objectives. The insights they received from this feedback encouraged Victoria and Gen not only to strengthen their existing programs, but also to develop a range of premium offerings, such as VIP levels, to further support their clients. They also used the findings to develop an automated email sequence that speaks to their customers' experiences throughout the customer journey. From the very first welcome email, Victoria and Gen direct their members on exactly what to do, how to navigate whatever emotional moment they are in, and how to access the different levels and layers of support that are available to them.

These insights pointed to another, unexpected opportunity: the community wanted help knowing where to buy tools that would help them on their journey to greater well-being and a healthier mindset. This prompted Victoria and Gen to develop an e-commerce arm of the business, offering products they already knew their community wanted, such as gratitude journals, healthy smoothies, branded apparel, and motivational quotes, all of which helped their members feel like part of a tribe. The result of all of this product innovation was an exponential improvement in program retention and the renewal rates of their customers. Meanwhile, statistics on their customers' results showed that their VIP clients were achieving twice the results of their regular members in the same timeframe. This equipped SuperFastDiet with the data to encourage more of their community to upgrade to a VIP level of support.

This combination of delivering great outcomes for their clients and connecting with them emotionally has produced a community of raving fans of SuperFastDiet. Clients regularly share their weight loss progress with the SuperFastDiet community, which creates a perfect opportunity for Victoria and Gen to capture testimonials and success stories. This process has been systematized to the point where Victoria and Gen now need a dedicated, full-time team member to keep up with the volume of wins available for them to capture. As soon as someone shares a win, this team member contacts them to ask whether they'd like to share their story as a success story for others. Written testimonials, before-and-after photos, and long-form video case studies now form an essential ingredient of every piece of marketing that the SuperFastDiet team puts out into the world.

As a result of the strategic moves they have made to strengthen and diversify their product offerings since joining Elevate, Gen and Victoria have tripled their revenue. In the last twelve months alone, they doubled their membership base from five thousand to ten thousand women, expanded their reach to the United States and the United Kingdom, and grew their total combined community to more than 50,000, a number that continues to grow. Their team has also more than doubled in size, and today Victoria and Gen have clearly delineated what each of them focus on: Victoria runs the business, while Gen dedicates her time to delivering world-class products, delighting their customers, and amplifying their innumerable success stories.

JACK AND TRADESQUARE REIMAGINE THE WHOLESALE MARKET

In 2020, Jack was approached by an impressive team, made up of some of Australia's leading tech-entrepreneurs, to invest in and sit on the advisory board of TradeSquare, a new brand they were forming.

While the brand was yet to launch, the caliber of the team and the vision of the organization were so compelling that Jack decided to join. TradeSquare's mission was to revolutionize how small-to-medium-sized businesses bought their wholesale goods. Historically, wholesale buying has been problematic for businesses that aren't large enough to order goods in huge quantities. Large wholesalers would either refuse to deal with them, offer prices that were so high they ate into their margins, or insist on terms that were so unfavorable to the business owner that the relationship wasn't worth pursuing.

For TradeSquare to solve this problem at scale, our first job was to understand the customer, so we could rapidly develop a high degree of product-market fit. The TradeSquare team talked to a range of buyers, including retailers, childcare businesses, schools, councils, and HR managers seeking corporate gift ideas. As we explored the ecosystem, we learned that most small-to-medium-sized organizations were buying their product from numerous different wholesalers all over the world. This meant they were operating on different contracts and multiple credit applications, adhering to varied terms, delivery dates, return policies, and even—when dealing with suppliers in different countries—tax systems, all offering quite poor customer service. As we dug even deeper, we found that most of these businesses were managing all their stock and wholesale buying through spreadsheets, which was manual, time consuming, and tedious. They weren't using any technology to monitor stock levels or to place new orders. In fact, their lack of internal management inside the business was *as problematic* for them as the buying challenges they often faced when dealing with wholesalers.

Adding an additional layer of complexity, TradeSquare wasn't just targeting small-to-medium-sized businesses. We also needed wholesalers to join our ecosystem and list their products for sale on the website—at prices and terms that were favorable for small businesses. People don't like change, so it stands to reason that one of *the most* challenging things to do with any new business or product is to change consumer behavior. At TradeSquare, we weren't merely setting out to change the behavior of one type of consumer; we were setting out to change the behavior of two. This meant that we were both asking businesses to abandon their tried-and-tested (albeit very clunky) method of *buying* wholesale *and* asking wholesalers to add a new digital channel to their *selling*, accepting a higher volume of smaller orders. This was certainly not something they were used to.

When a business needs to alter consumer behavior to become successful, the stakes of finding product-market fit quickly are magnified. To pile on even more pressure to the situation, being a new tech company,

Jack and the team needed to achieve this on a relatively short runway, before the financing from initial investment rounds dried up. This time constraint piled even more pressure onto the situation. The mountain we were climbing was both large and steep; we needed to change the entrenched behaviors of not one, but two, categories of consumer, develop product-to-market fit, and prove up the business model. And we needed to do all of this in a hurry, with the clock ticking.

Through obsessing about these problems every single day, and working around the clock to speak to as many prospects and wholesalers as possible, the TradeSquare team determined the three top value propositions for small businesses:

- Finding the absolute best prices
- Doing business on terms that suited them
- Buying most, if not all, of their product in a place that both helped them buy *and* had the technology to help them manage the whole process—no more juggling spreadsheets trying to manage multiple wholesalers on different terms

Our intention was for the TradeSquare technology to do all of this for them, in one place, with business-friendly terms, and a price guarantee that promised our prices would be better than anywhere else. If businesses found a better price elsewhere, we'd match the price and give them a saving. On the other side of our double-sided marketplace, the value proposition we presented to wholesalers was quite simple; to succeed, we needed to bring them more customers without additional headaches.

Obsessing over the frustrations, wants, and needs of both of our consumers took the team at TradeSquare months and months of product development. We ran down paths that led to dead ends, iterated constantly and made a lot of mistakes. Slowly, however, the product-market fit we were chasing so passionately began to emerge. As things began to click, we started to get real traction.

Building a product and an ecosystem that satisfied our core value propositions meant that we were delivering *and* delighting both of our avatars, on either side of the double-sided marketplace. As this approach began to scale, we captured testimonials, success stories, and case studies from small businesses and wholesalers alike, further strengthening the social proof we were able to convey through our branding, marketing, and messaging.

In its first twelve months, TradeSquare built an ecosystem of over 20,000 registered buyers, with in excess of 100,000 products listed for sale, making it Australia's largest wholesale marketplace. As this fueled rapid and product-led growth, TradeSquare caught the attention of investors around the world. In our second year of operation, we raised $28 million in funding from American investment firm Tiger Global. Tiger is headquartered in New York and specializes in investing in high-growth tech companies who demonstrate potential for global expansion.

When reflecting on the growth of the business, co-founder and CEO of TradeSquare, Einat Sukenik, said, "The old way of bringing wholesalers and retailers together was trade shows or overseas buying trips, but these disappeared during Covid. We can now think of TradeSquare as a 24/7 digital trade show, allowing retailers to easily discover and order wholesale products, and wholesalers access to retailers Australia-wide." Citing the importance of product-market fit, Einat went on to say, "Yesterday a gift and homeware shop in Dubbo placed an order from eleven wholesalers in one cart, with one invoice and 60-day credit terms. This is a game-changer. TradeSquare is a key player in making Australia's economy fairer and healthier by empowering the small businesses to easily discover and order wholesale products."

NEXT UP...

When your drive growth cycle brings together the marketing, sales, and product elements of your business, you create a self-perpetuating, upward spiral of growth. Installing the Drive Growth Cycle into our businesses, and those of our Elevate members, has propelled many of Australia's fastest-growing companies, both our own and those we serve.

When you bring these elements to life in your business, you have the keys to attract an almost infinite number of customers. This, however, brings a fresh challenge into focus. No longer is your growth constrained by reaching or converting enough customers; instead, the limiting factor is ensuring that the company can keep up with accelerated demand. At this point, operationalizing at a rate that *keeps up* with your growth is vital to your ongoing scalability and sustainability.

Enter Part III, the Enable Growth Structure.

PART III

THE ENABLE GROWTH STRUCTURE

B
y now, you should be excited by the prospect of tapping into the Drive Growth Cycle to bring your marketing, sales, and product together, generating an upward spiral of growth in your business.

Unless the growth you create is grounded on a solid foundation, however, it can soon spiral out of control, leaving you unable to serve all the new clients you've attracted to your business. This is why you need to devote just as much attention to the Enable Growth Structure of your organization.

The Enable Growth Structure complements the Drive Growth Cycle, demonstrating how operations, finance, and people lock together to provide a bedrock on which you can service the growth of your business. Operations is the glue that holds everything together, finance is the scorecard by which you measure your success, and the people in your business bring all of the other elements to life.

One thing you will notice immediately is that while the Drive Growth Cycle is circular, the Enable Growth Structure is triangular. Why is this? The triangle is an incredibly strong shape, frequently used in the construction of stable structures, and this is exactly what the Enable Growth Structure will allow you to achieve in your business. Driving growth is all about flow. Enabling growth, however, is all about solidity.

If you're naturally an enable-growth-focused entrepreneur, you'll feel immediately at home here. You love structure. If you're a drive-growth-focused entrepreneur, this model will likely articulate the aspects of your business that you already knew were lacking, but didn't know how to formulate or address.

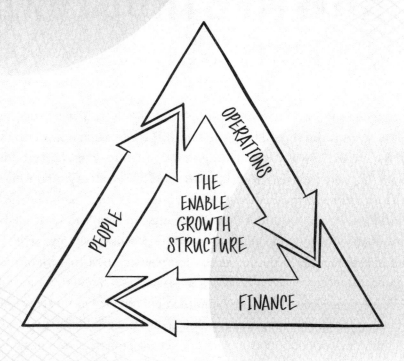

Figure E.1: The Enable Growth Structure

9

OPERATIONS

Build a Business That Can Work without You

"If I'm not across every detail, the work just doesn't happen to the standard it needs to."

This is just one of many frustrations new members bring to us when starting their Elevate journey. We also hear, "I want to be more strategic and look to the future, but I keep getting dragged back into the details of the day-to-day." Others will tell us, "I feel like I spend my days fighting fires, swamped with requests, and working *in* the business instead of *on* the business."

These are all versions of the same story, a story you're probably all-too-familiar with. You founded a business because you love creating something out of nothing, not because you wanted to get bogged down in detail. You love the big picture, not wading through what sometimes feels like endless small-scale problems. But if you're not across these types of problems, who will be? Breaking out of these cycles feels like an uphill task.

As you come up the growth curve and your business matures, you may well start to feel as though your mind is like an internet browser with a hundred open tabs. At some stage, your mental browser is going to slow down—some tabs may even disappear—and if you don't do something to reduce the load, eventually the browser will crash.

When you reach this point—and you almost certainly have—you may feel as though you're spinning out of control, and wondering whether you're the only founder whose business has become overwhelming. Don't worry, *every* high-growth business owner reaches this very point. It's completely normal to pass through this rite of passage as your business grows and outstrips your capacity to do everything yourself. During the startup phase, most business owners are rightly focused on the drive-growth side of their business, but what this means, particularly at and beyond the seven-figure mark, is that enable-growth functions such as operations become the things that hold the company back. We've all been there. The good news is, there's a solution to your dilemma.

WHAT IS OPERATIONS?

What do we mean by operations? In this context, we're talking about the internal workings of the business: the systems and processes that capture how things get done, the technology that underpins the business end-to-end, and the core metrics that highlight the performance of the business. Operations is the glue that holds the rest of the business together, ensuring that each of the Six Elements are talking to each other. It supports and enables all the other parts of the business, helping to keep things organized, manageable, and moving forward. While operations supports all the other parts of the business, however, responsibility for it cannot be spread across the departments. When something is everyone's responsibility, it ends up being no one's responsibility. For that reason, operations is often an orphan—a sadly neglected element of the business. For your business to be scalable and sustainable, it must become a function in and of itself.

That process—identifying operations as a unique function and supporting it accordingly—is what we'll cover in this chapter. When business owners don't recognize that operations is its own function, they spend the vast majority of their time spinning plates and holding the disparate elements of the business together with their bare hands. For a startup, this isn't necessarily a huge problem. The business is still small and processes are *ad hoc*. For a scaleup, it's a disaster. Best case scenario, you're exhausted with busywork and unable to focus your full energies on the development of the business. Worst case scenario, you're hemorrhaging customers and revenue while wasting huge amounts of time because your business is woefully lacking in systems and processes.

Ultimately, by the time you get to seven figures and beyond, if you don't have an operations manager, *you are one*. If you're comfortable with that situation, no problem, but for most entrepreneurs, this is not a role they want to play.

How do you move through this phase? Creating a robust operations team is absolutely key to building a business that can work without you. This shift will enable you to focus on the things that are most important. No longer will you be obsessed with keeping the engine running; instead, you'll finally be driving the car.

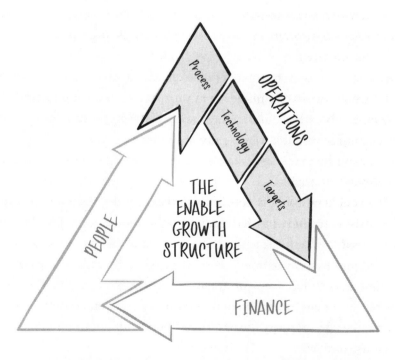

Figure 9.1: Operations Components of the Enable Growth Structure

In this chapter, we're going to explore the three main components of operations: **processes**, **technology**, and **targets**. We'll explain how you can systematize these components in a way that gets everybody on the same page. We'll also discuss how you can empower your team to make the right decisions and improve consistency across the business. By implementing the tools in this chapter, you'll streamline and simplify your business into a well-oiled engine.

MIND THE GAPS

When you compare the enable-growth functions of operations, finance, and people, against the drive-growth functions of marketing, sales, and product, one difference will become readily apparent: enable-growth functions are internally focused and often aimed at supporting the drive-growth functions. Nowhere is this more apparent than in operations. Operations focuses on supporting all of the other elements of the business. One of the key ways in which it does this is by bridging the gap between them.

What do we mean by this? Let's look at your buyer's journey and your customer's journey combined. Your prospect starts by interacting with your business as a result of your marketing, then moves through your sales process, and finally gets onboarded into a product or service. As they pass through all these stages, they need to move as smoothly and seamlessly as possible.

The problem here is that every transition represents an opportunity to drop the ball. There's a high chance that as your customer moves from one part of the business to another, something will get missed. Maybe some of your leads never make it through to your sales team. Maybe some customers never receive a product they have ordered, or purchase a service but never get passed on to the onboarding team. When customers fall into one of these gaps, you may lose them, undoing all your business's previous good work.

Very often, different parts of your business also speak in completely different languages. They focus on different things, use different acronyms, and think differently. While everyone in your team should be moving in one unified direction, your sales team is always going to have a different language and temperament to your finance team. As customers, information, and knowledge flow from one part of the business to another, you need to ensure that you have the systems and technology to facilitate information flow across departments.

This is the job of operations. These core operational needs exist regardless of whether a business owner recognizes them or not. If you don't address them, your business will leak morale, customers, and profit. The best way to handle these challenges is to recognize operations as a discrete function, and ultimately make someone responsible for that function. Otherwise, you as the founder will be saddled with that responsibility, a responsibility likely ill-suited to your interests and skills.

PROCESSES:
CAPTURING STEPS THAT PRODUCE A RESULT

Time and time again we see businesses that have experienced a period of growth and are now battling the consequences of that growth: more sales coming through, more customers than they can handle, and more team members to manage. Worse, everything needs to happen at once, and the team isn't fully trained or equipped to handle the multitude of tasks and decisions that need to be made everyday. We've been there as well in our own businesses. Topline everything is going great—more customers, more revenue—but underneath the surface it's chaos.

In any operation, there is a seemingly never ending list of potential decision-making points. Up to now, you may have felt the need to micromanage your team, telling them exactly what to do at any given moment. The problem with this approach is as the business grows, they'll *always* need to be told what to do. The greater your success, the less sustainable this style of leadership becomes. Processes provide you with an alternative; when you equip your team with a step-by-step process for how to complete a task or make an important decision, ultimately, they're freed from their reliance on you.

Most of the time, when a business owner or manager thinks they're delegating, they're actually *abdicating*. A new person or team starts and it's *assumed* that they will understand how to fulfill their role, complete core tasks, and meet expectations. A few months down the track, when they're not succeeding in the role, the business owner will conclude that the newcomers were not up to the job. In actuality, they were never set up to succeed. Most business owners significantly underestimate the level of instruction and training that people require to do their jobs properly. In our experience, this is the number one cause of organizational chaos at a company level, and nonperformance at an individual level.

The crucial principle to get you, your team, and your business organized, is this: *anything that gets done twice, gets systemized into a process.*

A process is a series of steps that outlines how something gets done. From the simplest of tasks to the most complex decisions, a good process will reverse engineer an outcome, highlighting the steps required for somebody else to replicate the result. Once you have created a process with the necessary accountability checks, you can expect the task or decision it relates to to be undertaken consistently, without the need for your intervention. The sooner you and your team start systemizing your business, the sooner you can delegate more effectively and step away from micromanaging.

Let's say that you notice your team members approaching you with the same type of question time and time again. Maybe they're asking you how to address customer complaints, or when to provide a refund. It's a situation that requires your team to think through a number of potential outcomes and come to a decision that aligns with the company's way of doing things—a perfect indication that you need to establish a process to guide the actions and decision-making of your team.

As an entrepreneur, you may believe that your team can't think through problems like you can. If you haven't taught them to, you're probably right. Establishing processes bridges this gap, allowing your team to tackle problems like you would (or better) and exponentially increases the capacity of your business to produce quality output. It's this type of seamless knowledge transfer that helps teams get unstuck and speeds up growth.

When developing a process, a key factor to consider is, "Is this a process that will be carried out by a person, or can it be automated using technology?" Increasingly, technology can handle more and more processes that used to require human intervention. When something can be automated, it is a huge operational advantage, because this makes the task infinitely scalable and removes human variability. As we discussed in Chapter Six: Marketing, deploying an email nurture sequence to thousands of prospects, each at different stages of their journey, would be a nightmare for a team of humans to manage. When loaded into an automated email sequence in your CRM, however, the technology handles multiple layers of complexity easily and effortlessly. Other systems, of course, are best fulfilled by humans.

This doesn't mean you need to craft every process yourself. Far from it. As you continue to elevate beyond technician and manager, part of the role of those who report to you is to take anything that will be done more than once and turn it into a process that others can follow. That's why we created a process for *developing* processes. Yes, you read that correctly, we (Jack, in particular) dislike writing processes so much that we created a process for creating processes, and just to mix things up we called it the "System For Writing Systems." In fact, the System for Writing Systems is the only system Jack has ever written.

In all seriousness, the reason we created the System for Writing Systems is that, as a leader, you want to encourage your team to build out the systems of the organization. This is not an optional extra, it's a nonnegotiable expectation. Why? Because as the company continues to scale and there's more to do, the team will change and grow. New people will join, some people will leave, and throughout all of these shifts, the same things must still get done. If a task is not documented into a process, it cannot be transferred. Therefore, it cannot be scaled.

As such, we've always found that providing our team with a structure for how to write systems gives everyone the confidence and competence to always document processes that strengthen our operations.

The System for Writing Systems

The System for Writing Systems is a simple, powerful framework for documenting processes, which we teach all of our members at The Entourage. A comprehensive system includes five key elements: what, why, who, when, and how. Let's go through each of those components in turn.

1. **What:** Name and explain what task is being done. What is the person executing the process trying to achieve?
2. **Why:** Explain why this task and following the system is important. Why is this task imperative and why is it critical that the system be followed?
3. **Who:** Identify the role in the business responsible for performing this process. It is very important to identify the *role* in the business, not the person, because people move around while roles remain the same.
4. **When:** When does this task get done? Is it triggered by an event such as a customer making a purchase, or is it done according to a regular cadence or occasion? How do you know when it's time for this task to be completed?
5. **How:** Detail *how* the system must be executed. What steps must be followed? There are three main methods of communicating how to undertake a process, each one effective in a different context. Let's take a look at each of them in order, from most simple to most complex:
   a. **Checklist.** When a process is relatively simple and undertaken in the real world—not on a computer—the best way to capture it is simply to use a list of steps. For example, "opening the store in the morning" or "setting up a product for display" are simple processes, best captured using a checklist.

b. **Screen-recorded video.** This approach is useful for any tasks carried out on a computer. It is incredibly effective, because it means that the next person to follow the process has a video outlining exactly what to do. When a member of your team executes this type of task, for example onboarding a customer or completing the steps at the end of a sale, have them open up a screen-recording software program and capture their approach. The tool just needs to be able to capture video and audio of your team member working through the process, and narrating what they are doing, step by step. There are a host of suitable options, from specialist tools like Screenflow and Loom to video conferencing tools like Zoom and Google Meet.

c. **Flowchart.** For more complex tasks and decisions, a flowchart is often the most useful tool to communicate how to get something decided and done. An example of a task best captured by a flowchart is determining whether to honor a refund request. This type of task will include many different scenarios and variables, as well as layers of authorization within your team. A flowchart needs to answer questions like, "When does the person completing the process have authorization to issue a refund?" and "When should a case be escalated to a manager for sign off?" A flowchart will inevitably capture both *who* is responsible for a decision, and *how* that decision should be made. When you're determining who is responsible for the *overall* system (as per point 3 in this section), it is whoever has *initial* responsibility for ensuring that the system is enacted. You then capture any escalation points—any managers who may need to be involved as the decision matrix progresses—within the flowchart.

You don't always need to fit *everything* into neat, small boxes. In the example of determining whether to honor a refund request, this process will essentially encapsulate a decision-making framework. At times, therefore, steps will require more detail than you can fit into a box or two. In this instance, you can open the "how" section of the system with a few paragraphs explaining what information to gather before commencing the flowchart, along with any other necessary instruction.

Some complex processes and decisions may require you to go into a great deal of detail at the "how" step. When this happens, you may find yourself using a combination of checklists, screen-recorded videos, flowcharts, and even good old-fashioned long-form instruction. At The Entourage, we have some all-encompassing flowcharts that cover four pages, and written guidelines that span six pages. The general rule here is that you want your process to be as simple as it can be, but not simpler.

When developing a flowchart, we advocate building them in Slides or PowerPoint. Again, it's best to keep the design as simple as possible, and ensure that it can be edited if anything changes later. It's far more important to make it easy for people to access and alter the flowchart than to create a design masterpiece using fancy software. A flowchart that looks amazing but confuses people isn't fit for purpose.

Once a process is developed, the person or team responsible for carrying it out needs to be *trained* on it. Once a process has been trained, it's best to assume that it's not going to get traction straight away. Often more training will be required, and the team will need to be reminded, *"we have a process for that now, jump in, give it a go and come back if anything's not clear."* From there, communicate that when issues or questions arise, you trust them to make their own decision on what the best course of action is. Only once they have read the process, tried their best to solve the problem, and still haven't been able to arrive at a solution, should they come to you for guidance.

The first step toward building a structure that enables your team to be more productive and autonomous is to have everyone in the organization developing great processes. In our own business, we've been developing and refining processes for decades; to see real-world examples of processes ranging from simple to complex, head to your Elevate resources section at www.the-entourage.com/elevate.

TECHNOLOGY: PERFECTING YOUR TECHNOLOGY STACK

Nowadays, every business runs on technology. Whether it powers your website, tracks the customer journey, or runs the internal operations of the business, technology is essential in underpinning the operations of modern companies.

The technology you use, whether it consists of two tools or twelve, is regarded as your technology stack. The larger your business grows, the more important it becomes to review your technology stack and ensure that you're making your business as efficient as possible. Ideally, you also want to streamline your technology choices, so that you're using as few tools as possible.

In the early stages of your business journey, you may reach for the most accessible technology—which is frequently also the cheapest. Through the startup phase, you will probably cobble together a number of technological tools. If some work better than others, or they're not wholly compatible, you'll tend to just make do. As your business grows, however, it becomes increasingly complex. Using different technologies that do their individual jobs reasonably well, but don't necessarily integrate seamlessly together, becomes less workable, draining your team's time and energy.

In practice, your technology journey usually goes something like this. You start out employing a low-cost marketing tool, such as MailChimp, which you use to gather emails and communicate with prospects. In the early days of your business, you settle on a low-cost website platform such as WordPress or Drupal, or you spend slightly more to host your site on Squarespace or Wix. You may also use a spreadsheet to manage new sales and customer notes. Even at this stage, you're operating three different systems. As you ramp up your marketing, you compound this discontinuity with an additional piece of technology that helps prospects move through your marketing funnel, then introduce another tool to power your e-commerce shopping cart. Soon, you reach a point where your growing customer numbers prompt you to subscribe to a CRM to manage customer delivery and relationships. Unfortunately, you never quite get around to optimizing the CRM so that it's tailored to your business, so most of your team simply choose not to use it. Nor do you bring the other functions, such as marketing and sales optimization, into the CRM, meaning you've got a tech-stack of five or six pieces of technology that are barely patched together.

Of course, marketing isn't the only element of your business. You'll want additional technology for handling product fulfillment or back-office operations, managing the finances of the business, onboarding, and handling staff.

This story is why we see business owners emerge from the startup phase with as many as twenty different pieces of technology for different parts of their business. They use one piece of technology to manage their marketing, another to manage their sales, and yet another to handle accounting, creating a patchwork that spans the business.

Like so many of the phenomena we detail in this book, this is fine in the initial phases of your business, when you clearly understand every aspect of it. Maybe you only have a handful of customers, can remember every promise you made to them, and know when every invoice needs to be sent. As the business grows, however, you start to notice that when different technological systems don't talk to each other, important information slips between the cracks. This results in lost customer notes, undelivered promises, and irregular payment cycles.

One way to address this is to try and stitch all of your systems together through patchwork integrations. This is extremely difficult, because different systems are built differently. It's like trying to marry a cow and a horse. You will reach a point—especially during the transition from startup to scaleup—where it's much better to concentrate on as few tools as possible, instead of cobbling disparate technology services together.

Technology underpins each function of your business. The key is to try and find technology that spans multiple functions. Your ultimate goal is to create great marketing, attract quality prospects, pass them through to your sales function, and manage the rest of the customer journey, all on as few platforms as possible.

This is important for two reasons. First of all, this type of technology stack makes the customer's journey feel seamless. Nothing is more frustrating for a customer than repeating themselves time and time again, because your technology stack isn't functioning optimally.

We're sure you've been on the other end of this scenario. Perhaps you called your phone company about a bill. After waiting on the line for an eternity, you're told that the department you're communicating with can't answer your question. You endure the delay of being transferred and waiting on hold for another several minutes. When you finally speak to someone else, you verify your information and explain your situation, only to be told yet again that you're connected to the wrong department. After this has happened a couple of times, you're about ready to throw your phone out of the nearest window. This type of scenario occurs when a company uses too many technology platforms to manage its different functions, and they simply don't integrate. When you streamline your technology, your customer's journey will become much smoother.

In addition to improving the experience of your customer, consolidating your technology also greatly improves the performance of your business. In Chapter Six: Marketing, we discussed developing an attribution model; something that enables you to trace every sale back to the marketing journey from which it originated. In this context, every time a customer moves from one system to the next, you risk losing the ability to attribute credit to the relevant parts of your marketing and sales process. Every break in the chain decreases your understanding of which parts of your marketing and sales engine work effectively. The only way to effectively track your return on advertising spend is for as much of the customer journey as possible to take place either within the same technological system, or across systems that integrate extremely well.

Because technology powers every element of your business, it is worth investing in. There will always be cheap, open-source versions of business technology available. But what you save in low user fees, you will invariably spend in user time, complexity, or errors within the business. To focus on the things that matter—marketing, selling, and delivering great products—we encourage you to invest in excellent technology that enhances every function of the business. When used well, technology will help you cut costs, get things done faster, and improve overall company performance. As such, you should always strive to employ the best technology you can afford.

Here at The Entourage, we are a technology-enabled business. Technology is our fourth highest expense, behind only people, advertising spend, and rent. Every single part of our customer journey is underpinned by the best technology we can find, from marketing to sales to product delivery. In fact, we spend about 5 percent of our total revenue each year on technology. In absolute dollar terms, that might seem astronomically expensive, but there's no way to achieve what we achieve without using the technology we use. Our investment in technology fuels our marketing engine, boosts sales performance, brings us new members, and ultimately drives business growth. We track every dollar that we spend across different platforms and different channels. Our marketing budgets run into millions of dollars, and the only way we can be comfortable allocating those types of numbers is by knowing exactly where that money goes and the return it achieves.

An effective CRM will allow you to power your advertising spend, your website, and your lead capture, then seamlessly pass prospective customers through to your sales team. From there, the team can manage people as they move from prospects or sales opportunities all the way through to deals. The same platform will enable you to manage the entire product or service delivery stage of the customer life cycle.

When the customer moves through the same piece of technology, and your team interacts with them via that same piece of technology, it's a much more seamless experience for the customer, and much easier for the team too, because they're interacting with just one tool, not a dozen. When you track data in the same place, you increase visibility throughout the customer journey, which enables smart decisions in other functions. For example, you can allocate marketing more effectively, and know which parts of your sales process work—and which parts don't.

The sophistication of this type of technology stack will make it more expensive than a system patched together from a collection of free and open-source tools, but the benefits *far* outweigh the costs.

Figure 9.2 shows a typical startup tech stack. Contrast this with the tech stack that we use here at The Entourage, shown in Figure 9.3, and you will immediately see a difference.

STARTUP TECH STACK

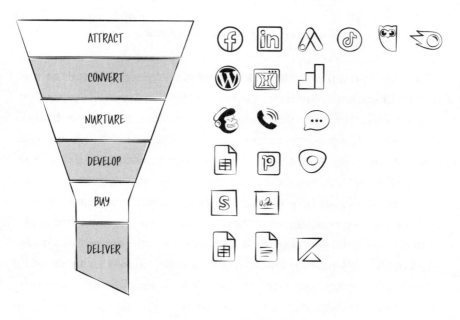

Figure 9.2: A Startup Tech Stack

SCALEUP TECH STACK

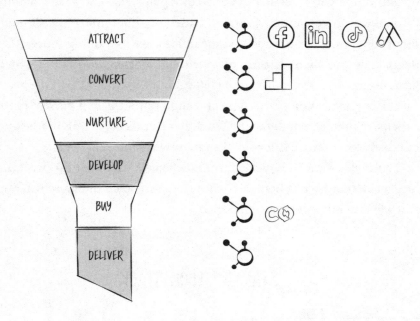

Figure 9.3: A Scaleup Tech Stack

A typical startup uses a raft of low-cost tools, each covering just a small part of the customer journey. The perennial problem with this situation is that the different tools don't communicate effectively with each other, which results in a poor customer experience. The business owner is then unable to make important decisions because they don't have a clear line of sight through different stages of the customer journey.

Compare this to The Entourage tech stack which is centered around one, best-in-class platform: HubSpot. Although we use other tools, HubSpot does the vast majority of heavy lifting and underpins almost all of our buyer's journey and customer journey. This gives us extreme visibility into every stage and provides the customer with a seamless experience. We then select the peripheral tools based on their ability to tightly integrate with HubSpot, which results in a tech stack that works together brilliantly.

TARGETS: PEOPLE PLAY DIFFERENTLY
WHEN THERE'S A SCOREBOARD

For every company, there are certain things that drive the performance of the business. These core things, when they happen, cause the business to thrive. When they *don't* happen, the business stalls and eventually declines. Chances are, as a founder, you are *very* in tune with the core factors that drive the success of your business. Having birthed and raised the business, you have both an intuitive and a learned understanding of the fundamental activities required to keep your business healthy.

The problem occurs when you, almost unknowingly, assume that your team shares this understanding, and that they are as invested as you are in hitting the core targets that drive business success. While these two things—your team fully understanding the core drivers of the business, and them being absolutely committed to making them happen—are absolutely achievable, they won't happen by osmosis, and they certainly won't happen by accident.

A hallmark of the startup way of operating is that everyone does everything and nothing gets measured or managed. Company objectives are opaque and individual targets are undefined. Not only is there no shared knowledge of precisely what the business needs to achieve, there is little understanding of what each individual needs to accomplish to enable the company's success.

One of the most critical and distinguishing factors of transitioning from a startup to a scaleup is capturing the core drivers of business performance in a few concise and meaningful metrics, and displaying those metrics on scoreboards for everyone to see. What gets measured gets managed, and what gets managed gets done.

A fundamental part of building a self-managing company is clearly defining what needs to happen at every level of the organization for the business to be performing. These numbers should cascade from a company level, to a team level, right down to each individual. First, you need to clearly define the core objectives of the company. These objectives will inform each team's targets. Last, the team targets will inform individual targets, highlighting exactly what each individual needs to contribute to achieve their team's target, and ultimately fulfill the company objectives. This not only makes performance both measurable and manageable, it also brings *accountability* to every layer of the organization, where previously there was none.

Business owners and managers often buy into the misconception that people don't like accountability. This isn't the case. While it's true that low-performers don't like accountability, A-players *love* it. When you start introducing performance metrics and targets to a team that is not used to having any, you may experience some initial resistance, simply because the new situation will be a change from what people are used to. When you communicate well and implement properly, however, the right people will quickly embrace targets and accountability, because these data highlight their success and indicate where they can improve.

Introducing visibility of performance also raises the intensity that everyone brings to their work. We humans love to keep score. It ignites our passion and competitive spirit, that we can then use to fuel us toward our goals. If you've ever played tennis—or any competitive sport—with friends, you already know how this works. Think about you and your friends on a lazy day, standing on a tennis court. Everyone's relaxed and warming up, not yet keeping score. You're lobbing the ball back and forth, probably laughing and chatting about nothing in particular. And then someone says, "Should we start the game?" All of a sudden, everyone gets into position and the *game begins*. Focus descends on the court, the intensity lifts, and even the level of skill each person brings to their game increases. Sure, you're still having fun and enjoying yourselves, but it feels different. Now there's a scoreboard and a game to be won. The key lesson here is this: people play differently when there's a scoreboard.

Scoreboards tap into intrinsic motivation. But even from an extrinsic point of view, you'll find it much easier to manage people toward clearly understood and visible goals. Whatever you're aiming to accomplish, a clear goal across the business—as well as within each department—makes managing your team much easier. The opportunity is to create a compelling, understandable scoreboard that is visible to everyone in the team, all of the time. You want to ignite competition in a positive way, so your team plays with a greater level of intensity and ultimately achieves more, both collectively and as individuals.

Therefore, you need a framework simultaneously simple enough to understand and adaptable enough that you can use it to track many different numbers and goals at once. The framework that we use religiously across all of our own companies, and help our Elevate members install into theirs, is objectives and key results (OKRs).

OKRs: An Upgrade on KPIs

Let's return again to our comparison between the startup phase of your business and the scaleup phase. At the startup level, you have a direct line of sight to almost everything that's happening; you're familiar with every role and can talk to everyone individually, on the fly. At this size, staying across the core drivers of success is relatively simple. At this level, a couple of well-promoted key performance indicators (KPIs) is probably all you need to get moving in the right direction. In fact, sometimes a single target, such as a revenue goal or a number of customers, can be enough to get everyone in your business on the same page.

The inherent challenge with KPIs, though, is that they often exist in isolation, disconnected from each other and sometimes even detached from evolving company objectives. While this will be tolerable in the beginning, as the business grows you will find yourself intuitively longing for a more comprehensive framework that captures *all* the drivers of the business in one place. Something that pulls everything together and ensures alignment to the most critical company imperatives. Something representative of the interconnectedness of the different elements of the business and the individuals that make them up. This is where OKRs come in.

The objectives and key results methodology stretches back to the mid-1960s. It originated at Intel, one of the most innovative companies of all time, before Google picked it up in the late nineties. Today, it's in use at some of the most progressive businesses around the world; companies such as Amazon, Dropbox, and of course The Entourage, along with our Elevate members.

OKRs: The Framework for High Performance

OKRs—as the name suggests—start with objectives. Throughout your organization, you are constantly striving toward a number of objectives. In the marketing department, for example, these can be things like, "raise our profile and brand," or "generate high volume, high quality leads." The objectives themselves aren't measurable; instead, they are qualitative. They represent a direction in which you want to move.

Let's look at how this might play out in practice. One objective for your sales function might be to generate sustainable, profitable sales. Another could be to develop an elite sales team. In your product function, you might want to improve the quality of your products and how you deliver them. In finance, core objectives might be tighter financial management or greater cost control. While these objectives aren't quantifiable, they are unifying, meaning every number that underpins them will be pointing in one consolidated direction.

OKRs always start with objectives. At the top level, you can collaborate with your executive team to determine a few company-wide objectives that you all want to align behind. You then cascade this approach into each department, settling on three to five objectives for each of the functions in the business.

There's a parallel here with a concept called *leader's intent*. Leader's intent is a delegation principle that ensures your team will be guided by your intent, and therefore be capable of making the right decisions in your absence. Aligning everybody around a high-level intent, not just a specific number, means that when situations arise and decisions need to be made, your team is *empowered* to determine the best path forward and get moving. While completing specific tasks and hitting numbers is critical, a leader's intent goes two steps beyond that, explaining both the purpose (*why* this task is important) and the end state (*how* the situation should look when the mission is complete). With this information, your team is equipped to execute in a way that is congruent with the highest company objectives, further alleviating the need for you to get involved in the details. Using the OKR framework, you then break down each objective into the specific key results that need to occur for the objective to be fulfilled. This is where more specific targets come into play. Key results represent achievable goals; when you hit them, you will inevitably make progress toward your objectives.

The best timeframe over which to set and assess OKRs is a quarter (three months). The reason this is the ideal time window is that it is long enough to get really meaningful things done, but not so long that it encourages procrastination; if your timeframe is three months and you lose a month, it will cost you significant progress.

It's also important to note that many objectives will extend beyond a single quarter. For example, a goal to develop an elite sales team may stretch over four quarters. This points to another key advantage of the OKR framework: objectives and key results can be placed on a spectrum, rather than simply a binary framework of "done" or "not done." In practice, you may be heading into a new quarter having achieved 50 percent of what you need to accomplish to develop an elite sales team, and the goal of progressing that number to 75 percent over the coming quarter.

Let's take a look at an example of an OKR framework in action, starting with the objectives dashboard. This captures all the objectives from each element of the business in one consolidated control panel.

YOUR CO. PTY LTD
OBJECTIVES AND KEY RESULTS

MARKETING	CURRENT		SWIMLINE	
Raise our profile and brand	77%		86%	
Sytemize our top funnel marketing activity	74%	75%	86%	86%
Maximize our return on advertising spend	73%		86%	

SALES	CURRENT		SWIMLINE	
Generate sustainable, profitable sales	80%		86%	
Develop an elite sales team	77%	79%	86%	86%
Implement best-in-class sales system and processes	87%		86%	

PRODUCT	CURRENT		SWIMLINE	
Improve the quality of our product	60%		86%	
Increase customer happiness and engagement	82%	77%	86%	86%
Capture and amplify customer happiness	65%		86%	

OPERATIONS	CURRENT		SWIMLINE	
Improve internal operations and processes	97%		86%	
Optimize our technical stack	100%	78%	86%	86%
Develop and engrain our OKR Framework	37%		86%	

FINANCE	CURRENT		SWIMLINE	
Grow profits	98%		86%	
Increase cash at bank	61%	86%	86%	86%
Tighten financial management	98%		86%	

PEOPLE	CURRENT		SWIMLINE	
Focus team on common goals	100%		86%	
Drive performance and culture	97%	92%	86%	86%
Improve employee documentation and OH&S	80%		86%	

Figure 9.4: The Entourage OKR Framework

As you can see from this dashboard, your OKR framework can also act as a perfect implementation aid for all the strategies we've covered in this book. OKRs are a great way to take strategy and make it *actionable*.

Each of the objectives on your dashboard then breaks down into several key results—specific goals that will be measured and managed to ensure each objective is achieved within the relevant timeframe. As an example, let's take a look at how the marketing objectives break down into key results.

MARKETING OKRs

Update 5/23/23

Raise our profile and brand — Score 77%

	From	Current	Target	Achieved
Featured in articles and other media publications	0	5	6	83%
Grow our customer testimonial library	6	11	12	83%
Finalize and launch new website	50%	82%	100%	64%

Systemize our top of funnel marketing activity — Score 74%

	From	Current	Target	Achieved
Grow our social media audience	15,000	27,300	30,000	82%
Number of social media posts over the quarter	0	127	180	77%
Organic leads generated	0	212	300	77%

Maximize our return on advertising spend — Score 73%

	From	Current	Target	Achieved
Percentage of online purchase data feeding into Google Analytics	30%	63%	75%	73%
Attribution modeling run in HubSpot for all acquisition spend	25%	111%	75%	68%
Increase 90-day ROAS on all acquisition spend	80%	59%	120%	78%

Figure 9.5: Marketing Objectives and Key Results

OKRs, while very much related to KPIs, take them to a whole new level. They allow you to define, see, and track all of your business's key initiatives in one place, and to distribute responsibility for their day-to-day management across the business. For business owners who usually have a good gut feel for the drivers of the business, but haven't previously been able to capture them in a way that gets everyone on the same page, doing this is incredibly cathartic. Developing your OKR framework enables you to define the most important objectives of the business, and tie every single key result to those objectives. This is an incredibly powerful framework to measure and manage the core metrics in your business, delegate the information in your mental browser, and ultimately empower your team to be at their absolute best.

Both The Entourage and our members use OKRs as our primary quarterly operational planning tool. We start by reviewing all the objectives for every function of our business and assessing whether each objective will stay the same. Oftentimes, especially if we've set our objectives well, there'll be very little change. From there, we look at the key results under each objective and map out each one. We chart where we are at the beginning of the quarter and where we want to get by the end of it.

You can use the same approach. Be aware that you should completely map the entire quarter's activity several weeks before the quarter starts. This will give you enough time to review every OKR across all the business's different functions, ensure your leadership team is aligned, and roll your chosen OKRs out to each individual team before the start of the quarter. By the time the game kicks off, everyone understands the objectives, and what they need to work on in order to achieve those objectives. They can get straight to work for the quarter and track their progress as they do.

If you'd like to apply the framework highlighted in the diagrams above to your business, we've developed a free template that will enable you to do that. Just head to www.the-entourage.com/elevate.

BUILD YOUR BUSINESS'S FOUNDATION
ON SOLID OPERATIONS

As your business grows, complexity will inevitably follow. This is a good thing. You *want* your business to get so big that you can't get your arms around it anymore. But when it reaches that point, you will need systems to simplify what would otherwise become chaos, so you can continue to scale.

Depending on your natural inclination, you'll find yourself in one of two situations. If you're a drive-growth-focused entrepreneur, you will most likely concentrate on marketing, sales, and growing your customer base. In this case, you will inevitably reach a point where you recognize that a lack of processes, technology, and targets is actually hampering your growth. Often, it's not until you've reached this point that you start to fully appreciate the importance of operations. As a drive-growth-focused entrepreneur, you want to genuinely appreciate the need for OKRs, green light your team to produce them, and—to the degree that your team requires—help shape them. Assuming that you *can* delegate the development and implementation, then you should.

Alternatively, if you're an enable-growth-focused entrepreneur, you will feel most comfortable in the inner workings of the business. If this is you, we encourage you to develop the structures as efficiently as possible such that you can delegate them. As an enabler of growth, you have a natural proclivity for developing and implementing OKRs, but probably need to be conscious of not burying yourself in detail. Based on your current workload, and the capability of your team, make a call on whether you want to delegate the development of OKRs, or implement them yourself. Your job is not to create layers of complexity so that you can live in it. It's to architect structural solutions so that you can delegate them. This is what will allow you to elevate into the position of a true CEO and entrepreneur, which is where you contribute the most to your business.

Every business owner wants to work smarter, not harder, to the extent that this is a universal goal for entrepreneurs everywhere. The question is: how do you do that? Without a strong operational infrastructure—processes, technology, and targets—you will repeatedly find yourself dragged back into the details. When this happens, you will have no choice but to grind harder. You don't want this. We don't want this for you. We want you to experience the freedom that comes from establishing strong operational foundations.

CASE STUDY: STEVE AND SIMON DIG FOR GOLD

We recently worked with a seven-year-old landscaping business at The Entourage that perfectly demonstrates the power of process. The two founders, Steve and Simon, founded the business in 2014 with the grand vision of creating quality environments, turning their clients' homes into havens. By the start of 2020, the business was averaging between $150,000 and $180,000 in monthly revenue.

But while the revenue and client base grew steadily, Steve and Simon found themselves stuck on the tools, day in and day out. During the day, they worked on-site, overseeing their team and the completion of projects and meeting with new clients to keep the business ticking along. At night, they worked away on the books, paid salaries, and managed every other element of the business. They were both putting in sixty-hour weeks.

Being tradies—Australian slang for laborers—by nature, they thought that working harder would get them more results. Past a certain point, however, that wasn't the case. The business couldn't grow beyond its existing limits, because the co-founders were too embedded in running it day-to-day. Their dilemma boiled down to one core problem: Steve and Simon didn't know how to run a business that grew sustainably past the point where they could do it all themselves. Their business lacked leverage and was all-consuming.

In early 2020, Steve and Simon joined The Entourage. After initial conversations with their business coach, they dived under the hood of their business. Very quickly, they realized that in order to elevate their business to the next level, they needed to reverse engineer everything that made them effective, turn them into processes, and delegate more effectively to their team.

Steve and Simon rapidly got to work, documenting everything they did into clear processes, bringing on new team members, and instilling structure where previously there had been none. In no time at all, they took themselves well and truly out of the day-to-day running of the business. Finally, they could focus on what mattered most to the growth of their company: searching for new business opportunities and looking after their existing clients.

Despite the COVID-19 pandemic, Steve and Simon hit milestone months in March and April of 2020. In fact, these two months were the most successful in the history of their business; they turned over an incredible $1.2 million. For comparison, their total revenue for the whole year of 2019 was $2.4 million.

Steve and Simon were stoked by their success, but their business wasn't just a money game for them. From previously doing sixty-hour workweeks, they cut their time in the business to just two days per week; even those days they worked because they wanted to, not because they *had* to. They were now working out of choice, not necessity.

Steve and Simon's success didn't come down to any pivot or quick change. Through insight and diligence, they rewired their entire understanding of what it meant to run a business. When they realized how much they could hand off to others, as long as they had effective processes in place to manage the transition, they quickly stepped up and discovered that many of the things they had assumed were their responsibility alone could be transferred to others using the power of leverage.

They now enjoy the time they spend working on their business, and have the luxury of spending more quality time with their families. Meanwhile, because they addressed the importance of operations to their business, their profit and businesses continue to scale, while they personally do less.

TIM CONTRIBUTES HIS ENABLE GROWTH SKILLS
TO GET THE OPERATIONS RIGHT

For the first five years of The Entourage, our main focus was on driving growth. In many ways, this led to strong results. We achieved rapid expansion, built a world-class brand, and developed a highly engaged clientele who wanted to turbo-charge their own growth. Having driven high-growth for five years, however, we found ourselves in the position so many drive-growth-focused businesses do after a period of sustained expansion; our challenge wasn't to attract more clients; it was to ensure that we were delivering at a high level for our existing clients. The time was ripe to build the enable-growth elements of the business to a more rigorous degree.

Synergy arrived when Tim joined The Entourage and brought his enable-growth focus to the business's heavily drive-growth-focused environment. With lots of customers and growing revenues, Tim was free to dive into improving the operational sophistication of The Entourage, for example by optimizing the CRM so that it was fit for purpose, establishing systems and processes, and improving visibility into targets and performance across the business.

Often, the strategic imperative for these initiatives came when—as we continued to grow and our demands increased—the old way of doing things no longer worked for the business. The rebuild of our tech stack to center around HubSpot, which we described earlier in the chapter, is a perfect example of this. Up to that point, our previous tech stack had worked well enough, but then, as we got laser focused on tracking the effectiveness of our marketing, we realized we needed a much improved and streamlined, technology stack to give us the visibility we needed.

Another step-change improvement came from the need to better manage a multitude of different priorities and initiatives across the business. By 2018, with The Entourage back in full-on growth mode after the tumults of the preceding years, this need was particularly apparent. We had ramped up our marketing, were welcoming members at unprecedented levels, and were rapidly rebuilding our team. There was a lot to deliver and even more opportunity ahead.

A consistent challenge, though—especially for Tim with his enable-growth focus and heavy involvement in the operations of the business—has been getting out of the details in order to strategize about how to best prepare ourselves for the future. A few years ago, Jack often found himself encouraging Tim to look further ahead. However at that time, Tim used to describe his role as keeping all the plates spinning, making sure none of them fell to the floor and crashed. He was so focused on those plates that he couldn't look anywhere else.

A big unlock came when we were introduced to OKRs by one of The Entourage's advisory board members. Here, at last, was a tool that we could use to organize, align, and oversee all of the different goals, projects, and initiatives of The Entourage in a single location—a single operational framework we could use to integrate every activity in the business.

Capturing the key drivers of the business using OKRs was an extensive project that took us several months. Tim adapted the framework to our methodology, incorporating the six essential elements of business. He also went through multiple rounds of iteration with our leadership team to align on their departmental objectives and the key results that would achieve them, as well as conduct a series of training sessions for the entire team on the importance of OKRs and how we would use them. Once we worked through the teething issues, incorporated the framework into our business, and delegated responsibility throughout our company structure, OKRs changed the game for us.

Making the improvements we've described in this case study didn't happen overnight. The path to strengthening our operations wasn't a simple matter of putting in place new systems and instantly seeing a leap in quality. Instead, it was an incremental process that involved making one or two significant improvements each year over several years. The culmination of all of these projects, however, is a business that today has the operational capability, tools, and team to support all of the other functions of the organization.

Tim no longer describes his role as keeping the plates spinning, because each department has taken responsibility for their own plates. Instead, he can focus on where The Entourage is going as a business, and finally look forward.

NEXT UP...

If the foundations of your business are shaky, just like a building, you will reach a point where you can't go any higher. A one-story house doesn't need much of a foundation; a skyscraper does. The higher you go, the deeper your foundations must be. The operations function is the lynchpin of those foundations. Now that we've addressed operations, let's move to the second element of the Enable Growth Structure: finance.

10

FINANCE

Manage and Maximize the Money

As business owners, we've all known that feeling of being riddled with indecision about our best next move. Should we hire for a particular role, or start to build out a sales team? Is now the right time to ramp up our marketing engine?

When you know what decision to make, but hesitate to make it, this is a good indicator that you don't yet have confidence in your numbers. While you might know the idea you want to pursue is good, and the business will benefit, underneath it all there's usually one of two concerns: either you're not sure whether the business can afford the cash, or cash flow is fine but you're not completely sure whether the move will be profitable.

Nothing slows you down like not knowing your numbers. Most business owners don't have a good relationship with the numbers side of their business, and this causes them to agonize over decisions that should be relatively straightforward. "I'm not a numbers person" is a phrase thrown around all too often in the business world.

Where does this poor relationship with the numbers originate? You guessed it; it's a hangover from startup. As your business expands, in several parts of your company the growth can be quite obvious, signposted by things like more customers, increased headcount, and even a bigger office. The financial side of the business, however, may catch you by surprise.

When your business grows from startup to scaleup, so do the numbers. Before you know it, the amount of money flowing into and out of your business goes from manageable to mind-boggling. At the same time, the business's obligations increase. You have a larger team to pay, bigger tax commitments, rent to meet, and customer payments to track.

With more revenue coming in and more expenses going out, a lack of financial management starts to cause serious problems and impede growth. Often, business owners don't fully appreciate the numbers until they've lived with the pain of financial mismanagement for an extended period of time.

In the startup stage, most business owners manage their finances through a combination of gut feel and their business's bank account. For a while, this strategy is usually tolerable. As the obligations of the business increase and numbers grow, however, managing on gut feel and bank balance alone becomes mentally heavy and increasingly risky. As with each of the previous elements of business, the key paradigm shift when it comes to finance is that the way you manage the money in the startup stage is not going to get you through the scaleup stage.

Let's be 100 percent clear: we do *not* want you approaching finance wearing the hat of the technician. It's not your job to do the bookkeeping or develop the financial reporting. In fact, when a business owner *is* doing these things—even when they are an accountant—it's usually the first set of tasks we help them delegate. You simply shouldn't be doing them. While getting involved in the numbers at the level of technician is certainly not your highest and best use, you do need to understand the finance element of your business from the perspective of the leader and the entrepreneur; what the core drivers of financial success in your business are, where the money comes from, where it goes, what to invest in, and how to manage a team to execute on the detail so that you can lead the business with confidence.

The bigger the business becomes, the more questions you simply won't be able to answer if you don't know your numbers. What products generate most of our revenue? How much margin do we have to play with? How much profit did we make over the last year or the last quarter? Why is our cash balance lower than the profit we supposedly made? What are our biggest expenses and how can we reduce them? When can we confidently hire for the next senior role? How much can we invest in more marketing, more stock, or new equipment?

To answer these questions with any sort of confidence, you need a fundamental understanding of your numbers. Good financial management will highlight the performance of the business in the past, present, and future: historical performance, your current position, and your forecasted future performance.

A lot of business owners live with a pervasive sense of anxiety brought about by a lack of clarity over the performance of their business. Many tend to neglect their finances until something goes seriously awry: a large contract falls through, they spend much more cash than planned, sales slow or grind to a halt for a period, or they need urgent financial projections for a business partnership or deal. These kinds of bumps in the road are an inevitable part of the journey we all travel as entrepreneurs. When something unexpected does happen, however, businesses that lack both the cash and the financial foresight needed to take their next step will be paralyzed by indecision.

In our experience, once an entrepreneur decides they need to understand the financial element of their business, even at a high level, it doesn't take long for them to embrace this function. As they start to understand the fundamentals and get on top of the numbers, they are infused with a renewed level of empowerment because they can see firsthand exactly how their business is performing, what their current position is, and different scenarios stretching out into the future. Now they can make financially informed decisions knowing that they are making the right decision. It's not to say every decision will turn out exactly how they anticipate, but that it was the right decision to make at the time.

Perhaps the most empowering thing about mastering your finances is that it forces you to understand your business. What is finance? It is the distillation of the Six Elements of your business into one coherent framework. In the most fundamental way, it is simply the output of what happens in marketing, sales, product, operations, and people. Finance is the language of business. It is the function that brings it all together, through the medium of numbers. When this framework is plotted out, it gives you a clear understanding of your business's past performance, as well as a clear roadmap predicting how your business strategy will play out in the future. Once you have this visibility, the clarity it brings is both therapeutic and empowering.

From this solid foundation, you can make informed decisions and be the leader you want to be. Let's look at the three components of finance that deserve mastery.

TODAY, TOMORROW, TEAM

In this chapter, we'll walk you through the fundamental building blocks of good financial management and foresight. As we've already explained, this is not a conversation about how to do the bookkeeping or develop financial reports. It's about equipping you with an understanding of the essentials, so that you can build a finance function that enables others to undertake these tasks on your behalf, providing you with the reports and forecasts that are going to be meaningful to you. This is finance from the perspective of the leader and the entrepreneur.

At its essence, good financial management is about understanding the financial performance of your business today, gaining foresight about the financial state of your business tomorrow, and enrolling your entire team in the numbers so everyone can make good decisions.

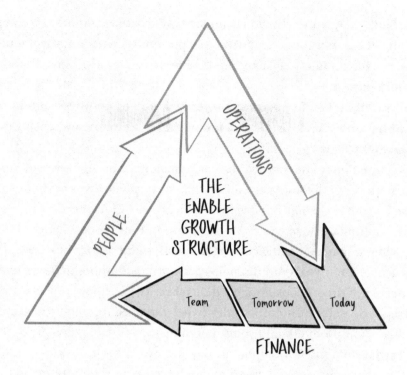

Figure 10.1: Finance Components of the Enable Growth Structure

This chapter will give you confidence in the current and future financial performance of your business. You'll be empowered to have your team develop a purposeful forecast that shows you how much money is coming in and how much is going out. Furthermore, we want to enable you to use that information to make growth decisions, especially to assess how hard you can drive and enable growth with the available cash and resources at your disposal.

TODAY: UNDERSTANDING YOUR CURRENT FINANCIAL POSITION

The first step toward mastering your finances is to get an accurate picture of your business's current financial position and performance. These tools enable you to go beyond simply looking at how much cash you have in the bank. They will enable you to understand where the money is coming from, where it is going, and—most importantly—what improvements you can immediately make to your business to increase profitability and unlock growth.

The three key financial statements you need to understand are your **balance sheet**, **profit and loss (P&L) statement**, and **cash flow statement**.

Your **balance sheet** shows the current financial position of your business. It lays out the assets: the things that the business owns or is owed. It also lays out the liabilities: what the business owes. From there, it provides the resulting owner's equity. At any point in time, your balance sheet provides a snapshot of the current financial health of your business.

Your **P&L** reveals the financial performance of the business over a period of time–for example, a quarter or a year. It lays out the revenues (gross sales); the cost of sales (what you need to spend to sell and deliver your product), and your operating costs (the ongoing expenses incurred from the normal day-to-day running of your business). After all these things are accounted for, you're left with the profit or loss of the business.

Finally, your **cash flow statement** shows the movements of cash into and out of your business, along with the opening and closing cash balances at the beginning and end of any period.

You may already receive these reports from your bookkeeper or accountant. The problem is that they're probably not presented in a way that is useful or meaningful for *you*. Let's say your accountant sends you your P&L statement at the end of each quarter. What do you do? You likely skip straight to the line at the bottom headed "net income," wonder where all the money has gone, feel disillusioned, and find something better to do.

Time and time again, we speak with business owners who either don't have access to up-to-date financials, or who do, but whose statements are laid out in a way that doesn't make sense to them. Please understand this one very important point: *Your financial reports are useful to the degree that they inform your decision-making.* They aren't about pleasing the accountant or the tax office (although pleasing the tax office is important too); they are about helping *you understand your business* so that you can make better decisions, faster.

TOMORROW: DEVELOPING YOUR FINANCIAL FORECAST

Your financial statements outline the current position and performance of your business, providing you with a snapshot of your business *today*. So long as they're up-to-date and accurate, you're already in a far stronger position than many business owners moving from startup to scaleup.

To truly push the business forward and execute your vision for the future, however, you need more than a picture of your current financial performance. You need a clear vision of the *future* of your business. You get this by developing a financial forecast.

A financial forecast will help you model potential inputs and outcomes for your business. Like any other part of the business, you achieve results by creating a goal, aligning activity and investment toward that goal, and then monitoring and adjusting as you go. This is a huge improvement on managing your business on intuition and gut feel. With no solid financial forecast, you can't possibly know how much you can afford to spend on growth activities, when to hire new people, or when you might be starting to get short on cash.

As an entrepreneur, operating a good financial forecast is crucial to architecting the future. As you and your team enter the inputs relating to your strategy, your financial model will illuminate the likely outcomes, bringing each scenario to life. For an entrepreneur who is always thinking ahead, looking into a meaningful financial forecast is like getting a glimpse into the future.

Forging Your Financial Forecast

To get a crystal clear view of the financial future of the business, you need a forecast that delivers your balance sheet, P&L, and cash flow forecast, all over a specific period of time. This is called a three-way financial forecast, because it is showing you the financial future of your business three different ways.

As we've already outlined, jumping into a spreadsheet and actually constructing a model like this is *not* your highest and best use of your time. However, you absolutely need to understand the core building blocks, as well as the process required to shape them into a meaningful format. Why? Because, in order for the model to be useful *for you*, it must be developed in a way that makes sense *to you*. This is an area where most business owners fall into the trap we described in the previous chapter; abdicating rather than delegating. While the actual *construction* of the tool should be delegated to your accountant or CFO (outsourced or in-house), the core inputs, preferred layout, and future scenarios must come from you and your team. Later in the chapter, under the "Team" heading, we'll explain in greater detail who should be constructing this model for you. When you understand the fundamentals that we'll take you through in this section, you will be well-equipped to work along-side them.

If you or your team do want to play around with a three-way forecasting template, in Microsoft Excel, Google Sheets, or a similar application, The Entourage has one that we use with our members, which we've made available in the Elevate resource center on our website. Go here to grab it: www.the-entourage.com/elevate.

To generate a forecast that is useful for you and your team, you will need to enter a variety of numbers from your business today, along with how you envision it taking shape in the future. To simplify what can feel like a complex concept, we first want you to think about three, key building blocks that you will need to create your financial forecast: revenue model, headcount, and operating costs. A good financial forecast will analyze all these things and spit out a balance sheet, P&L, and cash flow forecast that predicts your future financials over a specific timescale. This could be one month, one year, three years, or any other period you deem appropriate. Let's unpack these three building blocks in more detail.

Revenue Model

When you start directing the development of your financial forecast, begin by laying out the revenue model of your business. What is your revenue model? Think of it as everything you need to do to make sales and then, if you do those things well, the amount of revenue you will achieve as a result.

Your revenue model will include your marketing activities and campaigns, your business development initiatives, and anything else you are doing to acquire new customers. It will also include marketing spend, lead generation estimates, and conversion rate targets for each of these activities, so that you can determine the number of sales that will result from each. Finally, it will calculate the revenue you expect to receive from each new sale, allocate that revenue over the appropriate timeframe, and account for the variable costs of delivering that revenue, such as the cost of goods sold.

The purpose of laying out your revenue model like this is twofold. First, it will help you zero in on *how* you drive revenue and identify the activities that really matter. Second, once you have the model figured out and formularized, you will be able to use it to set your revenue generation targets.

A well-developed model will allow you to alter the marketing inputs and immediately see what impact that will have on revenue. For example, if you are currently spending $10,000 per month on lead generation and achieving a certain volume of sales, your model should be able to reveal what will happen if you increase that spend to $40,000 per month. It will also show you how your overall revenue will change as a result of increasing—or decreasing—your marketing and sales activities.

Once you achieve this, you can now use your revenue model to set your marketing, sales, and revenue targets. Let's say the $10,000 per month you are currently spending on lead generation brings in $2 million in revenue for the year, and next year you want to increase revenue to $3 million. Your revenue model will let you play around with your marketing activities and spend until you understand what combination will get you to your target number.

Later in this chapter, we'll go into more detail about how to use your financial forecast to plan out the future. For now, our key message is that you should spend enough time in this phase to get your revenue model right, as everything else will flow from here.

Headcount

The second building block of your financial forecast is your headcount projections. In most businesses, people are one of the top expenses. If you run a service-based business, as we do at The Entourage, and many of our members do, headcount will undoubtedly be one of your top three line items. Even if your business is based on products or manufacturing, headcount will certainly be a significant expense.

A good financial forecast will use ratios that you set to tie most of your headcount requirements to your revenue model. For example, it will automatically calculate how many more salespeople you will need to achieve a given increase in sales volume. As the number of customers you serve increases, it will also calculate the size of necessary increases in customer service staff, production staff, and any other team members whose roles can be directly tied to revenue generation activity, and the work that flows from it.

Of course, not all team members do things that can be directly correlated to revenue generation. Most finance and operations staff, for example, fall into this category. For these roles, there won't be a ratio or formula you can tie to the revenue model. You'll need to add details of these additional team members into the model manually, using your recruitment timeline and forecasted growth to predict when you will need them.

In addition to figuring out when you will need to bring on new people, the headcount component of your forecast will also include salary and additional employment expenses for all existing and future employees. This allows the forecast to generate your headcount expenses over any future period with the majority of it automatically flowing from any work that you do in the revenue model.

Operating Costs

The third and final major building block of your financial forecast is operating costs. This includes everything else that you need to spend money on over the relevant period of time and is usually the easiest of the three to forecast. When you're calculating your revenue, you need to think about how you want to increase it and what you need to do to achieve that goal. When you're figuring out your headcount, you need to consider who you need to hire to reach your objectives. When you're predicting your operating costs, however, you can often simply take your historical costs directly from previous P&L statements, figure out what percentage of revenue they represent, and extrapolate them out over the forecast period. Generally, spending a couple of hours on operating cost is more than sufficient to nail down those projections.

How to Use Your Financial Forecast

Once you've captured the three major building blocks of your financial forecast in a formularized template, either the one we've provided or one from your accountant, you get to have some fun. Start running different scenarios through the model and see how each of them play out into the future.

For example, try increasing your marketing spend to as much as you think you can possibly afford. What flows from there? Another area to tweak is your conversion rates. In Chapter Seven: Sales, we took you through a raft of sales strategies and tactics that you can use to improve your sales process. How much could you improve your conversion rates if you implemented just some of these strategies over the coming year? Experiment with different numbers and see what your financial forecast spits out. Play around with your headcount ratios too, along with your operating costs. With a well-developed model, you can change all of these things around and instantly get an insight into how the rest of the business is impacted.

Ultimately, you want to be able to run all your strategic ideas and initiatives through the forecast, and take a look at the numbers on the other side. Let's say that next year, significantly increasing the energy and money you spend on marketing activities is a key strategic priority for you. Great, punch the projected numbers into your financial forecast and see how revenue and profitability are looking. Alternatively, you may want to push much harder on a new product line, while pulling back slightly on an older one. Again, try it and see how things will look in twelve months' time. Another strategic focus might be delighting customers, which will involve investment in product delivery and customer experience. A good financial forecast will show you exactly how all of these scenarios will look in terms of revenue, profitability, and achievability.

What do we mean by achievability? As you implement your strategies into the forecast, you'll quickly be able to see how they translate in terms of marketing and sales activities, sales numbers, headcount, recruiting timeline, and a whole raft of other metrics. But that alone won't tell you whether your business can match those forecasts. The first test of achievability is your own sense of whether these numbers are attainable. Is your current sales team capable of achieving that number of sales? If not, and the forecast shows that you will need to recruit and train more salespeople in order to hit those numbers, do you think you can hire at the rate the forecast requires? The same goes for product delivery resources, office space to house everyone, and every other part of your business that is encapsulated in the forecast. After implementing all of your strategies into the forecast, and then carefully reviewing all of the numbers, do you think everything in there is achievable? Earlier, we discussed the importance of going beyond gut feel. We're not suggesting that your intuition shouldn't be trusted; it's just that it needs to be substantiated. That's what this model will do.

Another way to check the achievability of your plans is through the cash flow component of your three-way financial forecast. Until now, we have been talking about the profit and loss section of your forecast: looking at the revenues and expenses of the business from an accounting perspective. Of course, as most business owners know, cash flows differ considerably from revenue and expense flows. The moment you earn revenue from a customer may be long before they actually give you any cash. Likewise, you may incur an expense well before you pay for it.

The second vital tool in a three-way forecast, therefore, is the cash flow forecast. This takes your profit and loss projections and, using a series of assumptions that good financial models are capable of making, forecasts cash movements into and out of your business over a given period of time. Using this tool, you start to gain visibility into one very important factor: how much cash you have at any one time. Businesses that push hard on growth spend a lot of cash before they receive the commensurate return in revenue. The cash flow forecast tells you whether you run the risk of spending more than you can afford.

Consulting your cash flow forecast can give you tremendous confidence. When you model your cash flow forecast, you come to understand how hard you can push. Let's say you develop a profit and loss forecast that you feel is aggressive—it requires a considerable investment in marketing, sales, and headcount—but your cash flow forecast shows that you have the cash reserves to do it. In this case, you can move forward with assurance. On the other hand, if you develop an aggressive profit and loss forecast and your cash flow forecast shows that you could run very low on cash, or even go into the red, you may need to pull back or seek additional funding to execute the plan.

The third output of the three-way financial forecast is the balance sheet, which predicts the overall position of the business at any point in the future. The ability to foresee the financial health of the business one, two, three, or even five years ahead of time is useful for every business owner and shareholder.

In times of success, having a financial forecast is important. It will allow you to make confident decisions about where to allocate resources, and how much you can invest in driving the future growth of the business. In times of challenge, a solid financial forecast is even *more* important. When your business experiences a shock, whether it's a major contract falling over, a customer not re-signing, or even a global pandemic, a solid financial forecast can be the difference between surviving and not.

If things ever get really dire, a solid cash flow forecast can be your most valuable tool. Businesses suffering extreme challenges will often run projections that show them running out of cash. If you're in this situation, you should do everything you can today to kick that can down the road. If your cash flow forecast shows that you're running out of cash in four months, make short-term decisions to push that out to five months, then medium-term decisions to push that out to ten months. This extends your runway to get the business back into a position of profitability. When the threat of running out of cash has been worked through, you should return to making longer-term decisions.

LOCK YOUR FORECAST TO CREATE A BUDGET FOR YOUR TEAM

Of course, there's no point creating a financial forecast simply to frame it and hang it on your office wall. Its real power comes when you then translate it into a budget for your business. When you do this, you take the forecast that you've devised, codify it into a budget, and use that budget to set targets for your organization. This is where you start turning your plans into reality.

At The Entourage, our financial year commences in July, and we start doing our financial forecasting in February. We begin with strategy. Jack, Tim, and the leadership team come together to discuss what's working, where we want to scale up, what can be improved, where we perceive future opportunities, and whether there are risk factors that we need to take into consideration. Once we've developed a high-level strategy, we run different scenarios through our financial forecast, exploring the degree to which we can drive growth, and determining precisely where to invest to do that. Does each scenario bring us the top-line revenue, the bottom-line profit, and the cash position that we need to keep expanding successfully as a global business?

Next, we take the key scenarios to our advisory board and seek their input. By May, we lock the optimal forecast as our budget for the next financial year. That budget then becomes our yardstick for the year, and the job of the CEO and leadership team switches to ensuring its delivery. Once July 1 arrives, the entire business operates based on that budget. It informs every decision, from calibrating our marketing spend to determining our sales targets, from calculating our target member numbers to projecting our headcount and recruitment timeline.

Of course, things never go exactly to plan. We wouldn't expect to sail a boat in a straight line, and we don't expect our financial year to look identical in practice to the way it looks on the page. We can do as much planning as possible, and predict the route that will work best, but once we set sail, the market—and life—will surely dictate some changes. Some elements of the budget will work as we predict, whereas others won't. While it's important to have a destination in mind, we don't expect every single thing to go exactly as we plot it. We're comfortable going slightly off course, tacking back, veering the other way, and then tacking back again, making small adjustments as we go before finally reaching our destination.

Don't expect to execute your budget perfectly, but do use it to track performance throughout the year, and iterate constantly as things invariably go slightly wrong. A budget's power comes from the course it sets; you can always work back toward it. If you're ever under target in any area of the business, you can rapidly identify that shortfall, and then make decisions about how to bring yourself back on target. Conversely, if you're ever over target, you can strategize how to lock in the gains and continue to outperform the budget.

For a lot of growth-focused organizations, the challenge lies in achieving their growth targets. Often, they'll be slightly short on revenue because they aren't investing quickly enough. In this scenario, you might be under your revenue target but above your profitability target. But if you're looking to grow, that's not the ideal outcome. This discrepancy in your budget tells you that to grow, you need to push harder and invest faster. Conversely, if you are ahead of revenue targets but down on profitability, this means you are spending more without getting the commensurate return. It might be a good idea to slow down. This is the value of a strong budget. You can only make these decisions if you are regularly comparing your real-world performance with your projected budget.

The budget sets the course for your company, which it does its best to follow, even as winds and currents shift around it. To navigate through those changing conditions as effectively as possible, it's important to implement some other finance best practices for you and your business which we will explore now.

PROFITABILITY PRINCIPLES

As we've already discussed, your financial forecast is more of a guide than an exact outlook. You do want to stick to it as closely as possible, but in reality, you're going to over-perform in some areas and underperform in others. As long as you're monitoring and adjusting as you go, you should end up close to the position you set sail toward.

In our experience, the one area where growing businesses can often end up short on is profitability. Why is this? Because when you're short on revenue, you can always invest more to drive revenue up, but this in turn increases expenses, so it doesn't boost the bottom line. Conversely, if you're on track with revenue but have been spending too much, it's hard to pull back on your expenses without also decreasing revenue.

The way around this challenge is to build some wiggle room into your financial forecast, so that when you inevitably spend more than you plan in one area, you can offset it with savings in another.

At The Entourage, we have developed a series of Profitability Principles: key strategies to employ when creating a robust financial forecast.

1. **Build fat into your forecast**, by loading it with absolutely *all* the expenses you're likely to incur over the year. Don't cheap out. Don't skip things. Work diligently to include *every* potential cost, and then adjust your top-line revenue goals to ensure that you still achieve your desired profit. Chances are that when you get

into the action of the year, you won't get around to spending everything you've loaded into the forecast. This means that even if costs blow out in one area, they'll be counterbalanced in another area.

2. **When you overspend, save it. When you underspend, bank it.** This principle dates from many, many years ago, when Tim spent twelve months traveling around the world with his now-wife, Clare. To ensure their travels could continue for as long as they wished, Tim set a daily budget for each city, using the cost of local hotel rooms as a benchmark, and he and Clare were diligent about sticking to that budget. Whenever they overspent, they subtracted the same amount from the following day's budget. Whenever they underspent, they banked the surplus. Using this method, they spent a year traveling the world, working occasionally as they went, and returned with more money than when they departed. Tim has since adapted that same cost-saving principle to The Entourage and embedded it into the business of countless members. If you overspend *anywhere*, you need to save it somewhere else. If you underspend anywhere, bank it, because you never know when you'll need some extra cash to cover something else.

3. **Inject cost consciousness across the business.** Let's make a key distinction: cost consciousness is not about saving money at all costs. Rather, it's about spending where it's important and saving elsewhere. Important spending helps to drive revenue and drive the development of the business. Spending that simply boosts the ego, or comes from a place of impulsivity, is usually wasted. One interesting principle that business owners rarely appreciate is that for each dollar of revenue generated, only a portion accrues to the bottom line. Every dollar of costs *saved*, however, goes straight to the bottom line. Therefore, combining a focus on driving top-line revenue with strong cost management has a potent effect on increasing your profit. To inject cost

consciousness across your business, you need to regularly talk with your team about the importance of sticking to budgets, spending where it matters, and avoiding wastage everywhere else. Later in this chapter, we will go into detail about enrolling your team in the numbers, which is also essential for creating awareness around the importance of cost management.

4. **Sweat the big stuff.** In every business, a couple of large expenses, like headcount, rent, technology, and raw materials, weigh disproportionately on the bottom line. When the time comes to commit to or renegotiate these expenses, sweat them *hard*. One example from The Entourage: When we moved offices, we entered intense negotiations to get the best possible deal. The outcome? Savings of about $400,000 compared with what we would have spent if we simply accepted the sticker price. Another example of negotiating well dates from a few years ago, when we rebuilt our technology stack as we outlined in the previous chapter, consolidating from dozens of tools down to fewer than ten. This cut our technology expenses by more than $200,000 a year, while *improving the quality* of the tools that underpin our business. This is why it's so important to push hard on the big stuff, especially when you're negotiating with a larger company that won't be overly affected by your ask. One strong piece of negotiation can save you hundreds of thousands of dollars.

Sweating the Big Stuff: Negotiating Secrets from the Frontlines

What exactly do we mean by sweating the big stuff? Let's get into it.

First, whenever you are forming any business relationship or supplier agreement, it's critical that the deal is a win-win for both parties. Achieving an outcome that disadvantages either side will not be sustainable, and therefore will end up costing both parties more in the long run. When you approach any potential arrangement seeking a win-win, people will want to do business with you and will champion the best deal possible on your behalf.

Seeing inside thousands of small-to-medium-sized businesses each year, we get a firsthand perspective into how many are spending more than they need to on key expenses, particularly with their larger suppliers. In every instance, this situation results from suboptimal negotiation at the outset, or from the business owner not returning to the negotiation table when they know they should.

Because negotiating thoroughly does take time and skill, it's important that you're selective about when and with whom you choose to do this; this is why we encourage you to *sweat the big stuff.* Pushing for a better deal, particularly with your larger suppliers has a huge impact on your business's bottom line. And don't worry, your larger suppliers aren't going to do anything that disadvantages them—they usually know that they can afford to give you a better deal.

When Tim sweats the big stuff, he employs a couple of key strategies. First, he is transparent that he will be seeking a good deal. Second, he enters with a low offer and doesn't accept whatever the other company comes back with. Third, he aims to negotiate at length through several rounds of offers and counteroffers, without burning bridges. When concluding a negotiation, a good rule of thumb is to win the respect of the other party; they should know that they gave you the best possible deal, that was still a win-win for both parties.

Don't be intimidated by large suppliers. Stand up for yourself, do your homework, and be transparent about your process. Tim tells all vendors and agents he speaks with about his criteria, including price, as well as sharing that he's speaking with other people. He talks them through his process, and when he whittles his selection of potential vendors down to the last couple, he tells them that he needs to get down to a certain price point for it to be viable. When you're negotiating the big stuff in your business, it's only sensible to take a similar approach. Sweat it hard, and reap the rewards.

TEAM: BUILDING YOUR FINANCE TEAM AND ENROLLING THE COMPANY IN THE NUMBERS

When it comes to building out a finance team, business owners benefit from a clear plan of who to hire, when, and—even more importantly—what each person will do. You may have some financial assistance, such as a part-time bookkeeper, but the chances are it will be someone you engaged in the early stages of the business. Now that everything is bigger and more complex, they don't have either the ability or the bandwidth to keep everything in order.

You may also employ an external accountant. A complaint we hear regularly from business owners, however, is that their accountant is purely reactive, waiting to receive instructions or be asked for information rather than proactively providing insight, information, or advice.

Breaking free of this situation is difficult, because we all find it hard to recruit and direct people who perform roles in areas where we ourselves don't have expertise. For most entrepreneurs, bookkeeping and accounting fall into this category, which is why it can be so difficult to bring on the right people to provide support in this area. To help you navigate these challenging waters, we have developed the following section on who to hire—and when to hire them—to manage the money in your business.

Who Does What?

The first finance position that every business owner should fill is a book-keeper. A bookkeeper logs the everyday transactions of the business and ensures they are entered correctly into the company's accounting software. Your bookkeeper can also send out invoices, keep track of accounts receivable, process payroll, and prepare month-end and year-end accounting reports. The bookkeeper does the basics; the granular tasks, so they need to be someone with a high attention to detail, who loves process.

Bookkeeping is fundamental to keeping your accounts in order, so we encourage you to bring someone in this role as soon as possible. Your bookkeeper will likely start on a part-time basis—as little as one day per week—and gradually increase their hours as your business generates a greater volume of transactions. Additional tasks that will also drive up the time commitment you will need from a bookkeeper include managing payroll, sending and tracking payment of invoices, and preparation of reports. Whether your bookkeeper is engaged on a part-time or full-time basis, local or offshore, it's important that this person is neither you nor your life partner. Your bookkeeper should be a professional, employed for the sole purpose of keeping the day-to-day accounts of the business fully up-to-date.

At The Entourage, we see many business owners try to do the books at night or on the weekend, working overtime to track the numbers and send out invoices. Occasionally, a potential new member will seek us out because they're running out of cash only for us to discover, when we look closer at their financials, that this is because they haven't sent out invoices. When we ask why, they tell us they don't have time for this essential task. This is why it's so important to have a bookkeeper.

The next financial role that you need to fill is a tax accountant (alternatively called a tax lawyer, tax agent, or tax preparer) who can take the day-to-day accounts prepared by the bookkeeper, prepare and file tax returns, and ensure that your business is meeting all your tax obligations.

For most startups, and even scaleup stage businesses, this tax accountant will be an external professional who you engage to ensure your tax compliance on an annual basis. The biggest frustration we hear from our members about their tax accountants is that they "just don't get it." The entrepreneur is focused on growing their business and identifying all the things that *can be done*, while the tax accountant is focused on rules, regulations, and all the things that *can't be done*. When choosing a tax accountant, therefore, ensure that they have had extensive experience with businesses at your stage of growth and that they can demonstrate they understand your business and its objectives. Your key selection criteria are appropriate qualifications *and* an understanding of growing entrepreneurial businesses—they may be a sole practitioner or a member of a small-to-medium-size accounting firm.

A good accountant should also be able to help you develop your three-way financial forecast. If you already work with an accountant, have a good relationship with them, and think their business acumen is strong enough to help you develop a forecast, inviting them to scope and quote the work is often the fastest, most effective way to get it done. If you don't think your existing accountant is up to the task, another option is to engage a more experienced accountant or accounting firm specifically to develop your financial forecast. This may be relatively expensive—usually between $5,000 and $20,000, depending on the complexity of your business—but it's a worthwhile investment to gain clarity into your financial future. A good forecasting model, developed specifically for your business, should last you at least three years, so remember to factor that life span into the cost-value equation when scoping the work.

As your business grows, another role you might consider is an internal business accountant. This is a different role from the tax accountant, as an internal business accountant focuses much more on the internal workings of your business than on external tax requirements. For this position, you will want someone who is an expert in accounting and, preferably, has experience in your industry.

A clear sign that you might benefit from an internal business accountant is the realization that—despite having both a bookkeeper and a tax accountant—you personally are still spending a lot of time on finance-related tasks. Responding to emails, providing information, approving staff expenses, running reports, developing expense guidelines and policies—these are the kinds of financial activities that tend to slip between the cracks and land on the business owner's plate. If you find that you are spending considerable time on any of these tasks, you are probably ready for a business accountant.

Last, ascending up the ladder of finance roles, you will reach a point where you need a virtual or full-time Chief Financial Officer (CFO). The key indicator that you have reached this point is when you find yourself wanting more sophisticated, strategic input from your finance function. If you are no longer satisfied driving the delivery of the financial strategy, instigating each financial initiative, or reviewing every financial decision, those are strong signs that you need to bring on a senior financial executive.

For most scaleup-stage business owners, the first step into this territory is to engage a virtual CFO. As the name implies, a virtual CFO will sit outside your business. You should, however, absolutely expect them to dive in and understand the entire workings of the organization, so that they can take many of the higher-level financial tasks and projects off your hands. A virtual CFO will provide your internal accountant and bookkeeper with direction, liaise with and guide your tax accountant, and improve your internal accounting and reporting procedures. If you haven't developed your financial forecast by the time you bring on a virtual CFO, they can also help you with that, as well as scoping out and providing recommendations on any other financial initiatives in the business.

The next step up from a virtual CFO is a full-time executive, who can be your go-to person for all things financial and commercial. This is someone who can own and execute your strategic plan alongside you, day in and day out. A full-time CFO will take on responsibility for the financial performance of the business, ownership of your financial forecast, and leadership of your finance team. They will be the point person for all things finance within the business, and will help you to liaise and communicate with stakeholders, such as your board of directors, shareholders, the bank, and even—when you are required by size or regulations to prepare audited accounts—auditors. This is a significant span of responsibility, and you can expect to make a corresponding investment in the right person. Nonetheless, appointing a full-time CFO is one of the biggest steps you can take toward elevating out of the day-to-day of your business.

ENROLLING YOUR TEAM: CREATING A PROFIT-CONSCIOUS CULTURE

In addition to recruiting the right people to manage the finances of your business, it is also essential to enroll the rest of your team in the numbers. This is because the majority of your broader team won't have a background in finance and this will likely cause challenges as the business grows.

What kind of challenges are we talking about? One that we see on a regular basis is employees knowing what a company generates in terms of revenue, but having too little understanding of all the other expenses that are incurred. The result? They think the business owner is pocketing all the revenue and shortchanging everyone else. "If only they knew!" is the catch cry of the business owner who is yet to train their team on profit-consciousness. As leaders, it's our job to help our teams better understand the economics of the business.

Another more nuanced challenge is expecting employees to act in the financial interest of the business when they have little understanding of what that looks like. Even for us as business owners, it can be hard to understand how all the numbers work together—for example, how sales today lead to revenue tomorrow, or how spending more than we've budgeted for in one area means we can't afford to do something in another—so we shouldn't expect our teams to understand this unless we train them in it. The result of training your team in the numbers is that they gain a greater appreciation of how the finances of your business work, and start to make good decisions.

Another benefit of enrolling your team in the numbers is creating a shared sense of ownership of the business's financial goals. Say you want to increase revenue from $6 million to $10 million next year and have made a detailed plan for how the business can achieve this. Now, imagine you tell your team just the top-line numbers and nothing else. You can understand why this may not transfer the level of confidence and certainty the team is seeking from you.

Compare that with sharing with them how much you are going to increase the marketing budget by, the additional salespeople that you will be hiring, and how you expect sales and revenue to increase at a high but realistic rate as a result of this increased investment. Your team's confidence in the numbers and their ability to achieve them will be significantly improved, which in turn increases the business's chances of achieving them. The same goes for all the other areas of your business—the more insight you give your team into the numbers that underpin each of your targets, the more they will embrace them.

At The Entourage, we employ multiple strategies to enroll our team in the numbers. Before each financial year, we run the entire team through the key numbers in the financial forecast. In this session, we talk through the revenue model for the coming year, our headcount plans, and the major expenses. We don't get bogged down in the details of the spreadsheet itself, instead we go through a summary document of the most important numbers, paying particular attention to the areas where we are investing more—and, in turn, expecting greater performance from—than previous years.

Each month we then track and report on the key numbers at both a departmental and company level. We discuss these numbers in the leadership team meeting and also with our advisory board to ensure visibility and accountability right across the mid to senior layers of the business. We also provide, at minimum, quarterly updates to the entire team on how we are tracking against revenue, profit, and other key performance metrics such as active member numbers. This level of transparency into the finances of our business means that everyone on the team understands how we are performing, whether we are ahead or behind target, and what is expected of them and their department next.

Last, we train our team on how to read and interpret financial statements. This benefit translates immediately to our members because it means that everyone in our team can have meaningful discussions with members about what is going well in their business, what should be improved, and what can be done about it. We do this training on a team-by-team basis, working through real profit and loss statements, balance sheets, and financial forecasts, discussing what is going on in the business, running scenarios, and devising strategies to drive further growth through the numbers.

FINANCES UNLOCK YOUR FUTURE

For a lot of entrepreneurs, fulfilling a vision is a more powerful motivation than making a lot of money. That being said, the financial health of a business is one of the main scoreboards that will underpin your success. The more financially healthy your business, the further it can go, and the more impact you can make. A business that is not financially sustainable, and is operating from a place of survival, is not fun for anyone.

As you can see, your finance function really is just a distillation of each of the Six Elements of your business. While this is an area that too many business owners avoid for too long, falling in love with the numbers makes you a more confident CEO, a better entrepreneur, and a much more informed leader. Becoming acquainted with the financial performance of your business helps you make better, faster decisions without the angst, because every decision you make is financially informed.

Instead of shying away from the numbers, every entrepreneur should embrace the finances of their business. When you have a clear picture of where you stand and where you're going, you build confidence. You know how hard you can push, and when, what you can invest in, and who you need to hire. There are dozens of things that you want and need to do within your business. When the numbers are taken care of, you will have the solid foundation and freedom to focus on growth.

CASE STUDY: EVERYTHING GOES OKAY...
UNTIL IT DOESN'T

Zooming out from the details and thinking about finances at a macro level, we frequently see business owners who feel entirely comfortable with their finances. That is, until something goes wrong. They're working well, the cash is coming in, and everything seems great. Then, they make a mistake–or have one thrust upon them. Seemingly out of nowhere, there isn't enough cash to cover all their expenses. At this point, what do they do? Usually, they panic. How did this happen? Where did the money go?

What are we going to do? Ironically just when they need answers, they are flooded with unanswered questions. Their previous state of ignorance seems blissful, but unfortunately they can't return there.

This is exactly what happened to one of our Elevate members recently, an extremely successful high-end interior design and home renovations business. They were coming into their eighth year of business with an established team, multiple awards under their belt, and an enviable reputation. Up to this point, everything had been going extremely well. Projects were delivered on time, customers felt happy, and they had plenty of cash in the bank to show for their success. So much cash, in fact, that they'd been able to draw out good amounts of money through their trust structure over the years, always with enough left to pay the bills and grow the business.

This idyllic state didn't last forever, though. In the move to a new contract management system, somehow they missed a payment to a builder. Not a small payment either; more than $400,000. Still, in the world of renovation, this number wasn't astronomical, so it took a couple of months before the oversight surfaced. In the interim, the founders had decided to pivot slightly and focus more on the design services side of the business, rather than the capital-intensive construction side. In normal times, this move wouldn't have been too scary. But at a time when they'd just discovered they owed a supplier an unaccounted for $400,000, suddenly the pathway forward for the business became alarmingly narrow.

In fact, it was worse than that. What had seemed like an easy decision just a few days prior was suddenly a major problem. Should they put the money back into the business? Should they pause their plans to pivot? Was the business actually sound enough to support either—or any— strategy? If they missed this, what else could they have missed?

Fortunately, as Elevate members, they were able to schedule a strategy session with The Entourage executive team, which they used to sit down with Tim to plan the way forward. The first thing Tim asked for was their financial statements: at least their profit and loss and balance sheet, ideally their cash flow statement and forecast.

"Yeah, we don't really have any of those," they replied sheepishly. "We've always just managed the business on cash, and by having a really good understanding of what's coming in and out. We have very detailed project budgets, but not much at the company level."

"What about your accountant?" asked Tim. "Would they have some of this?"

"Not really," they answered. "We have a part-time bookkeeper who's been with us for years, but to be honest, we've known for a while that the business has gotten too big for her. She's just not keeping up. We never speak to our accountants. The bookkeeper just sends in our end-of-quarter and end-of-year accounts, and they handle submissions and payments to the tax office. We asked them both for some numbers to send to you, and it took us less than a minute to see that they were all wrong. So really, we're flying blind."

"Okay," replied Tim. "I know this is a tough place to be in, but I don't want you to be concerned or embarrassed. We see countless members in the same position and there is a clear roadmap from where you are now to where you need to be."

Having been in a similar position at The Entourage, we knew exactly how to advise these members. The first critical step was developing some certainty around their current financial position and future. They had enough personal cash to put back into the business and pay their supplier, but they had no idea whether they were still in a position to execute the pivot to design services at the same time. The first step was to engage some proper financial assistance to figure out exactly where they were, and also develop some kind of forecast for the new model.

They agreed with this diagnosis and our proposed remedy. Through The Entourage Growth Services, we brought in one of our expert partners to conduct a detailed review of their books, clean them up, model the options available to their business, and establish methods to maintain quality financial practices going forward.

This process revealed that the situation, while dire, wasn't the existential threat they first imagined. Going through this kind of rigorous audit clarified the pathway forward, reinforced the viability of a greater focus on design services, and uncovered one particular opportunity that has now become a fundamental pillar of the new business model.

One of the big question marks surrounding the pivot to design services was the high cost of skilled draftspeople, who command considerable salaries in Australia. After identifying this as a key challenge to overcome —as we shared earlier in the chapter, headcount costs are always a major expense in service-based businesses—we introduced the business to another of our growth partners, who specializes in engaging full-time offshore resources.

Today, a little over a year later, the business has recruited seven draftspeople based in the Philippines, along with a senior designer, also based in the Philippines, to manage this team. These talented draftspeople help them support the existing Australian design team for a fraction of the cost of local resources. What kind of cost savings are we talking about? Top-level Filipino resources generally cost about one-third of the equivalent mid-level role in Australia. In total, the business spends roughly $20,000 per month on these eight remote staff members, a saving of roughly $40,000 per month compared to hiring the same number of staff locally.

The business went from discovering an unpaid bill of $400,000, to regaining confidence and seeing a clear pathway forward, and ultimately to saving more than $400,000 every year through smart resourcing decisions. Not only did they solve their big challenge, they reengineered the economics of their business model forever, facilitating a complete turnaround and a powerful uplift, all brought about by diving into the numbers and experiencing the empowerment that comes from looking into the financials when most business owners look away. As the icing on the cake, the business has now also recruited a full-time business accountant to keep an eagle eye on every aspect of their numbers and ensure they never again end up confused and anxious due to a lack of insight into the financials.

THE ENTOURAGE LEARNS HARD LESSONS,
AND TURNS THEM INTO A BRAND NEW BUSINESS

We've discussed the dramatic events of 2016 several times in these pages, and we'll explore them in even greater depth in Chapter Twelve: There's Always a Play. There's a reason for that: the shift in government regulations was perhaps the single most impactful event in the history of our business. You're already aware of the bad—we came perilously close to folding—but that period also catalyzed crucial lessons that have shaped every aspect of today's Entourage.

During Zen meditation training, masters reputedly hit their students with sticks to keep them totally focused on the present moment. Whenever the student's attention strays, even for a moment, the master gives them a whack. It's a brutal corrective, but it seems to work. The loss of our accreditation arm was our Zen stick. It woke us up, hard. It also demanded that we put in place best-in-class financial practices—anything less would have been insufficient to keep The Entourage alive. All the hard work ultimately had an enlightening payoff, however. Once we had instilled these practices and pulled ourselves out of danger, we realized they were so effective that many other businesses could benefit from them.

A healthy business usually displays a financial forecast on a month-to-month basis. In a distressed position, however, a business might start and finish the month with a positive cash balance, but slip into the red somewhere in between. A monthly forecast won't flag this. That's the position we were in. We needed to ensure that we knew exactly when we would enter and exit a negative cash position, which meant moving our cash forecast to a week-to-week model. When things were at their most dire, we even went to a *day-to-day cash forecast*, so that we could monitor our cash position with forensic detail. That's how bad things were. At the time, Jack lived constantly in the week-to-week (sometimes day-to-day) cash flow model, which, as you can imagine, is not a fun way to live.

For the next two years while we were in the rebuild phase, we managed the entire business on that cash flow forecast. The north star, as it always is when you're in distress, was simple: don't run out of cash. Around 2018, once we moved back into growth mode, we could start managing the business more on the profit and loss forecast, focusing on driving up revenues and profit margins. To map out our path to success, we engaged a top-tier accounting firm to develop a renewed three-way forecast for The Entourage. This then allowed us to turn our attention more to the balance sheet, increasing the overall value and assets of the business.

The principle we followed was this: When in distress, look at cash more granularly. When your situation alleviates, you can begin to look more broadly and further into the future. Today, we fully plan out our next financial year using a three-way financial forecast, which also extends three years into the future.

Our experience of creating financial forecasts that serve us in even the most distressed situations has instilled some important lessons. We take the level of rigor that we developed at our lowest ebb and apply it whenever we enter a new market or start a new venture. Financial models are an important aspect of our decision-making—we don't *start* with a forecast, but it is a key piece of the planning process before we green light a new project. Despite their value, however, we never allow financial forecasts to replace strategic thinking. We could punch any inputs into a financial forecast; that wouldn't mean they were sound, and it certainly wouldn't be a solid indicator that they would play out in reality. Our first port of call is always rigorous strategic thinking: then, once we think we've got a solid direction (for an existing company) or a strong value proposition, grounded in market demand (for a new company), *then* we sense check our assumptions using a forecast, to ensure we can make the numbers work.

Our hard-won financial expertise has played a vital part in our work with thousands of founders, the vast majority of whom have wanted to develop a greater level of understanding and certainty in their companies' finances. In almost every case, these members recognized that a lack of proper financial visibility of current and future performance was hampering their ability to confidently make moves in their business. To make matters worse, many told us that their accountants were hindering the situation more than they were helping it.

Given our commercial experience of scaling companies, along with our vast experience of managing finances to a forensic degree, we realized that we were in an ideal position to assist business owners with this prevalent problem. The lessons we had learned through overhauling and refining our own financial function were applicable in a far wider context. Over several months, we set out to better understand the bookkeeping and accounting landscape, along with the role played by outsourced chief financial officers (CFOs) and how we could deliver an enhanced service. As we became more and more familiar with this terrain, we developed a strategy to enter this market with The Entourage Accounting & Advisory—a strategy that we naturally verified using the financial forecasting tools we've outlined in this chapter! Our vision was, and remains, *to make money matter for business owners*. We do this by building their entire finance function, from bookkeeping, to accounting, to CFO strategy. We train their existing team on integrating these principles into the business, and coach the founder *only* on what they need to know, from the perspective of the leader and entrepreneur.

Whether we're building forecasts for our core business, for new projects, or for the clients we serve, we find that the most profound benefit of diving into the numbers is often the way it forces us to surface the key activities and corresponding metrics across each of the Six Elements: What **marketing** activities will we drive? What cost per lead do we anticipate? How can we take those leads and run some early tests to determine our expected **sales** conversions? Based on those numbers, how many salespeople do we want on the project initially, and how quickly do we want to ramp up the revenue model? Assuming our sales and marketing projections hold true, how many customers will we onboard onto the **product** each month? If we resource those marketing, sales, and product activities appropriately, what sort of **operational** support will the project require? Transferring all of those inputs into **finance**, how much do we need to invest into the project, and when will it begin to break even? How much potential do we think it has for future growth? Finally, what kind of org chart do we want to start with, and what's our desired recruitment timeline to build out a world-class team of **people**?

As we said at the beginning of the chapter, finances are simply a distillation of the Six Elements. To *truly* understand our business, we need a firm grasp of the numbers. They guide us on how we anticipate a new venture will pan out, and—once we launch—our forecast gives us an objective benchmark against which to measure each month's performance, ensuring that we are delivering on core objectives, and resourcing the project in a way that is commensurate with its growth.

As you can see, whether it's getting granular to manage through distress, or aiding our strategy when launching new high-growth ventures, finances have become a tool that enable us to feel confident in any environment. We know exactly what we're spending and where, along with what we expect to generate in return for that investment. Effective forecasting allows us to understand just how much we can invest in any business in order to really drive the growth that will enable us to continue serving more and more business owners around the world.

NEXT UP...

We've now covered five of the Six Elements that make up every business. From the **marketing** and **sales** that initially attract customers, to the quality **product** that wins their trust and repeat business. From the **operations** that make the whole company function smoothly, to the **finance** that allows you to keep the score. There's just one element left—the **people** who bring each of these elements to life.

Process and structure are vital. As we've shared, it's near-impossible to build sustainable growth into a company without them. But every business is ultimately fueled by its people. If there is *one* skill the world's greatest entrepreneurs share, it's knowing how to recruit and lead great people toward a shared vision. In the next chapter, we'll outline how to hire—and inspire—the right people.

11

PEOPLE

Assemble Your A-Team

You're it. You wear all the hats. You pull all the strings and put out all the fires. Every problem is your problem, and every solution involves you. While you may have a few trusted people in your inner circle, in most businesses that still operate like a startup, the one or two founders are by far the most in-demand people. From strategy to culture and decision-making, the company revolves around you. This creates a paradox: you are simultaneously the linchpin and the bottleneck when, ultimately, you don't want to be either.

A truly scalable and sustainable business requires a team capable of not only sharing the load, but of achieving more together than any one team member—even you—could accomplish on their own. Throughout this book, we've explored the idea that the key ingredient to becoming a great entrepreneur is leverage. The people element of your business is perhaps the foundational building block to achieving this. As we've discussed, when you operate like a startup, you lack the revenue and cash flow to build a great team; therefore, you need to do everything yourself with zero leverage. In startup, one unit of input equals one unit of output.

As your revenues grow, however, you have the opportunity to build a fully functioning team that can exponentially multiply the productivity of the business, one great person at a time. As such, the job of the entrepreneur is to get the business to a point where it can afford to start building a great team. This is how you build leverage into your organization. Take The Entourage, for example: right now we employ a team of a hundred world-class people. If you assume that each person on our team works an average of eight hours a day, it means that every single day, we produce eight hundred hours of concerted and concentrated output, all pointing in one common direction.

TO GO FAR, TRAVEL WITH OTHERS

The core message of this chapter is that a great team will make or break every element of your business. To improve any aspect of your company, you will inevitably need to build teams that enable parts of the machine to operate without your constant attention. Once you've developed your business to a point where it functions smoothly without your day-to-day involvement, you will be able to massively multiply the value of your contribution to the business. Have you ever seen a domino run? It starts with someone pushing over one domino, which sets in motion a chain reaction. This is what will happen when you have a great team in your business, aligned with a shared vision. When you contribute one unit of input, it will have a ripple effect and the business will produce 1,000 units of output. *That* is leverage.

Some business owners are concerned that if their business grows too big it will become all-consuming. If they're trying to scale while still operating like a startup, they're right. It will be exhausting and unsustainable. But when they transform their business into a scaleup with a capable team, leadership group, and structure, scale equals freedom. This is one of the most counterintuitive truths of scaling a company: the larger your business grows, the greater its potential to become self-managing, meaning that it grows faster while you do less.

In summary, assembling your A-team is an essential part of the transition from startup to scaleup, and that's what we'll show you how to do.

This is the final element of our Enable Growth Structure, and indeed the last of the Six Elements, because people are the force that brings every element to life. In this chapter, we'll explain exactly how you can craft your company identity, attract and hire the right people, and inspire them to work together in service of common goals. These three aspects of the chapter fall under three headings: **define** your DNA, **recruit** your A-team, and **lead** your people.

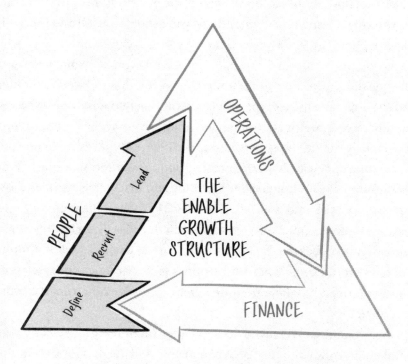

Figure 11.1: People Components of the Enable Growth Structure

To define your company DNA, you will need to dig deep into your organization's vision, mission, and values. Once you do that, you'll have a clear cultural blueprint, enabling you to identify and recruit the right people. Once you have put together a team, of course, you will want them to fulfill the roles you intended, doing great work and achieving your company's vision. Let's get started.

DEFINE YOUR DNA

When we talk about the DNA of a company, we're referring to the fundamental essence that makes your business unique. By the time you reach the scaleup stage, or are on the cusp of this transition, your business will already have developed a distinct core DNA. The problem is that most businesses never truly define it or capture it. Organizational DNA consists of the culture you have created, the direction you and your team are working toward, and the standards you expect yourself and everyone else to uphold. In other words, who are you as a company?

As you progress into scaleup, it's imperative you know the answer to this question. If you don't right now, however, that's okay. We'll guide you step-by-step through the process of finding that answer. Maybe you already have a pretty good idea, in which case now is a great time to consciously define the values and principles you may have been communicating unconsciously. Deliberately bottling this formula enables you to communicate it through your branding and marketing, use it as a tool to recruit people who are truly aligned with the heartbeat of your business, and lead and manage your team with purpose. Even if you've been through this process in the past, we encourage you to revisit it. Culture will and should evolve as your business grows and new people come in, so you need to take a periodic check that you are attuned to your core DNA.

There's another advantage to doing this. Identifying and clearly communicating your company DNA can become a vital tool for developing clear behavioral expectations, and thereby setting you free from the day-to-day operations. When you trust your team to uphold essential aspects of company culture even while you're away, you will gain that elusive ability to work *on* your business, not *in* it. Your business DNA comprises three core ingredients: vision, mission, and values.

Defining a clear and compelling company DNA is the very essence of what sets founder-led companies apart from large corporations. Great entrepreneurial companies capture their vision, mission, and values in such a way that it permeates their culture, brand, marketing, and the very fabric of the organization. While large corporations may have more resources, perceived credibility, and stature, they cannot imitate your unique and authentic entrepreneurial spirit. This energy and focus that flows from the founder, when acknowledged and amplified, can become your *number one* advantage.

Finding Your Vision

As Steve Jobs famously said, "If you are working on something exciting that you really care about, you don't have to be pushed. The vision pulls you." Vision is arguably the most potent and essential foundational principle of your business. Your vision is the North Star toward which you're constantly orienting. It must inspire you *personally* and represent the shift you want to create in the world. It must be a light bright enough to steer you through the inevitable chaos and murky waters. As a founder, your number one role is to lead people. You can't do that if you don't know where you're going, and why.

Your vision represents the ultimate purpose pursued by your organization, which should be defined by the impact you can make. Your vision is not a self-centered, company-oriented goal. It focuses on the *contribution* your organization can make to your customers, other people, your industry, or the world at large. Your vision expresses your loftiest future aspirations for your company. It is your picture of the future and your company's purpose in that future. What difference will your company make? Crafting a clear vision is about knowing where you are going, getting everyone on the same page, and inspiring them toward one common purpose.

Getting this right allows you to tap into an energy far more powerful than business alone. A purpose bigger than yourself will transcend day-to-day operations, and attract people who want to embark on the same journey. Just like Steve Jobs said, you will no longer be pushing people; instead, you will offer a vision that pulls people toward it like a magnet.

Crafting a Compelling Vision

Settling on a vision that defines your company can take time. It may come to you straight away, or it may take shape more slowly. We've worked with business owners who felt crystal clear on their purpose, even though they hadn't previously defined it. We've also worked with business owners who needed weeks of thought and meaningful discussion to land on their perfect vision; that's normal and often necessary. This foundational step will provide the platform on which you build all subsequent steps, so take the time to do it well.

To zero in on your vision, ask yourself these fundamental questions:

- What emotions does our product or service elicit in our customers?
- How does what we do improve people's lives?
- Why is this important to us?
- What difference can our business make?
- What will it contribute to the world?

The answers should give you some clear signposts toward your vision. Once you have written them out, your next step will be summarizing the highlights into a concise, yet powerful and inspiring sentence.

Examples of Captivating Company Visions

- **The Entourage**: Move the world forward through entrepreneurship.
- **Canva**: Empowering the world to design.
- **Apple**: To make the best products on earth and leave the world better than we found it.
- **Airwallex**: To empower businesses of all sizes to grow without borders.
- **LinkedIn**: Create economic opportunities for every member of the global workforce.

When you read the examples above, do you experience a visceral response? Great visions elicit an emotional reaction or even a physical one. They speak to the heart, not the head. Your vision should be big, bold, and capable of generating this gut-level response in your customers and clients. Because your vision is future-focused, it may not be fully measurable. There's no metric for calculating how much Canva has empowered the world to design. That's not a problem. Your vision provides direction, not detail.

Also notice that each one of these visions is focused on the *impact* the company can make, not on internal business goals. There is absolutely merit in defining company-centric goals—we do this in the strategic plan and when we formulate OKRs—it's just not what the vision is. The vision is contribution-centric; it taps into the company's deeper purpose, a reason for existing that goes beyond self-interest.

Once you have identified this fundamental building block, which represents what your company strives for in the big picture, subject it to the vocal test. You'll be saying it a lot, so make sure it sounds right when you speak it aloud. Check in with the people closest to you, to ensure that it resonates. When you truly, madly, deeply love your vision, then, and only then, can you move on to the next step: mission.

Turning Your Vision into a Mission

If your vision captures your big-picture purpose, your mission focuses on who you serve and how you serve them today. It incorporates the daily objectives you must meet to reach your future vision. Your vision is the mountaintop, and your mission is the path that leads you up to the summit. Your vision is inspirational, and your mission needs to be actionable. Every day that you accomplish your mission takes you one step closer to the actualization of your vision.

A good mission will root your future-focused vision in the present moment, giving your team a tangible goal to strive toward. Your mission encapsulates what you and your team do every day to achieve the vision. Your vision should be lofty and aspirational, but your mission should be achievable and measurable. Your mission should clearly and compellingly explain what your business does, and how it impacts your customer, while inspiring your team to perform at their best. It should still strike an inspirational note, but should feel more grounded than your vision. A good sign that you've got the right mission is you find yourself using it to guide your team and ensure they focus on the right things. This is an indication that you've created a worthwhile mission that complements the overall direction of your vision. Your vision won't be specific enough to do this, but your mission should be.

Generating an Actionable Mission

Similarly to creating your vision, you don't want to rush your mission. Once it's in place, you'll use it almost on a daily basis to calibrate your activities and guide your team. Here are some crucial questions to connect you with your mission:

- Who do we serve, and how do we serve them?
- What inspires me and my team to progress every day?
- What is the emotional effect our product has on our customers?
- When the going gets tough, what inspires you and your team to keep progressing every day?

Once you have answers to these questions, you can begin summarizing them into a concise, actionable company mission.

Examples of Powerful Company Missions

- **The Entourage**: Empower entrepreneurs by giving them everything they need to build great businesses and live meaningful lives.
- **Canva**: To empower everyone in the world to design anything and publish anywhere.

- **Apple**: To bring the best user experience to customers through innovative hardware, software, and services.
- **Airwallex**: With technology at our core, we build global financial infrastructure and applications to empower businesses to operate anywhere, anytime.
- **LinkedIn**: Connect the world's professionals to make them more productive and successful.

You'll know when your mission is complete because it resonates with your entire team, and makes you feel proud and confident when you say it aloud. It's the bridge from where you are now to where you want to be, so it needs to walk the line between inspiration and realism.

Once you've defined your vision and mission, the next step is to capture the principles that set the standards you and your team aspire to reach every day.

Determining Your Key Company Values

Values communicate your company's unique personality or characteristics. They articulate a set of principles, which guide *who you must be* to demonstrate the mission and achieve the vision of your company. Which expectations, beliefs, and behaviors are pervasive in your company? As an individual, strong values help you define what's right for you. The same is true of your company culture. Values play an essential role in self-governance, a quality that is magnified when you're leading and managing a team.

Another key point: your company may have several divisions, each one with its own vision and mission. At The Entourage Accounting & Advisory, our vision is, "To make money matter for entrepreneurs." At The Entourage Growth Services, it is, "To make businesses move faster." Whereas each branch of your organization can have its own vision and mission, however, your values should apply across the board.

As your business grows, it's critical to have a solid set of values in place, so you can recruit people who are aligned to those values and thoroughly induct new people as they join. If your values provide clear guideposts, many of your growth challenges can be addressed. For example, let's say you value speed over perfection. In that case, identifying and communicating that value to everyone will help individuals make the choice most aligned with your company values when they encounter a situation where there may be a trade-off between speed and perfection. By the time your business reaches the scaleup stage, you will certainly have developed an informal set of values. However, you may never have clearly defined them or written them down.

Your values aren't a manufactured set of principles; they are an authentic representation of the true heartbeat of your organization. You're not necessarily looking to create your values; rather, your aim is to *discover* them. Building a great company culture relies on aligning with and living those values on a day-to-day basis. Great organizations have a soul, and values reflect and represent that core.

A word of warning: your values must authentically represent who you are as a company, so people hold themselves and each other accountable. Like many things in the business world, values have sometimes been bastardized by corporate misuse. One infamous example is Enron, who listed integrity as one of their top four values, until their executives ended up financially and morally bankrupt, and doing time in prison. Many successful startups that became unicorns have been tripped up by values that promoted aggressive growth, to the exclusion of a well-balanced company culture. If your values are nothing more than empty platitudes that nobody at the company lives, you'll encourage the wrong behavior and keep attracting the wrong kind of people.

Discovering Your Company Values

Your values need to capture what makes your company unique. They need to be memorable and remarkable, in a literal sense—you want your values to represent concepts that people can easily remark upon. As such, you probably don't want more than seven values. For most businesses, the ideal number to strike the balance between defining enough values to truly capture the essence of the organization, and not having so many that they are hard to remember and discuss, lies anywhere between four and seven. More important than how *many* values you have is that they *feel* like you.

To identify your values, ask yourself these probing questions:

- What is our company's unique culture?
- When we look at our top people, what attitudes, communication styles, or behaviors do they consistently demonstrate?
- Conversely, when someone is not culturally aligned, which attitudes, communication styles, and behaviors do they exhibit that we want to eliminate?
- Are there aspects of our ideal culture that would boost performance and well-being, which we would like to see more of, or that don't yet exist?

To capture your values we suggest you write down all of the answers to the above questions in a free-flowing way. Don't try to edit your answers or word them perfectly, just get them out and get them down. Once you've done this, you'll be able to see patterns in the attitudes, communication styles, and behaviors you want to see more of, and combine similar values into core groups. From here, the final step is putting them in a cascading order of importance, from most to least essential.

Examples of Compelling Company Values

The Entourage	Canva	Apple	Airwallex	LinkedIn
Be wow	Make complex things simple	Accessibility	Customers first	We put members first
Lead innovation		Support education.	Intellectual honesty	We trust and care about each other
Education matters	Set crazy big goals and make them happen	A planet-sized plan.	Obsessive curiosity	
Make it happen		We're all in	Craftsmanship	We are open, honest, and constructive
Come from the heart	Be a force for good	Privacy is a human right.	Inspire and be inspired	We act as one LinkedIn
Become world's best practice	Empower others	Racial equity and justice	Make impact	We embody diversity, inclusion, and belonging
Be happy: bring quirk				We dream big, get things done, and know how to have fun

Define Your DNA before Recruiting

One of the core reasons it's critical to capture and communicate your company DNA is so that you can build a team of people who feel a strong connection to the vision, who are willing to fight for the mission, and who embody the values. In the absence of a well-defined company DNA, you will build a team of people who don't fully represent the culture you want to create, who lack a set of common values that bond them together.

How can you tell when your vision, mission, and values are singing? When you're willing to hire for them, fire for them, promote and encourage for them. When you're building a team, everything from recruitment to induction, from how you lead to how you manage, should all center around your vision, mission, and values.

We know that at times it feels like you'll never break free. We've been there. But it is possible, so please don't shortchange yourself. Make sure you figure out the DNA piece before you consider hiring new people. Experience tells us that by now you already know firsthand how important it is to hire and onboard capable team members, who are proactive and will take a load off your shoulders. This will happen only if you're first clear on your vision, mission, and values, so you can attract well-aligned, high-performing team members, with a long-term commitment to your company's purpose. Let's talk about how to do that.

RECRUIT YOUR A-TEAM

In a small but growing company, every new hire has an outsized effect on your trajectory and culture. Of course, it's expensive to keep hiring and training and firing the wrong people, but more importantly, it slows your momentum. This is why it's so crucial to get it right the first time. We've hired hundreds of people, and dozens of them have said the same thing: "I've never participated in such an involved recruitment process."

Time and time again, we discover that recruitment is a weakness for our Elevate members, a trend that holds true across industries and company sizes. The process we employ isn't all that complicated, but it does take more time and effort than most other approaches. It's worth it. In this section, we're going to share that process in depth, so you can install it into your company.

We know from years of experience how many companies get it wrong, with boring job ads and half-hearted screening processes, which is why we're giving you all the tools you need to do better. The main principles break down into two areas: the recruitment ladder, which dictates who to hire and when, and recruitment strategies, a toolbox to dig into each time you're hiring someone new.

The Recruitment Ladder

To achieve your vision and mission and to live your values, you'll need a group of people collectively moving in a common direction to achieve shared goals. For this reason, every company is a recruitment company. The bad news is that most founders and startups aren't great at recruiting, because it's one of those business-specific skillsets that don't come naturally to many people. Chances are that right now, you've got a lot to learn, just like we did.

One common mistake we see among founders is that they look for people with whom they share a rapport, as opposed to complementary capabilities or the expertise to succeed in specific roles. This makes them exceptionally bad recruiters. Bottom line: you don't need more people like you. You need people who can do the things you can't or don't want to do. Compounding this issue, many founders find recruitment incredibly boring and tedious, and fail to give it the attention it deserves. As a result, many companies don't invest enough in finding the brilliant people they need to elevate the business to the next level. In most seven- or eight-figure companies, the main bottleneck is that they lack a broad executive leadership team of senior people. We don't want this to happen to you.

We've previously introduced you to the Four Hats model. With the Six Pillars mapped across it, this model applies equally to our recruitment process. The Six Pillars correspond to teams and departments, and the Four Hats correspond to levels of management within the business. We use this model at The Entourage and recommend it to our clients. It provides a good starting point for developing your own organizational chart.

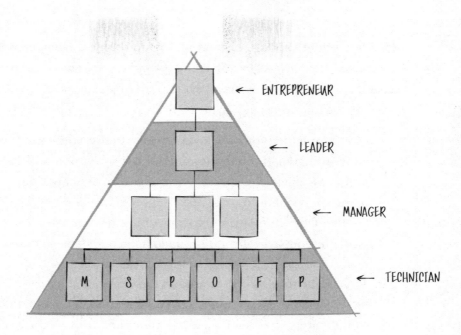

Figure 11.2: Organizational Chart Over Four Hats Model

Once you've used this model to create your basic organizational chart and plugged the roles of your existing team into the relevant boxes, the gaps and empty spots will be obvious. Your next challenge will be determining the order in which you should hire. It's tempting to go overboard and try to hire everyone at once, but since we all have limited budgets and time, the key is to build your team incrementally.

Let's say there are currently five people in your business: you, the founder, in charge of driving revenue through new customer acquisition, three people responsible for interacting with existing customers and delivering products and services, and one part-time person doing back-office jobs, to support you and the customer-facing employees.

While there's undoubtedly some overlap of responsibility, this isn't enough people to cover the myriad tasks required to keep the business running. Of course, as the founder, you assume the dubious privilege of picking up all these extra tasks in your nonexistent spare time, so you're likely distracted by processing payroll, maintaining the website, and providing admin support, instead of driving revenue. Dragged down by minutiae, higher-level tasks fall by the wayside. So, what are the core recruitment principles to ensure you build the right team at the right time? Start with the following guiding principles:

1. **First, you'll hire your weaknesses; eventually, you'll hire your strengths.** If you're a founder who is strong in marketing and sales, for example, the first teams you build out will be in the areas where you are weakest: product, operations, and finance. Once those teams are flourishing, the next phase of elevating yourself will require you to build out teams in the areas where you are strongest: marketing and sales.

2. **First build bottom-up, later build top-down.** In the early stages of building out your team, you'll want to build from the bottom up. Start with low-level positions and work your way up —first technicians, then manager roles, then leadership positions. Whenever a low-level role is taking up too much of your time, you can almost always begin by hiring a technician. Once your overall team has grown, and your revenues are higher, you will probably benefit from building any new teams top-down. First, hire the senior leader, then give them the budget and responsibility to build out a team underneath them. The real determinant here is *cash*. If you have the available cash, it will be more effective and efficient to hire top-down. However if you don't yet have sufficient cash reserves, then hire bottom-up until you do.

While every company is slightly different, this sequence works effectively for the majority of our members.

SEQUENCE	HIRE	OWNERSHIP
6	PEOPLE	A leadership team that can manage and lead each of the below elements without your operational involvement
5	SALES	Converting prospects to paid customers following the "Our Company Way of Selling," increasing conversions and average customer spend per sale
4	MARKETING	Producing and distributing content, building funnels, generating leads, crafting nurture sequences, measuring and optimizing conversions
3	PRODUCT	Onboarding, customer support, developing and delivering the product or service
2	FINANCE	Bookkeeping, reconciling accounts, developing financial reports and forecasts
1	OPERATIONS	Administrative support, running errands, inbox and calendar management, developing processes

↑ RECRUIT IN THIS ORDER

Figure 11.3: Recruitment Ladder

Ideally, you and other senior leaders should handle recruitment. This is a self-reinforcing process. Once you start building out your senior leadership team, they will become your greatest resource in finding future recruits for the most critical roles. Your best hires will hire your best hires.

If you have a choice between drive-growth-focused people and enable-growth-focused people to run the recruitment process, choose the latter. They will adopt a more scientific and calculated approach to recruitment, wading through applications, conducting multiple rounds of interviews, and keeping on top of the inevitable and tedious work. They're also less likely to rely solely on their gut to make important hiring decisions.

Effective Recruitment Strategies

The cost of bringing on the wrong person, especially in senior roles, can be huge, so while our recruitment process is involved and comprehensive, it still has the net result of saving us time, money, and headaches.

The first principle of good recruitment is to consciously drop every assumption regarding the person across from you. It's tempting to want the person in front of you to be the right candidate so badly that you adopt a positive hypothesis out of the gate. In this case, it's wise not to trust your intuition. Your intuition is important, but mostly in a negative context. If your gut tells you no, definitely listen. If your gut tells you yes, that's only the first hurdle.

We call this the null-hypothesis principle. Assume the person sitting in front of you is the *wrong* person for the job, until they've proven through the steps outlined below that they are the right person. You need the right candidate to achieve much more than just an intuitive connection; you need them to demonstrate a strong cultural fit and the ability to do the job you're hiring for, brilliantly. Over the years, we've hired hundreds and hundreds of excellent people. We've learned how to rapidly identify candidates who thrive in an entrepreneurial environment, can handle the ambiguity of a growing business, and perform at an extremely high standard in a fast-paced organization. Below you'll find the exact steps that make up our recruitment process, from choosing the right person to leading it to selecting the ideal candidate.

1. **Nominate the most senior person feasible to manage the recruitment process.** In our experience, the more senior

the recruiter, the better the results. This person will need to devote considerable time to the process, so you'll need to weigh the costs and benefits of having them focus on recruiting for a large chunk of their time. For a startup or scaleup-stage business, we recommend an internal, rather than external recruiter, because you're often looking to hire for a position that has never previously existed. While external recruiters are great for large corporations, this situation calls for a senior internal leader who brings the necessary understanding of the company.

2. **Ensure the recruiter possesses real-life, intimate knowledge of the role they're hiring.** Your recruiter should have worked in the position themselves or, if it's a newly created role, have spent a considerable amount of time diving deeply into its requirements, to gain a genuine understanding of the essential skillset and the problems that will need to be resolved. At The Entourage, for example, Tim spent six months directly managing our sales team before starting to recruit for the senior leader, to ensure that he understood the role and the type of person who could succeed at it.

3. **Write a clear and compelling job ad, focusing on your ideal candidate, not your company.** Many of our applicants tell us that they felt our ad was talking specifically to them. That's a result of values-alignment and role-alignment. We expend considerable time and effort on making our job descriptions as precise as possible, focusing on our ideal candidate, details of the role, and what success looks like for them. We also include the company values that they will most need to demonstrate to excel in this particular role, so the potential candidates get a real insight into our DNA. You are free to piggyback on our hard work by stealing the job ad templates you'll find in our website resource section at www.the-entourage.com/elevate. Uninspiring, company-centric job ads bore applicants and

discourage them from applying. To attract the best possible candidates, do the opposite of that.

4. **Advertise the position in the right place.** In terms of popularity and candidate numbers, platforms rise and fall. Instead of dusting off our crystal ball, we advise you to do some basic research. Take a close look at your usual job-ad platform. Is it still delivering the quantity and quality of candidates you expect? If you have no baseline data, ask colleagues and mentors for their favorites. Also, consider niche factors such as geography and the specifics of your industry. Maybe there are platforms dedicated to your needs. You also want to advertise job openings to your audience—the followers who already know you and love what you do—so consider where you already have an engaged audience. Even if your followers aren't in the market for employment, they may refer quality candidates.

5. **Think carefully about whether to advertise salary ranges.** As a general rule, we prefer to be transparent about compensation. When advertising, however, this can be complicated. Your team will see the ads you publish, so if positions are advertised at a higher range than those in similar roles currently earn, you should have the necessary conversations upfront to prevent any misunderstanding. On the other hand, if you decide not to share any salary range at all, then you may miss out on excellent candidates, or interview great applicants who end up falling outside your price range. Take the time to address this aspect of recruiting carefully, so you'll spend your time hiring people rather than dealing with an internal mutiny.

6. **Rate and choose applicants.** Instead of immediately contacting candidates as they roll in, we wait a few days to get an idea of the total candidate pool. Once we have about fifty applications for popular roles, or twenty-five for slightly more specialist roles, we use the internal rating tool of the job platform itself to assess them. Then, we identify the first group of candidates we want to

speak to, casting the net wide enough to include everyone we think might fit the role, and only exclude those who definitely lack the experience or skills we need. Resumes and online profiles only convey a limited amount of vital information, so don't be too quick to dismiss people. On many occasions, we've found that the best candidate for a role wasn't the strongest one on paper, but when we interviewed them, it quickly became apparent that their capabilities far outweighed applicants who looked better in theory.

7. **Initial thirty-minute phone or video screen.** This part of the process is a bit like speed dating. We advance roughly 30 percent of candidates to this stage, which can be a lot (usually around twenty to thirty people). For the best possible results, however, it's effort well spent. If we get it right, we rarely lose candidates further down the recruitment funnel, when both they and we are more heavily invested. We want to get an initial insight into each person, while giving them an overview of our company and the role. How smart are they? Have they been able to demonstrate they have the necessary skills for the role? Are they a good fit for the culture? The best candidates will have multiple options, so a good recruitment process is about finding the person who is the best fit for our company, and also helping them assess whether our company is the best fit for them. This initial call is not a deep dive into skills and experience— we leave that for the next round.

8. **Getting serious with a select few candidates.** Following the first round of interviews, we narrow our pool down to five or six people we think are a good fit. At this point, it's time to put them through our rigorous interview process. We invite mid-level candidates to a face-to-face interview, where we dig into their skills, experience, and expertise. For higher positions, such as heads or directors of departments, we arrange two face-to-face meetings, plus an intensive project requiring them to put

together a detailed presentation, knowing that the right candidate will relish the opportunity to show what they're capable of delivering. When we're running this process, we explain to the candidate that the interview process is a practice run for working together on an actual project. We'll give the applicant access to real data, deliberately providing too much so that they need to show they can filter through and determine what's most relevant. We'll direct them to areas that require attention, as well as those that are lacking information or a clear strategy for improvement. Then, we give the candidate four or five days to dig into the content, cut out the fluff, and develop a presentation. As part of the practice run for working together, we explain to the candidate that if they have any questions or need further information, they should simply ask, just as though we were already working together. In the follow-up session, the candidate presents their case study, including their observations, opportunities for improvement, and specific examples of how they've achieved similar outcomes in their related work experience.

9. **For the cream of the crop, panel interviews.** The process in step eight is a lot to ask, which is why it works. Some people come back with rudimentary ideas and presentations, but usually two or three will wow us. By doing this, they show us that they know what they're talking about and have the experience and thoughtfulness to go the extra mile. We invite these final candidates to present to two or three other senior people in the company. These last sessions generally follow the format of ten minutes of meet and greet, thirty minutes of the candidate delivering their presentation, and twenty minutes of Q&A. In the end, it's almost always obvious who is the best fit.

10. **Check references.** Finally, we ask each of our top candidates for two or three references and follow up on all of them. Naturally, every referee will say nice things, so we focus only on one

question: if this person came back to you today, would you hire them again? If the response is an immediate and emphatic yes, that's a good sign. If we hear even the slightest hesitation or the response is lukewarm, we will probe further to see if we can uncover any issues or red flags.

As we said earlier, *every* business is primarily a recruitment business. On the road from technician to entrepreneur, the key paradigm shift here is: *you build the team and the team builds the business*. For this reason, investing the necessary time and effort into a rigorous recruitment process, *especially* when recruiting senior leaders, is one of the key areas you should be focusing on once you have altitude. Your culture, and therefore your overall brand, start with recruitment.

LEAD YOUR PEOPLE

Once you've defined your DNA and are recruiting great people into critical roles, you need to ensure that the team has the leadership necessary to drive high performance. As the business is growing, adopting proven and effective leadership principles is crucial to building a culture that is not reliant on you and your energy. Without these principles, you risk leaving your team behind, but harnessing them will bring you one step closer to achieving the next stage of your business growth.

Equally vital is understanding the distinction between leadership and management. Where leadership provides heart and inspiration, management offers detailed day-to-day support and guidance. Effective leadership should keep people connected to what you're doing as a company, and—more importantly—why you're doing it. Efficient management ensures people know how to do their role, and where this fits into the rest of the organization. In a well-developed company, leadership and management coexist and support each other. As a founder, you don't want responsibility for managing your team on a daily basis, but you do want a strong management structure in place. If you have excellent leadership skills, but don't task anyone with adopting and implementing sound management principles, the company will experience wild fluctuations in performance. Let's explore the principles and practices of these complementary disciplines in turn.

Leadership Principles

Champion the Vision

The best way to lead your team is to constantly champion the vision you identified in the DNA exercise earlier in this chapter. It's your job to infuse the company vision into every interaction, meeting, and conversation, repeatedly and passionately. If you're a driver of growth with the ability to imagine the future that created your company, *seeing* this vision will come naturally to you. The risk, however, is that because the vision is so evident in your head, you may under-communicate it to others, expecting everyone to have a similarly tight grasp on it. Unfortunately, this is not how teams work, especially bigger ones of thirty or more people. You absolutely must talk about the vision all the time. This is one instance where you should embrace sounding like a broken record.

Embed Cultural Rituals

Your vision, mission, and values must come to life in practical ways, otherwise they will be meaningless. A framed mission statement on the wall does nothing to encourage your team on a daily basis. They need to experience the company's vision, mission, and values as tangible influences on their working lives. Every Monday at The Entourage, we kick off the week with a morning meeting, priming the team for what's ahead in the upcoming week and month, and prioritizing our goals. This speaks to our value of being outcome-oriented. Every Friday, we meet at 4:30 p.m. for a celebration called the "Made It Happen Circle."

As we mentioned previously, one of our values is "Make it happen," and this all-staff meeting recognizes everything we've achieved that week. It's a free-flowing forum, where anyone can speak up at anytime, calling out instances where they have seen someone really embody our culture or demonstrate our values that week. There are few rules, which makes it chaotic and entertaining. Members of the team might share something big, like, "I've got a 'made it happen' for Sarah. This week she spent a lot of time coaching one of her members on the sale of their business, and she was so successful that they've just signed off on the sale for $4.5 million. Sarah really went above and beyond to ensure this member knocked their sale out of the park." Alternatively, they might pick a small yet significant moment, like, "I've got a 'made it happen' for John. This week he checked in on me when he could see I was struggling; he really came from the heart, and I appreciated it." The point is not to heavily structure these rituals, but to block out some time for regular touch points, where you plan, reflect, celebrate, and connect. You don't need a ritual for every value, and there will be some overlap, but make sure you have enough for your team to feel connected to the values.

The Culture Pulse Survey

Every quarter, we gauge our entire team's mood by sending out a brief, anonymous survey, sometimes as short as three questions. We ask everyone how they're currently feeling in their role, offering a choice of emoji in response. This is not designed to be a full and comprehensive cultural report, but simply to give us a regular snapshot of the overall satisfaction of our team members. We also ask them to name one thing they're proud of from the previous quarter, and one thing the company could do to improve their experience. This is very valuable feedback. In the best case, it allows us to make good experiences even better. If things are going wrong, it helps us to course correct, before minor issues become big problems.

Hold a Regular Founder's Address

At The Entourage, Jack addresses the entire team regularly. This is consistently the cultural ritual that receives the most positive feedback, so we aim to hold a founder's address quarterly. The founder's address is designed to do one thing: reconnect the team to their "why" for being at The Entourage. During these presentations, Jack shares his thinking with the entire team through the lens of our vision, mission, or values. Jack might update or underscore his vision for the future, or speak to the direction of the company. He may interview some of our members and facilitate their stories, to highlight how we are bringing our mission to life and remind the team of the outcome of their work. Or he may speak to values, recognizing where the team is demonstrating the values well and shining a spotlight on places where certain values could be amplified further. The founder's address is an effective way to get everyone on the same page and reignite the entire team's passion for being here.

Use Leaders to Create Leaders

In growth-stage businesses, few things are more critical than continually building out leadership at every level of the company. Every leader must be responsible for identifying and fostering leadership potential at their level of the company. As a founder, you need to lead by example, demonstrating a consistent focus on building out your executive leadership team across the Six Elements. They will then build out their own teams, and so on. To build a culture that is self-managing and not reliant on you, it is critical to develop layers of leadership in your company.

Force Yourself Out of the Detail

As a founder, you must protect your time and energy to think *about* the business, not work *in* the business. It was Henry Ford who said, "Thinking is one of the hardest things to do, and that's why so few people do it." As an entrepreneur, learning how to *think constructively*, solve big problems creatively, and implement innovative solutions, is one of the most important skills you can develop. If you don't do this, you can't fulfill the number one leadership principle of championing the company vision and moving the company forward. As you move from startup to scaleup, you must actively force yourself to pass on some of your responsibilities. You must develop a team willing to take those responsibilities from you, so that you have time to dedicate to strategic thinking.

Who's Got the Monkey?

One of our favorite timeless pieces of leadership advice comes from a 1974 *Harvard Business Review* article titled "Who's got the monkey?" written by William Oncken Jr. and Donald Wass. Once you get past the outdated language, the advice remains valid and actionable almost half a century later. The basic premise of the article is that every team member has problems to solve and priorities to take care of (the monkey on their back). Many people are tempted to pass their monkeys off to others, or take care of other people's monkeys, but a leader's goal must be to empower everyone to deal with their own monkey. If a monkey must be passed on, it should only move *down* the chain, never up.

This principle speaks to the importance of not automatically accepting monkeys from those who report to you. If you do this, all the monkeys move up the chain, with the result that team members never get to experience solving their own problems and learning from their mistakes. This type of dynamic, which is rife in most organizations, undercuts people's development, and overloads leaders with problems they should be delegating to their team. Resist taking monkeys that aren't yours, so that you can spend your time where it is needed: working *on* your function, not always *in* your function.

The article mentions a helpful hierarchy of initiative and explains what to expect from team members, from junior to senior-level. These levels ascend from least to most desirable:

1. Waiting to be told what to do
2. Asking what to do
3. Making a recommendation
4. Taking the recommended action
5. Taking action and informing others immediately
6. Acting on one's own and routinely reporting to others

No one in your business should be allowed to operate at level 1 or 2. The baseline for any team member should be level 3, with those in management positions operating at least at level 4. Anyone in a leadership role should be at level 5 or 6. Next time someone tries to give you their monkey, politely decline. "I'm happy to give you some suggestions, but that monkey is yours to take care of."

Management Practices

Translate Strategy Into Action

The most effective tool for translating strategy into action is the OKR framework we introduced in Chapter Nine: Operations. As we described in that chapter, you will need to nominate a champion within your organization to take full ownership of driving the adoption of OKRs, and spearheading their regular use across the business. We augment this approach with an annual strategic planning process, undertaken by each department, that details specific tactics and timelines for achieving that department's unique goals.

Create Clear Position Descriptions and Responsibilities

In startups, position descriptions are often redundant, because everyone is responsible for everything and wears multiple hats. Many people working in startups perceive position descriptions and responsibilities as something only big corporations do, believing that they undermine the entrepreneurial dynamics and agility of early-stage ventures. This approach may work well for a time in early stage ventures with a flat structure, but once you employ ten or more people, company activities quickly descend into chaos, with no one knowing for sure where their responsibilities begin and end. Once you begin building a hierarchy into the company, you need to create levels of management and assign clear responsibilities. At this stage, the challenge is to ensure that tasks are completed to an agreed-upon standard, by people who take accountability for their specific domains. To scale your company effectively, people must know exactly what is expected of them.

Focus on Effective Onboarding and Training

We've discussed our comprehensive recruitment process, but getting the right person through the door is only the first step toward adding another great team member to your company. Even the greatest candidate won't contribute much on their first day. They are at the beginning of a steep learning curve about the company, the DNA, their specific position and responsibilities, and what they'll need from their management team to succeed. The better your onboarding and training process, the sooner your new hire will become an effective, contributing team member. Based on the position, we estimate different timeframes for effective onboarding and training—four weeks for a junior role, and about eight weeks for a mid-level hire. Senior-level people, such as heads of departments or executives, won't understand *all* the drivers, nuances, and rhythms of their department and the business for at least six months. This is why we invest so much effort in recruiting. We don't want to waste all that time developing the wrong person.

Organize Regular Performance Reviews and Feedback

At The Entourage, we hold annual performance reviews for every role in May. This allows us to review positions, promotions, and compensation increases in June, in time for our new fiscal year that starts in July. This is a reliable sequence, of which everyone is aware. It keeps us all on track and minimizes employee questions, such as requests for promotions or salary increases outside our regular cycle. When we review performance, we're looking for evidence that people fulfill the responsibilities of their role while also looking for opportunities to go above and beyond. As a growing, innovative company, we're always looking for new ideas, strategic development insight, and new customer initiatives. These new opportunities constantly create gaps that an engaged employee can identify and fill. Those who do this are thought of first and viewed favorably when requesting promotions, expanded titles, or remuneration increases.

Schedule One-on-Ones Between Managers and Direct Reports

These meetings are not a forum for managers to chastise or criticize their direct reports. They are primarily for junior people to bring their concerns to managers and receive guidance and support. As a rule of thumb, we suggest weekly meetings between managers and every direct report, ranging from thirty minutes to one hour. Generally, we find that the more junior the report, the more frequent and shorter the meetings. With more senior-level reports, some projects take a couple of weeks to progress, so we extend the cadence to every two weeks but increase the meeting length to an hour, so we can cover more ground. This approach requires managers to step back from trying to control the meeting agenda, and direct reports to come prepared with issues and solutions to discuss. Overall, we aim for a 90/10 split: talk about what the direct report wants to discuss 90 percent of the time, and what the manager wants to discuss 10 percent of the time.

We encourage people to request help dealing with their monkeys, but only ever to give them to someone else when the problem is so great that it needs to be escalated. This format and cadence prevents the scenario of a report popping their head around the door and saying, "Hey manager, got a minute?" followed by unloading a problem (monkey) on the manager, who can't provide any actionable insight in such a short time frame. Bam! Suddenly the manager has accepted a monkey and feels responsible for delivering a solution, whereas the report feels like they don't need to do anything until they hear back. These one-on-one meetings clarify who's responsible for the monkey (usually the junior) and who provides guidance on how to take care of the monkey (usually the senior). No manager should find themselves trapped in an office having inherited four or five monkeys at the end of a day. Only at the very end of a meeting do we encourage managers to give their report a few pointers on what to focus on, or how to improve.

BRINGING IT ALL TOGETHER

As a founder, you have a big vision. You started a company because you want your vision to travel and impact the lives of as many people as possible. For that to happen, you'll need a team around you. Ultimately, business is a team sport, and you can achieve only so much on your own. With others around you, however, rallying around that vision, you can take your vision so much further.

Of course, locating, recruiting, and leading those people is a skillset in and of itself, particularly in the early phases of the business when you're trying to do everything else as well. That's why we've given you the keys in this chapter.

When you define the DNA of your business, you take the vision that seems so clear to you and you turn it into something concrete, so that others can understand it and commit to it. You distill it into a mission that team members can get behind and be willing to fight for. You make it tangible and measurable, so people know when they're making progress. And you codify all those elements into clear values, so that you have a framework of shared language and behavioral norms.

With your vision, mission, and values in place, you have a fantastic foundation for bringing on amazing additions to your team. Recruitment based on your vision, mission, and values invites people to self-select, applying only when they feel a strong affinity with your organization. It also gives you defined principles for screening their suitability. The recruitment ladder featured in this chapter equips you with a framework for helping you determine who to hire and when, and providing you with specific steps to take when recruiting.

Once you've defined your DNA and recruited the right people, you need to lead them effectively. This is where you need to get your head out of the day-to-day operations and find ways to keep them connected to the reasons they want to be part of the business. You likely don't want or need to be directly involved in management, but that doesn't mean you can ignore it altogether. You need a strong leadership team behind you, who can take on the responsibility of managing and supporting people throughout the business.

Ultimately, our ambition for all our members is to move them away from tinkering and toward leadership. We fully understand, however, that this can seem like a long road at first. The strategies in this chapter bridge that gap, taking you from confusion and uncertainty toward a clear understanding of what to do and in what order. When you define your DNA, recruit the right people at the right time and lead them well, you will give your business the solid people foundation it needs to scale.

CASE STUDY: SUNIL KUMAR PERFECTS HIS CULTURE TO SKYROCKET BUSINESS

Sunil Kumar is a perfect example of someone who leveled up his people game to grow his company. Sunil founded his real estate business, Reliance, in Melbourne, Australia, in 2011. For the first few years, however, in a steeply declining national real estate market, he had to fight tooth and nail simply to stay in business. Every week, Sunil worked at least six days in an effort to pay his mortgage and provide for his family and newborn baby. At best, he was keeping his head above water. He wasn't bringing in significant profits or paying himself. Many times over three long years, he considered throwing in the towel and going back to a safe, steady job. Each time, he redoubled his determination and focused on bringing in new business. Eventually, by 2014, Sunil started to see some progress.

As his business finally began to grow, Sunil succeeded in claiming a little bit of breathing room, which allowed him to see that he'd been stuck in technician mode for three years, enmeshed in daily operations and the minute details of every aspect of his business. Desperate to continue his upward trajectory, Sunil asked himself two questions: What am I exceptionally good at? What made me successful in this profession in the first place?

Sunil had always thrived when he focused on prospecting, selling, and nurturing clients, but he wasn't spending most of his day on his highest-value tasks. Instead, he had gotten stuck doing everything *but* listing and selling properties. Attracting new clients, building his brand, and growing his team had all fallen by the wayside. In short, he had been working *in* the business, not *on* the business.

Sunil went back to basics and cut down on low-value tasks, such as unnecessary meetings, handling supplier relations, and indirect networking activities. He delegated those tasks or eliminated them, doubling down on his most productive and valuable work—generating income by focusing on new client acquisition and taking excellent care of existing clients. Once again, he started cold-calling fifty prospects a day and within two months began serving new clients and producing new revenue.

Shortly afterward, Sunil started working with The Entourage. Having resolved his immediate revenue challenges, one of his top priorities was to lay out his twelve-month plan, including quarterly focus areas to attack. One of his first core tasks was to crystallize the purpose and culture he wanted to instill in his company. As an immigrant to Australia, he quickly realized that he had a passion for helping new residents buy their first homes. This core purpose came to inform every aspect of the company. Sunil hired several first- and second-generation Australians and crafted company values centered around community and neighborliness, reflecting the immigrant community his business serves.

With his company DNA firmly in place, Sunil worked to build out his leadership team, which today consists of a general manager, directors for each branch of Reliance, and several executives in operations and finance. Back in 2016, Sunil realized his company needed a central hub from which to direct the growth of the business and additional employees to bring his vision to life. He set up a headquarters staffed with some of his key executives to work on his big-picture strategy. Most of these executives are developed internally and have moved through the ranks and departments, consistently accepting new responsibilities and excelling as leaders. Sunil used The Entourage's recruitment process to find suitable external candidates for several positions necessary at different stages of company growth, such as a head of rental, executive assistant, and HR advisor.

Sunil ensures every hire is a good fit for the culture. If crucial leadership team members want to move on, he digs into their motivation: are they making a life-stage decision, or is there an issue with the company that impacts job satisfaction and needs to be rectified?

Filling key roles with capable leaders allowed Sunil more time to work on the company itself, onboarding and training staff, focusing on high growth, and developing his leadership philosophy, including seven fundamental leadership principles:

1. **Vision**: Define your vision and structure your business to achieve alignment.
2. **People**: Find the right people, train them properly, and take care of them. Your team members help you succeed, serve your clients, and represent your company.
3. **Leadership**: A strong leader empowers others to become leaders and contributes more than they take.
4. **Culture**: Creating a culture of communication, idea sharing, celebration, and fun will attract and keep people who will help your company flourish.
5. **Execution**: Actioning your ideas is as important as developing your vision. Designing efficient processes, delegating tasks, holding effective meetings, and awarding responsibility to others all support proper execution.
6. **Marketing**: Communicate your message to your target audience through efficient channels to support your branding and marketing efforts.

7. **Growth**: Adopt a growth mindset to continuously evolve and move your business forward to reach new heights.

Fast forward to 2017, and Sunil's relentless passion and work ethic were paying off big time. Reliance had become the fastest-growing real estate company in Australia. By 2020, Reliance made the list of Australia's fastest-growing companies for the third year in a row. During that period, annual property sales increased from two hundred to more than a thousand, while his sales team exploded from fifty people in one office to 150 people in ten offices. Yearly revenue, meanwhile, skyrocketed from $1 million to $16 million over the same three-year period.

After a decade of hard work, more growth is on the agenda. As Sunil has supported the immigrant community, they have supported him and Reliance.

For Sunil, Reliance, and the community they serve, this is only the beginning.

JACK AND TIM REMEMBER THE IMPORTANCE OF THE FOUNDER'S ADDRESS

One lesson we keep relearning is the importance of the founder's address. In the chaos of business, particularly during an especially volatile time such as the COVID-19 pandemic, it's essential to keep team members connected to the larger vision of the business. As we described in the Lead Your Team section of this chapter, one of the best ways to do this is through the founder's address. We know this from long experience, and yet sometimes circumstances arise that interrupt this cadence, and we go too long without reengaging the team in this much-needed ritual.

During the founder's address, often we will look ahead at least one year and as much as five years. Our goal is to share where we're going, how we're planning to get there, and how everyone's role is important. Every single time we do this, we're flooded by responses from the team saying how inspired they are, how they love seeing a picture of the future we're creating together, and how they're reinvigorated because they can see how their role plays a part in realizing that future.

With the daily grind of figuring out how to adapt to the ever-changing circumstances of the COVID-19 pandemic, the importance of the founder's address was pushed to the side. Prior to March 2020, we had established a good rhythm of holding a founder's address every three to six months, with the most recent just before the first wave. After March 2020, it was all hands on the pump, as Australia went into lockdown for several months. Emerging from that period in August, we were primarily focused on a hard charge toward the end of the financial year. Then, just as the situation appeared to be stabilizing, a new variant sent us back into lockdown for another four months.

This second lockdown really took the wind out of our sails. We thought we were through the worst, and all of a sudden we were back at square one. The whole country felt deflated. As a small-to-medium-size business, serving other small-to-medium-sized businesses, we were at the forefront of the frustration engulfing the country. Although we made a big effort to ensure that we supported team members, through clear communication, virtual team activities, and even resilience training, we couldn't completely insulate them from the general malaise. Everyone worked just as hard as before, but we lacked the same spring in our step. Instead of focusing on the reasons why we chose to work at The Entourage, we found ourselves grinding through the days. Was this ever going to end?

By the time we got around to holding another founder's address it was early 2021, almost a year since the previous one. After that, we went almost another year before the next one, in early 2022. On each occasion, we realized afresh how deeply the team values these moments.

Naturally, the two of us were strategizing consistently during the entire pandemic, so we had a clear idea of how we would address the challenges, determine the future of the business, and turn that future into reality. Insights that seemed obvious to us, however, were opaque to many of our team.

Following the address, we received an exceptionally strong, positive response. It turned out that after two years of global pandemic, people were desperate for an opportunity to get their heads out of the grind and align with a larger vision. Almost universally, people told us that they felt a deep sense of relief and reinvigoration, because they could finally look up again and see their contributions in terms of something greater. It's important to note here that we didn't use the most recent founder's address to discuss COVID-19. It was barely a footnote. Instead, we talked about where we're going as a business, with a focus on inspiring our team to remember why we do what we do.

The incredible positivity unleashed by this founder's address occurred within the confines of a ninety-minute session. It transformed the sense of apathy that many people felt due to the long privations of the pandemic into a feeling of excitement.

The period following March 2020 has been described as the Great Reshuffle, with thousands of people deciding they want to leave their boring corporate jobs and find more meaningful work. As the kind of organization many people aspire to be part of, we found that the Great Reshuffle was predominantly a brilliant recruitment opportunity. We strive every day to live and breathe our vision, mission, and values, making us a magnet for people who want to work for a company that connects team members to a greater purpose.

Recognizing this element of The Entourage's business, AFR BOSS recently named us one of the Top Ten Best Places to Work in Australia, in the professional services category.[10] Restarting the founder's addresses was like breathing life back into the business. As a company, it helped us refocus and remember our center of gravity. We recommitted to our purpose, which energized us to shift our focus back to what lay ahead. Post-pandemic, more and more people are determined to be part of an organization that matches their values and stands for something in the

---

[10] "AFR BOSS Best Places to Work 2022: Top professional services firms," *Consultancy.com.au*, May 1, 2022, https://www.consultancy.com.au/news/5384/afr-boss-best-places-to-work -2022-top-professional-services-firms.

world. Connecting your team to your vision, mission, and values can be a crucial differentiating factor.

NEXT UP...

We've reached the end of Part III of this book. By now, you're developing a clear picture of how each of the Six Elements currently function in your business. You're getting a picture of where you're strongest, where you're weakest, and what you need to prioritize to break through the roadblocks that are currently holding your business back.

Part IV will bring that picture into even sharper focus. It combines everything we've discussed so far, in a single chapter. We wrote this part both to galvanize you and to reassure you that whatever state your business is in right now, there's a path forward. It's a distillation of all our best strategies, in a format that will enable you to quickly diagnose where you're at, what you need to focus on first, and how you can make a difference most rapidly.

PART IV

THE FUTURE

We've spent much of this book examining the existing state of both your business and your personal entrepreneurial toolbox, to give you everything you need to diagnose your current strengths and weaknesses. We've also shown you how to plan ahead, imagining what your business can become and anticipating what you must do to take it there.

There's a reason we encourage you to project your business forward. As entrepreneurs, we spend our lives tinkering with a universe that doesn't yet exist. We are architects of the future. As an entrepreneur, you must stake a claim to the potential of your business and take an active role in shaping it how you see it. Success comes to those who can see what *might* be, enhance the picture so it becomes high resolution, and then marshal the people and resources necessary to make that picture a reality. Great entrepreneurs are great leaders, and the people you wish to lead must buy into your vision and trust that you have both the professional and personal qualities to enact it.

Think of business like a game of chess. The beginner is still learning the moves of the game. The intermediate player thinks in tactics. The master is constantly plotting three to five moves ahead, envisaging potential scenarios and figuring out how to make an advantageous move in any one of them.

For the entrepreneur, learning how to make the right moves is a crucial first step. Where is the leverage in your business? When you pull different levers, what impact does that have? It's impossible to win at chess if you don't understand how the pieces move, and how to use them. The next step is mapping out *sequences* of moves. How do the pieces work together, and which are most valuable in different scenarios?

When you truly master the game of business, your vision will be so clear that you can identify the state of play at a glance, and instantly see which moves will be most effective. That's the path we want to take you on in this final part—and final chapter—of the book.

12

THERE'S ALWAYS A PLAY

Navigating the Different Seasons of Business

As an entrepreneur, you will inevitably voyage through every season imaginable. You will be forced to wrestle with the stresses and pressures of rapid-expansion as you try to keep up with the speed of your own business. You will sail through smooth seas of steady growth, momentarily catching your breath and enjoying your surroundings. You will navigate through periods of challenge, extended plateaus, and intervals where you're weathering the stormy waters of extreme distress trying to keep your ship afloat. In business, one thing is for sure: a skilled sailor needs to be able to chart the best possible course, regardless of the conditions they find themselves in.

Even with everything you've already learned in this book, you may still be laboring under the belief that some situations are unsalvageable, or that how your business develops is ultimately out of your control. We talk to a lot of business owners who feel hopeless, uncertain how to turn the ship around, or simply confused about their next move. The unfortunate reality is that most business owners spend their entire lives feeling stuck.

With a shortage of quality advice available, they gather feedback from the wrong places: well-meaning friends, their accountant, insolvency practitioners, or underqualified business coaches. They may talk to people who see the stress they are under, but not how much the business means to them, or those whose livelihood depends on wrapping up distressed businesses, and who don't understand the entrepreneurial mindset. Very rarely do they have seasoned professionals to turn to, who can both identify with their situation and show them the path to a healthier, balanced business.

Unfortunately, this approach tends to be self-defeating. If you *believe* that you're trapped by your challenges, your success, or simply by boredom after your business begins to stagnate, you won't commit to making the changes that can pull your business into a new phase. It's only when you come to believe that there really *is* always a play that you'll do whatever it takes to seek out the play that works for your company and to execute it. Whatever state you're in right now, whether distressed, challenged, growing, or booming, you can take it from us that there's a route to a better, more structured version of your business.

How do we know this to be true? Throughout this book, we've examined case studies from our own businesses and those of our Elevate members, outlining how we've navigated every conceivable terrain. We opened the book by describing our own extreme challenges of 2016, when regulatory changes almost killed our company and required us to shift our entire business model. Throughout those years, regardless of how dire the situation looked, one of the phrases we used to remind ourselves we *would* get through was, "There's always a play." The seismic shock of 2016 and the years that followed were the hardest of our lives, but they gave us an opportunity to sharpen some very powerful tools.

TOUGH TIMES MAKE TOUGH BUSINESSES

The first crucial message of this chapter is that whatever scenario you find yourself in right now and in the future, however uncertain you might be about the path forward, *there is always a play*. The fact is that hard times create better businesses, because they force good behaviors. This philosophy is backed up by hard statistics. Counterintuitively, during the years of Covid lockdowns and restrictions, we saw small- to medium-sized companies make more progress than during any other period. When put under pressure, either by rapid growth or sharp decline, businesses no longer have the luxury of procrastination and complacency, so they start to make the improvements they've always known they needed to make.

The second key lesson from this chapter is that going it alone is *hard*, and business leaders who become part of a supportive, like-minded community fare far better than those who don't. Illustrating this, the tendency of small- to medium-sized companies to adapt successfully to the challenges of COVID was even more pronounced among our members. At the peak of COVID, we surveyed 2,430 business owners who *weren't* members of our Elevate program, and asked them what category their business was in: ***distressed***, **challenged**, **growing**, or **booming**. At the very same time, we surveyed our Elevate members and asked them the same question. Figure 12.1 highlights the disparity in performance between those who were receiving business coaching and those who weren't:

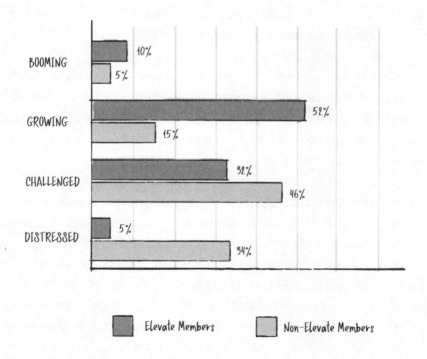

Figure 12.1: Elevate Members Versus Non-Elevate Businesses During COVID

Across the pandemic, one of the most challenging periods small businesses have ever known, our Elevate members outperformed the market by 310 percent. They proved that it's not what happens *to us* that matters, but how we *choose* to respond. And that's the third insight we want to convey in this chapter. It's not about circumstance, it's about strategy. It's never about environment, it's always about execution.

Why did our members outperform their competitors? Because, within a month of the crisis hitting, we were sitting down with each of them to develop a tailored strategy according to where *they* were as a business, what category they were in, and focusing them on the moves that were going to have the biggest impact. While the rest of the business world was scrambling, each of our members had a renewed operational roadmap across each of the Six Elements—marketing, sales, product, operations, finance, and people. They knew exactly which levers to pull and what key initiatives to undertake to turn adversity into opportunity. When an industry, or the world, is going through big changes, entrepreneurs have a tremendous advantage: once we know what to do, we can move quicker than anyone else.

Why and how were we able to guide our members through the storms of the pandemic years with incredible results? Because whether they were navigating rapid growth or working out what it would take to come back from a near-fatal blow, we knew how to chart the best course of action. Not in theory, but in practice.

The adversity of our circumstances in 2016 forced us to develop our playbook for becoming a bullet-proof business that can navigate any environment. As COVID started to take hold in 2020, this playbook allowed us to lead our members through unprecedented and uncertain times, regardless of how their specific business was affected by the changes. The only constant for business owners is change. Being nimble, flexible, and quick on your feet are the hallmarks of the modern-day entrepreneur. It's no longer the big that beats the small; today, it's the fast that beats the slow.

That's what we'll teach you in this chapter; we'll outline how to steer your ship through the different seasons you will inevitably face. Regardless of which scenario you're experiencing right now, and whatever may happen in the future, we want you to know one thing: you are *never* stuck. If you know what strategies to employ, there is always a play. Knowing how to navigate extreme growth, stormy waters, and every point in between, is one of the most important skills an entrepreneur can develop. One day, this skillset could very well become the difference between the life or death of your company.

Now, we're going to provide you with a framework for making decisions when the pressure is high. Let's dive deeper into the four categories we mentioned above: distressed, challenged, growing, and booming, to get really clear on your starting point.

IDENTIFY WHERE YOU ARE: THE FOUR STATES OF PLAY

When strategizing the best path forward, your first step must be to accurately assess where you are right now. Too often, we see business owners displaying a lack of clarity about the current state of their business. In most cases, they do this either by romanticizing—seeing things as better than they actually are—or by catastrophizing challenges and seeing things as worse than they really are. Both skewed attitudes breed the same problem: an inability to accurately diagnose the true issues in their business.

Exact knowledge of both your starting point and your desired endpoint are a prerequisite of picking the right strategy. Imagine you want to drive to a particular destination and need directions on how to get there. You can't possibly chart a course until you know your starting point. Worse, if you *don't* know your starting point, any directions you try to use will lead you to a place you don't want to be.

At The Entourage, we've coined the phrase Four States of Play as a guide to help you figure out where your business currently is on the map. Think of them as a ladder. At the bottom, you have a lot of climbing to do. In the middle you're making progress. At the top, you've got to where you want to go, but unless the ladder is stabilized, it may start to wobble. We'll discuss the Four States of Play from bottom to top, because that's the order in which we climb a ladder. See Figure 12.2 for a description of each category and to find your starting point.

CATEGORY 4 Booming	Your business is experiencing rapid growth that is hard to keep up with.
CATEGORY 3 Growing	Your business is experiencing good growth. Sales are increasing, and your ability to deliver on your promises is growing proportionately.
CATEGORY 2 Challenged	You have fewer customers coming in and more customers going out, but if you manage it well, your survival shouldn't be threatened.
CATEGORY 1 Distressed	The survival of your business is being threatened, and you need to make fundamental pivots in order to survive.

Figure 12.2: The Four States of Play

DRAW UP YOUR PLAY: DEVELOP THE STRATEGY

Depending on what category your business is in, it's going to have different strengths, weaknesses, opportunities, and threats. Managing a business in distress is a vastly different proposition from leading a rapidly growing company. Now that you've identified which category your business falls into, we'll show you how to go from understanding your current position to developing a custom strategy that's right for you. Depending on your starting point, you will deploy different initiatives and priorities across the Six Elements.

Every business has resource constraints. More specifically, the *category* your business is in will largely determine the resources you do and don't have. When discussing strategy in a small-to-medium-sized business, we're really discussing *resource allocation*: how to balance the competing needs and priorities of the business, and determine the course of action that generates the highest return on investment. At its heart, strategy is how you choose to allocate limited resources against unlimited options.

In the following section, we will map the Six Elements against each of the four categories: distressed, challenged, growing, and booming. In each category, we will outline the optimal order in which to address each element, the main issues you will need to tackle, and the practical initiatives to deploy. While you're only in *one* category right now, we encourage you to read through the different plays for each of the categories. This will develop your *range* as an entrepreneur, giving you foresight that will help you manage through different seasons when the time comes.

Category One: Distress—the Only Way Out Is Through

A distressed business is one that is losing cash rapidly, and therefore is at risk of running out of money in the next twelve months. There are various reasons why a company may find itself in distress:

- **External factors.** Examples include a recession, regulatory changes, such as the shift in government directives that impacted The Entourage in 2016, or the various COVID restrictions and lockdowns of 2020 and 2021.
- **Financial mismanagement.** A lack of financial management, visibility, and foresight can cause a seemingly sudden cash crisis. If your business operates without the necessary financial reporting, you won't see the iceberg until it's too late. In which case, it's only a matter of time until you crash and sink.

- **Client dependence.** Relying too heavily on a single client can spell disaster if they fold or go elsewhere. Even for consulting businesses, where it's standard practice to work with large clients, ensure that no single client represents more than 40 percent of your revenue.
- **Poorly diversified activity.** If you're betting solely on one particular project, the failure of that project can send your company into a tailspin. As with clients, diversification of projects is vital.

If your company is in distress, here's how we recommend you apply The Six Elements in prioritized order:

Applying The Six Elements to a Distressed Business

1. Finance: Know your position, reduce costs, and drive revenue.

When in distress, start with cash. How much is going out and coming in? How much runway do you have before you're out of money? It's critical to create a clear cash forecast that offers visibility into your cash position in any given week. Your cash forecast will highlight how much you need to reduce costs and increase revenue to get the business back to profitability. Fully understanding your financial position will dictate your most important tasks ahead.

Once you have visibility of your future cash position, you must proactively communicate with creditors. When challenging times hit and cash is low, it's understandable that you feel like shutting down and talking to nobody. Understandable, but not effective. Doing this will kill your business and your reputation. Resist the urge to retreat; instead, lean in. When creditors don't hear from you or get the runaround, they become nervous. In our experience, if you communicate honestly about your financial position, what you are doing to fix it, and when you expect to resume payments, most creditors will be supportive and cooperative.

Remember that if your business goes under, each creditor will see cents on the dollar at best, and nothing at worst. It's in *everyone's* best interest to cooperate with you and work out a payment timeline, provided you are honest and communicate openly. As we mentioned in the introduction of this book, after years of extreme distress following 2016, The Entourage repaid every dollar owed to every creditor. If we'd stuck our heads in the sand and not been forthcoming in communicating our plan, it would have been a *very* different story—we wouldn't have written this book and you certainly wouldn't be reading it.

2. Product: Pivot, but only if you need to.

When your business is distressed, you need to generate cash rapidly, which means a strong focus on sales and marketing. However, if the business is distressed due to a lack of product-to-market fit, or environmental factors affecting your ability to *deliver* your product (such as COVID restrictions), then a product pivot needs to precede sales and marketing efforts. There's no point in investing more into sales and marketing to drive prospects to a product they don't want, or one that can't be delivered.

If you already have excellent product-to-market fit and you're confident in your ability to deliver, don't worry about pivoting or improving your product. Your time and effort are much better spent selling and marketing your existing product suite.

3. Sales: Drive revenue and kick the can down the road.

When your company is in distress, your main objective should be to kick the can down the road. In other words, buy yourself some breathing space by bringing in cash as quickly as possible, and minimize how much money is going out by reducing costs or negotiating with creditors to pay them later. Keep lengthening this runway and use the time you've bought to restore the company's health. Once you have a clear financial forecast and a product you can sell, your next step is to aggressively move your attention to sales.

In times of distress, you need to become a sales-focused founder leading a sales-focused team, paying attention to both quality and quantity.

Achieve better *quality* by auditing your sales process and finding areas of improvement to increase conversions. Attain higher *quantity* by moving as many team members as possible to focus on sales and marketing activities.

4. Marketing: Focus on immediate lead generation.

When businesses get into trouble, they often cut marketing budgets, a move that usually sends the company into a death spiral. Even if you think you could spend less to generate the same number of leads, resist this temptation. If this is your situation, you are far better off using your existing budget to generate more leads rather than finding ways to cut the budget. During periods of distress, an aggressive focus on sales and marketing is paramount to your survival.

Your focus at these times should be more on immediate lead generation, as opposed to brand building or audience growth. The exception here is if your audience growth translates into sales within a thirty-day window. In that case, go for it! Otherwise, focus on generating enough leads to ensure you hit sales targets. You also need to emphasize conversion rate optimization (CRO). Audit your overall marketing funnel, and the conversion rates between each step, to determine which ones you can optimize for higher conversions.

5. People: Make the hard decisions and communicate honestly.

During periods of distress, it's essential to be open with your team. Avoid exaggerated optimism—being excessively positive will make your team think you're lying, dumb, or both. Be truthful about the current state of your business, while also explaining what you're doing to get back on track. You may be pleasantly surprised at how mature your team can be when you treat them like adults and communicate honestly.

In the most extreme instances, layoffs will be necessary. Cutting costs is a fundamental part of surviving periods of distress. While you always want to avoid letting people go, in times of serious distress the reality is that either some people lose their jobs now and the business has a chance of survival, or you do nothing and the company fails, costing everyone's jobs. The hardest thing about navigating distress is that there are no good decisions. There are only bad decisions and slightly less bad decisions. For many entrepreneurs, periods of distress are the first time they learn how to make the hard calls, even when that means being unpopular.

6. Operations: Get comfortable with operational imperfection.

When you're trying to survive, operational excellence should not be a priority. At this point, don't worry about perfecting systems and processes, unless you're streamlining work to get it done faster and cheaper. Postpone any major organizational efforts until you've come back up for air. Right now, you need a relentless focus on cash. When in distress, you must triage what is and isn't essential. As such, get comfortable with operational imperfection.

Category Two: Challenged—Getting the Plane to Take Off

If your business is not performing well but you're not quite desperate yet, or you're experiencing an extended plateau, you fall into this category. There are many reasons you may find yourself here, for example if you've experienced a reduction in revenue or a blowout in costs, meaning that your business is barely breaking even or losing money. The difference between distress and challenge is that you're not yet fighting for survival. Your losses may be manageable because they're less severe, or because you have greater cash reserves. Whatever the reasons, managing this situation effectively will prevent you from slipping into distress.

If your business is challenged, here's how we recommend you prioritize the Six Elements, and the key initiatives to undertake in each.

Applying The Six Elements to a Challenged Business

1. Finance: Identify the problem and how to fix it.

Just as if you were in distress, your top priority when in a state of challenge is getting your finances in order. There are two reasons for this. First, you want to make sure you're not in worse financial shape than you think you are. To be confident of this, you need to understand exactly what's going in and out, every month and every week. Start with developing or updating your three-way forecast, because understanding your current and future financial position is the bedrock for *every* other step you take.

The second reason is that getting a clear picture of your financial performance allows you to identify and fix the problems. The numbers will tell you a story of underlying issues. Are your costs too high relative to the appropriate ratios of your business model? Are your costs reasonable, but you're not pulling in enough revenue? Whatever's going on, the financial data will help you determine whether you have a cost problem, a revenue problem, or both.

2. Sales: Increase conversions to spike revenue.

Finding yourself in the challenged category usually points to a sales problem. On the basis that your business is challenged but not distressed, it's likely that your product is good enough, and there is a demand for it. Your marketing or word-of-mouth must be at least moderately successful to feed the existing sales. When you're in the challenged category, therefore, most of the ingredients for success are in place; you're probably closer to pulling out of the slump than you think you are. The first and most impactful lever you can pull is to increase your sales conversions. Doing this will give you a much-needed revenue boost, without increasing your marketing and sales activity. You will have the same number of leads, and the same number of opportunities, you will just be *converting* more of them. Once you've increased conversions, the next step is to increase volume; deploying more effort, resources, and time to drive sales up.

We speak to many founders who suffer from *Field of Dreams* syndrome. They wrongly believe if they build it, people will come. This only works in Hollywood. In the real world, you must build it, and then focus on sales, improve conversions, and create a sales engine that can operate at volume —this probably wouldn't make for a very good movie quote, but you get the point. Founders who underestimate the focus and effort required to drive up sales often create challenges and plateaus for their company.

3. Marketing: Prove profitability and scale spending.

Once you've optimized sales performance and are satisfied that you're converting your existing leads at an acceptable rate, you need to increase the number of leads you generate. Do this by creating two or three foundational marketing funnels and obsessing over conversion rate optimization (CRO). Once a funnel proves that it can profitably generate leads that convert to sales, increase spending on that funnel until you see diminishing returns. Counterintuitively, when your business is challenged and cash is tight, you want to work out how much you can profitably invest into your marketing to generate sales, and then *invest that much*. This is how you get the plane to take off.

4. People: Create a culture of performance.

Many companies don't have a high-performance culture, meaning the founder and team don't fully appreciate the importance of driving bottom-line performance. When your business is not performing at its peak, it's best to be upfront with your team. Let them know you need to orchestrate a shift in focus and communicate your new expectations clearly. Seek your team's input about performance issues, both at a company level and a personal level. Ask for their feedback on potential fixes. Once you've agreed on a strategy, transpose it into your OKR framework for the next quarter and clearly communicate what success and failure look like to each team member.

When your business is challenged, you may need to make layoffs to reduce costs. However, the calculus isn't always straightforward. Consider the human impact on the employees you're thinking of cutting, and the cultural implications for those who remain. If you don't *need* to fire people, a less harmful measure is enacting a hiring freeze—not adding more people to the mix until the current model and team are operating profitably.

5. Operations: Find efficiencies to cut costs and increase speed.

In this context, operations should be viewed as a way to find inefficiencies that increase speed and decrease costs. One way to achieve both of these outcomes is to audit your current business end-to-end, to determine what current manual tasks could be automated. Where is your team doing heavy lifting that could be streamlined, sped up, or performed for a far lower outlay than the cost of manual human labor? When you're in the challenged category, it's not the time to pursue operational perfection. Instead, focus on operations to the degree that enables you to achieve your strategic imperatives faster and more cheaply.

6. Product: Double down on marketing and selling your existing products.

When companies are challenged, they often introduce new products in the belief that this will solve their problems. It rarely does. The reason for this is that their challenges aren't usually caused by a lack of product-market fit, but by insufficient effort in *taking* their product to market. If anything, it's their focus *on* product—to the detriment of sales and marketing—that is creating their decline or plateau.

Exacerbating this issue, the vast majority of founders underestimate what's required to introduce a new product and take it to market. When you are thinking about launching a new product, you need to consider how you're going to integrate it across *all* Six Elements: How are you going to market it, and will it detract from the **marketing** of your core products? How will you sell it, and to what degree will it interfere with **sales** of your existing offers? What extra work will it take from your **product** team, and do you risk confusing or frustrating existing customers? In terms of **operations**, how will you integrate the new product into the business's current tech stack, to ensure that it gets proper traction throughout the business? From a **finance** perspective, how much do you need to invest to get this new product off the ground, and at what point does it break even? Finally, how will you communicate the change to your **people** and ensure that everyone knows exactly what to do?

For over a decade, a persistent conversation Jack has had with Elevate members has been encouraging them to focus on their core products, rather than launching new products and new businesses. Most business owners find it difficult to sustain their focus. They are painfully aware of the challenges of their current model and product suite, and remarkably unaware of the inevitable challenges that will come with creating a new model or developing a new product suite. In their minds, the grass is always greener somewhere else. This pattern causes some entrepreneurs to spend their lives jumping from one shiny thing to the next, never going deep enough in any direction to make it work.

In a state of challenge, it's particularly important that you resist the temptation to immerse yourself in the creation of a new product. Instead, double down on marketing and selling your core products, and develop your Customer Journey Map to ensure you're looking after your new and existing customers.

Category Three:
Growing—How to Scale Sustainably

If you're in this category, you're experiencing meaningful yet manageable profit growth. Your business is also *cash flow positive*, meaning that in each period your net cash position increases by a material amount.

Category three is a great place to be, and is where most founders want to live. One of the hallmarks of this category is relative harmony between how strongly the business is *driving* growth, and how well it is *enabling* growth. As you've seen, when your business is distressed or challenged, you need to place an urgent emphasis on driving growth. Conversely, as we'll show in category four, when business is booming, you are most likely scrambling to *enable* growth. Category three is like the perfect porridge in *Goldilocks and the Three Bears*: not too hot and not too cold. As we apply the Six Elements in category three, you'll notice that you can adopt a fairly balanced approach, without veering too much in one direction or another. This is the perfect time to optimize across each of the Six Elements, thereby building a business that is both scalable and sustainable. At this juncture, you're free to put in place the building blocks that will enable you to create longevity and build a self-managing company.

If you're growing, this is the order in which we recommend you apply the Six Elements and what to do in each.

Applying the Six Elements to a Growing Business

1. Finance: Where does the money come from, and where should you invest it?

Once again, finance is top of the list. What can we say? Cash is king. Knowing your financial performance and forecasts is imperative for making sound decisions about what you can, can't, should, or shouldn't do. In Category Three: Growing, you start with finance because you must determine the answers to four questions. As always, we'll position these questions to encourage you to think from the perspective and using the language of the leader and entrepreneur hats:

1. Where is the money coming from? Which revenue streams and products are performing well? This is most likely a key indicator of where you can expect future growth to come from.
2. Which revenue streams and products are underperforming? This is an opportunity to eliminate these products, thereby reducing operational drag and freeing up capacity to double down on the products fueling growth.
3. For the next year, how profitable do you expect to be, and how will your cash position look at the end of each month? These forecasted metrics will tell you how much you can *invest* in building your senior team and fueling further growth.
4. Are you able to pay dividends to yourself? If the business is profitable and has enough surplus cash to fund your new hires and growth initiatives, why not pay yourself some of the profit? While this might sound like you're compromising the future growth of the business, we find that companies that pay dividends are often the best-run companies, and in turn continue to be the most profitable. Why is this? Because paying dividends makes founders more financially focused. When a founder hasn't taken a dividend out of the business, it can feel like they're playing with Monopoly money. Once they start to pay dividends—or even *consider* paying dividends—the finances

feel more real. They become more profit conscious, a healthy shift that benefits the entire business.

2. People: Develop your recruitment timeline.

If your business is growing well, you need to focus on sustaining that growth long term. Take advantage of an expansion phase to develop a strong organizational structure and build out your senior leadership team. This is your opportunity to put in place the people and building blocks necessary to help you elevate from technician and manager to leader and entrepreneur—an ascension that lifts the *entire* business.

Sustainable growth requires you to recruit experienced leaders who can be responsible for driving the commercial outcomes of each function, developing their own teams, and creating a scalable engine in *each* of the Six Elements. To determine who to hire *first*, consider each element of your business and ask yourself:

- Which element promises the most opportunity for accelerating growth?
- Which element presents the biggest challenge to growth?

You'll probably find that these are the two areas where you're spending the majority of your time. Therefore, these two elements—the highest and lowest performing—are the places where your business can benefit the most from bringing on senior leaders who can take commercial responsibility for accelerating or developing these functions.

With this distinction in mind, take a look at your current org chart and imagine what you want it to look like both one year from now and two years from now. From there, develop a recruitment timeline, planning which roles you will hire for and when.

3. Product: Create a delivery engine that runs without you.

Your product function may very well be an element that meets the above criteria, making it ripe for a leader. As businesses grow, we often see owners still buried in product delivery. When a business's product function relies excessively on an increasingly busy founder, there is usually a significant drop in quality. This, in turn, results in customer attrition and a decline in brand equity. This makes product one of the first elements where founders do well to hire an executive.

When you're growing is also the optimum time to develop a meaningful Customer Journey Map, to ensure that you are delivering to and delighting your customers, while also capturing and amplifying success stories.

If you're growing at a healthy rate or are nearing customer capacity, now is the perfect time to increase your prices. When you do this, every extra dollar you earn goes straight to the bottom line. If the following conditions apply, give serious consideration to raising your prices:

- You're near capacity for customer numbers
- Your sales conversions are strong
- You haven't raised your prices in twelve months

When you do decide to raise prices, it's important to introduce a *meaningful* increase, not a paltry 5 or 10 percent. Assuming you meet the criteria above, we recommend a 20 to 30 percent price increase. If this makes you cringe, remember that customers wouldn't be beating down your doors if your product wasn't incredibly valuable.

When considering price increases, one factor business owners often miss is if you increase your price by 30 percent and conversion rates or customer numbers drop by 20 percent, this is both a net gain for the business financially and a win in terms of resource allocation. Under this scenario, you can deploy fewer staff and lower resource levels to serve fewer customers, even as you earn more profit.

4. Sales: Drive hard and expand the team.

When you're growing, it's easy to get complacent about your sales function, but this is the ideal time to transform it into a highly tuned sales engine, complete with a defined process, objectives, key results (OKRs), and commission structures.

Hopefully, you've already hired a senior executive, as laid out in the people section, with the necessary expertise to drive outcomes in this area. Once you have a structured process in place and a leader at the helm of this function, this is the perfect time to train and expand your sales team. A solid sales team will ensure your growth rate holds steady or increases, ensuring continued sales performance and strong future revenues.

5. Marketing: Increase conversions and decrease Cost per Acquisition (CPA).

Once you're profitable, cash flow positive, and experiencing growing sales, you can start to thoroughly audit your marketing funnels, to ensure they are fully optimized. This audit should help you determine how to increase conversions, driving lead volume up and CPA down. When you're already growing, take the opportunity to fine-tune your marketing funnels to become even more profitable.

In addition to this, now is the time to start investing more energy into building your brand and audience. Implement the Content Blueprint from Chapter Six: Marketing, to become the most visible brand in your industry. Scaling your audience of people who like and trust you will bring longevity to your marketing pipeline and lead generation.

6. Operations: Build foundational structures throughout the business.

While we're describing operations as the lowest priority while your business is growing, it's still an area where proactive investment will yield excellent future results. Enjoy riding the wave, but find out what's fueling it before it dissipates. Use this time of growth to translate best practice into processes, streamline the business using technology, and capture the key drivers of the business in OKRs and scoreboards. Your overarching goal should be to closely examine what is driving and enabling the growth of the business, and translate these aspects into a standard operating model. When your business is in the growing category, you want to put in place the operational building blocks that will allow you to create an engine that can run without your hands-on involvement.

Category Four:
Booming—Keeping Up with Turbo-Charged Growth

When your business is booming, you're experiencing hypergrowth that is hard to keep up with. While many business owners fantasize about being thrown into this category, the reality is that it brings complex challenges of its own. The struggle is real. The stress of expansion and the pressure to *enable* growth at a relentless pace require you to be on top of your game. You must closely manage cash, constantly recruit new people, and ensure that supply meets demand; all while keeping your sales and marketing engines humming, to ensure you don't suffer a costly dip in revenue at a time when your business requires a lot of cash.

If your business is booming, here's the order in which we suggest you approach the Six Elements:

Applying The Six Elements to a Booming Business

1. Finance: Growth devours cash—know your forecasted cash position.

Yes, it's eyes on cash at all times. Once again, we start with finance for two main reasons. The first is that growth devours cash. When you're spending to keep up with a steep growth curve, cash disappears quickly—especially if there is a time lag between purchasing supplies or delivering product and receiving payment from your customer. Therefore, when you're growing at breakneck speed, you need visibility into both historical performance and forecasted performance. Counterintuitively, many companies go out of business during a hyper growth phase, because they fail to manage cash flow correctly.

The second reason for placing finance at the top of your priority list is that growth requires continuous investment. To keep the party going, you must reinvest quite considerably back into the business. To give yourself foresight into how much money you can safely invest into the business at any given time, be certain to come back to your three-way forecast to determine your rolling cash position over the next twelve months.

2. People: Recruit the best talent you can find.

When you're experiencing hypergrowth, your main objective is to stay ahead of the curve, or at least keep up with it. The lynchpin of these efforts is the expansion of your team, while ensuring that you hire the right people. You must emphasize and proactively develop a recruiting, onboarding, and training process for new hires. You also need to deliver the same training to your existing team to ensure that everyone is on the same page, with the knowledge and skills they need to fulfill their tasks.

A word of caution: massive revenue can mask many problems. Even when you're booming, monitor and manage your company's objectives and key results (OKRs), and continually upskill your team. Raise your sales targets, incentivize strong performance, and pay your key people exceptionally well.

3. Product: Invest heavily to take care of your customers at scale.

When you're booming, product development and delivery will be the business function experiencing the most intense pressure. For this reason, it's crucial to scale your product delivery as fast as your customer acquisition. You must divert adequate resources to ensure that supply keeps up with demand. Otherwise, your rapid growth will translate into more unhappy customers and scathing Google reviews. Don't be that company, or else your growth will be short-lived, quickly followed by a sharp decline that damages your brand and your business.

In periods of hypergrowth, you must learn to care for more customers at scale. Do this by thoroughly strategizing and implementing your Customer Journey Map from Chapter Eight: Product. In addition to this, you must hire the best talent you can afford—a senior leader who can build a scalable product delivery engine. You should also expand your product team, implement clear OKRs, and document customer satisfaction and feedback. Finally, your product and operational functions must work together closely, to ensure that the product team is leveraging all available technology and processes to scale quickly.

4. Operations: Establish strong operations to minimize your personal involvement.

When you're experiencing high growth, operations can make or break you. As we covered in Chapter Nine: Operations, your operations function deals with process, technology, capturing and measuring core metrics across the business, and collaboration among all the other business functions. These are the factors that are essential to managing and sustaining growth.

The key to handling this period is to maximize the time you spend wearing the hat of leader, and avoid getting sucked into technician mode. To do this, you'll need a senior executive leading operations. This executive should have deep operational experience in the same industry or similar business models, along with the ability to develop rigorous operations across the entire company. They must also be committed to robust reporting standards, providing you with visibility into the health and performance of each of the Six Elements.

5. Marketing: Build your brand and grow your audience.

When your company is experiencing turbocharged growth, it's often because of too much demand. If you have honed your marketing engine, however, you should be able to turn your lead generation on and off like a tap. You must control your marketing tightly, so that if you become overwhelmed by customer demand, you can turn down the volume on your lead generation.

The best way for your marketing to contribute to the longevity of your growth is to invest in brand and audience creation. Scaling your audience of people who like and trust you is a massive long-term driver of growth and competitive advantage. When you're experiencing hypergrowth, now is the time to turn your marketing function into a marketing engine that runs without your operational involvement, a move that requires a defined marketing strategy, clear OKRs and budgets, and a well-resourced team.

6. Sales: Deliver on your sales promise.

We've put sales last in this category because, during phases of hyper-growth, you should only drive growth as far as you can keep your sales promises and take care of your customers. Most of your attention should go toward enabling growth rather than driving growth. If you focus on the elements we've discussed previously—finance (not running out of money), people (expanding your team), product (ensuring you can deliver), and operations (fine-tuning the engine)—you may reach the next level of increased capacity. Then, and only then, should you pivot back toward driving growth.

THE EIGHT-FIGURE ELEVATION FRAMEWORK

Throughout the journey from startup to scaleup, you need to develop an operating *rhythm*—a way to consistently schedule the right behaviors and systemize your success. Mastering this cadence will ensure that you are continually wearing the hats of leader and entrepreneur, and therefore maximizing your impact.

There's a huge amount of information in this book. This exercise will help you to determine how best to make use of that information, based on the state of *your* business. We call it the Eight-Figure Elevation Framework, and it brings together everything we've covered in these pages, in one simple process. You'll notice that the first three steps come from Chapter Five: Craft Your Roadmap, step four references the OKRs we covered in Chapter Nine: Operations, and the meeting cadence in step five comes from Chapter Eleven: People.

Using the Eight-Figure Elevation Framework

Step one: Determine where you want to be in three to five years. Work through the North Star sections in your one-page Growth Roadmap:

- Revenue
- NPBT

- Team
- Hats
- Hours per week

Step two: Determine your starting point. Using the Four States of Play, identify what category your business is in, and therefore your biggest challenges and your greatest opportunities. As a reminder, the four categories are:

- Distressed
- Challenged
- Growing
- Booming

Step three: Develop your Twelve-Month Operational Plan. This will enable you to capture your key initiatives across the Six Elements:

- Marketing: Attract, Convert, Nurture
- Sales: Develop, Buy, Ascend
- Product: Deliver, Delight, Amplify
- Operations: Processes, Technology, Targets
- Finance: Today, Tomorrow, Team
- People: Define your DNA, Recruit, Lead

Step four: Translate your Twelve-Month Operational Plan into OKRs for the next quarter.

- Take The Entourage OKR template that we introduced in Chapter Nine
- Transfer the strategic goals from your Twelve-Month Operational Plan over to the objectives section in each part of the OKR template
- Identify the key results that will enable you to make progress toward these goals over the next quarter
- Set targets for each of the key results

- Review each section of the completed OKR template with your senior leaders before presenting the completed document to your entire team

Step five: Monitor, measure, and manage. Conduct the following:

- Quarterly strategy sessions to develop and revisit strategy
- Monthly advisory board meetings to measure company performance against your OKRs and financial forecast, and to ensure the company is progressing the right initiatives
- Weekly one-on-ones to measure individual performance against targets and OKRs, and ensure everyone has what they need to succeed in their role
- Put key reports and scoreboards in place for you and everyone else on the team to monitor performance daily

Over the years, we've noticed that when businesses begin to plateau or see a decline in performance, it's often because they don't have an operating rhythm that keeps them on course. Conversely, when an entrepreneur joins our Elevate program and installs this operating system, it ensures the ongoing performance and profitability of their company.

Let's take a look at a company that having scaled, didn't have the structures and operating rhythms in place to sustain and manage their growth, and how they ultimately turned the situation around.

CASE STUDY: TROY AND MICHELLE PULL BACK FROM THE BRINK

Troy and Michelle, the husband and wife team behind construction company BE Projects, learned that there's always a play the hard way. Their journey from startup to scaleup was catalyzed by a catastrophic event that threatened their survival and forced them to uplevel their game.

After founding BE Projects in 2010, Troy and Michelle drove the company to a point where, by 2016, they were doing $11 million in annual revenues with strong margins. They had built a business that looked from the outside to be highly successful, and in the process outstripped their most ambitious goals. In a story we see far too often, however, their strong growth rates were not underpinned by a solid structure.

Although they had scaled the business, they didn't have an operating rhythm. Although they had built a team, they didn't have comprehensive OKRs. Although they were working on a diverse range of projects, they hadn't defined best practice or captured it in defined processes. Troy and Michelle had employed some managers, but they hadn't put in place detailed reporting or scoreboards. And while BE Projects had a good working culture, they hadn't defined their DNA, or leadership and management practices, so transmitting and maintaining that culture was entirely reliant on them.

None of the above was their fault. Troy and Michelle were highly talented entrepreneurs, who had never been taught to build a well-structured business. Like so many business owners, they were great at *delivering their product,* but as their organization grew, they unknowingly continued to operate like a startup. Looking at their strong revenues and good margins, they were under the impression that they had *done it*; surely, they thought, they had built an enduring business, and could afford to take a step back. Unbeknownst to them, without the foundations we've described throughout this book, the business still relied on their involvement and exertion for its survival. As Troy later shared with us, "We got there without any structure in place. So, when we started to take our hands off the wheel, performance started to plateau and then decline."

In 2017, Troy and Michelle metaphorically left the building. They didn't depart the business entirely, but they created enough distance to lose touch with its day-to-day running. The factors that once drove the growth of BE Projects began to dissipate. They hadn't successfully captured and transferred the ingredients that made the company successful, and the more distant they grew from running it, the more those cracks started to show. All of a sudden, the company was winning fewer clients, revenue was dropping, costs started to bloat, and their cash position was getting squeezed.

As they began to eat into their overdraft, their bank noticed a reversal in company performance. Steadily at first, the bank applied pressure on them to reverse this trend, until one day Troy and Michelle were told, "Enough is enough, we need you to get this balance back into the black." The overdraft was converted into a loan, which was secured against both Troy and Michelle's home *and* Michelle's father's home. As company performance continued to worsen, and without the availability of an overdraft, the company well and truly ran out of cash. They had tipped over into category one: distress.

Perhaps the most sobering moment—literally—came when Troy was driving home on a Friday afternoon. Michelle, knowing that Troy loved to stop and pick up a beer on his way home on a Friday, called him to say, "See you when you get home. Just so you know, you're not going to be able to buy a beer on the way home." Troy and Michelle had gone from being on top of the world, to not having enough money for a beer.

The business was in ruins. "It felt like we had failed," Troy reflected, with understandable emotion in his voice. "From a personal point of view, people had trusted us, and we'd let them down. I remember thinking to myself, 'What has become of us?'"

"That's when I reached out to Jack and said, *'I can't pay my creditors. What do I do?'* Having been in that situation before, Jack was able to tell us exactly what to do." At the time, Jack was still working through the distress of The Entourage, and was only about eighteen months ahead of Troy and Michelle. Although he hadn't fully documented his playbook for navigating distress, he was able to draw on the key strategies—still very raw in his memory—that had worked for him.

Years later, Troy looked back on that first pivotal conversation. "Jack's advice on how to deal with creditors was invaluable. He told us to, 'Reach out to them and communicate. Let them know you're developing a plan, and enroll them to work with you. They'd much rather work with you than deal with an administrator once the company goes under. They'll know that, if that happens, they won't get cents in the dollar." Jack worked with Troy and Michelle to develop a plan to reinvigorate performance, one that matched the distressed situation they found themselves in. He showed them strategies to work with their creditors, coached them on how to manage the relationship with the bank, and most of all reassured them that, no matter how bad things get, *there is always a play*. "The creditors were so surprised to hear from us," Troy shared. "They were completely receptive, and many actually told us they had been in similar scenarios throughout the years. One by one, they each agreed to work *with* us."

Troy and Michelle categorize their strategy from that point on as, "a return to the basics." They developed their three-year strategy and north stars, outlining exactly where they wanted the business to get to. This strategy then informed their Twelve-Month Growth Roadmap. Once they knew where they wanted to go, they set to work capturing the core drivers of the business and translating these into ninety-day OKRs. And they agreed on a clear operating rhythm: instead of holding quarterly check-ins, they decided it was necessary to move to a monthly cadence. This meant they were discussing performance-to-strategy every month, while holding key one-on-ones with each other and the rest of the team every week. "Now, everyday we know how we're performing, rather than just seeing the financials six weeks later." Troy told us.

More recently, utilizing the recruitment process we outlined in Chapter Eleven: People, Troy and Michelle have started building out their leadership team. Having defined their vision, mission, and values, and implemented their management and leadership rhythms, they have structurally ingrained the culture they want to create in their business. The effect, as Troy explains, is powerful, "It used to be that we brought all the energy," he says. "There's now other leaders who bring energy and drive performance. It feels great knowing that the culture is no longer reliant on us."

For Troy and Michelle, the impact of their comeback has well and truly translated onto the financial scoreboard. From doing $11 million in 2016, and then navigating two years of distress, BE Projects is on track to record an annual revenue of $40 million in 2023, with higher margins than they earned back in 2016. Like so many businesses, their journey from startup to scaleup was catalyzed by adversity—the near-collapse of their previously successful business forced them to uplevel the way they operate. Today, they have bottled what makes the company successful, and proactively manage these levers to grow sustainably. Reflecting on the journey from the strong position they are in today, Troy says, "We lost our heart and soul, and The Entourage gave it back to us. We wouldn't have survived if we didn't engage in the Elevate community."

THE ENTOURAGE MANEUVERS THROUGH EXTREME DISTRESS: FROM SCALEUP TO STARTUP AND BACK AGAIN

The playbook we've outlined in this chapter was forged through hard-fought experience over two decades in business. Nowhere is this truer than the strategies we've learned to deploy when a business is in distress. We've mentioned our seemingly calamitous experience in 2016, which galvanized us into reshaping and growing The Entourage. Now, let's look in detail at how we maneuvered through that catastrophe, and the steps we took to turn our hardest adversity into our greatest teacher.

When the regulatory change of 2016 hit the accredited education sector in Australia, The Entourage went from **booming** to extreme **distress** in a matter of months. As a reminder, let's flash back to the situation we were in, as we outlined in the Introduction of this book:

> On October 1, 2016, I walked into my office to a newspaper sitting on my desk. "Government to Axe Skills-Based sector. 478 Vocational Education & Training (VET) Courses Won't Be Eligible," screamed the headline. The second unforeseen announcement had arrived.
>
> In an effort to drive hundreds of thousands of students back to large traditional education institutions, the government was introducing significant policy changes, which would ultimately make it unviable for the vast majority of private providers to continue. The new regulations were due to take effect on January 1, 2017, giving us and everybody else in the industry a mere three months' notice of a reversal that would prove catastrophic. When this

second policy change came into effect, we would lose 70 percent of our revenues instantly, bringing us to the brink of collapse.

We were like a sinking ship taking on more and more water. There we were in October 2016, having built an institution around our VET delivery that would become obsolete in three months. We were already carrying more than $4 million in debt due to the government's earlier decision to cut off payments to new entrants, and now, following the announcement of the policy change, we were three months from taking a monthly loss of $800,000.

Those two government announcements arrived roughly nine months apart. First, the decision to cut off payments to new entrants—of which we were one—closely followed by the policy change that was designed to bankrupt the industry. These two decisions hit us like a one-two boxing combination; the first shot knocked us off center, while the second delivered the knock-out blow. Once we came to, we were forced to shake off the grogginess, get to our feet, and move incredibly quickly.

In the space of those nine months, we went from an eight-figure company with a defined business model, to a seven-figure company with no choice but to iterate our way toward a new viable model. In essence, we took the opposite journey to the one we've been describing in this book. We went from scaleup to startup, and needed to act like it. The overnight move from peacetime to wartime flipped our priorities on their head, almost reversing how we needed to manage and lead the business. The whiplash was so immediate and extreme that we were all disoriented.

What exactly did we do next? As we outlined in the playbook that makes up the majority of this chapter: when you've been dealt a near-fatal blow, start by checking your vital signs. In business, your vital signs are your *finances*, without them, nothing else survives. Our financial position was so distressed that it was screaming at us to start there.

Understanding our cash position, and being able to visualize our future cash runway, was everything. Jack's first priority was simple: based on the new information at hand, quantify how far in the red the company was going to go. This involved running forecasts using the new revenue model, and assessing how this information flowed through to both P&L losses and—most importantly—cash losses and our rolling cash position. In step one, Jack's method was simply to get everyone focused on the macros; the big picture. He didn't want to get fancy or concern himself with the minutiae—that would come later. In this case, the first fundamental that everyone needed to understand was simple: *how deep does the hole get?* That would quantify the problem and set the bar for every decision, large or small, thereafter.

As we revealed earlier, it turned out that the hole in the forecast got pretty deep; $800,000-per-month deep. Jack and his team rapidly converted the boardroom into a triage unit, where he, his COO, and his CFO drew plays up onto a whiteboard for three weeks, figuring out whether the patient was already dead, or whether there was a chance of resuscitation. Before we could even dig into strategy and attempt to build a roadmap back to health, the first week was simply about executing on essential immediate financial decisions to give us a *chance* at survival.

The first move was the most painful: layoffs. We needed to go from a team of ninety to a team of forty, knowing full well that although this wouldn't resolve all our problems, it would strip us back to the bare bones, where we would at least have a fighting chance. We needed to execute on the layoffs quickly, but it was an agonizing experience. How could we decide who stayed and who left? Who did we tell first? Those who were staying, thereby potentially ostracizing, even insulting, those who were about to depart? Or those who were leaving, in the knowledge that they would talk to the rest of the team, perhaps alarming those who were staying, and who might believe—even momentarily—that their role was next?

Given the extreme distress we found ourselves in, we needed to retain those who would help drive cash back into the business, along with just enough support staff to enable those activities. In deciding *how* to enact the layoffs, we developed a system. While that might sound cold, counterintuitively it was the most humane approach we could have taken. We started by addressing the entire team, explaining the situation and communicating the necessity of layoffs. We also told the team that in the interest of everyone's well-being, we would be speaking to everyone that same day. We stationed Tim, Jack, and other executives in different rooms, where they held the necessary conversations, both concurrently and compassionately. Doing it this way meant that everyone in the team understood their situation as swiftly as possible, minimizing the time for worry, gossip, and speculation. Perhaps most poignantly, most of the individuals who were losing their job expressed deep gratitude for the opportunity to work at The Entourage, and reaffirmed their belief in our future.

Once we had communicated the harsh news to the team, our next step was to connect with creditors. Remember, at this point, we still didn't have a plan—we were buying ourselves fourteen days to *make* a plan. These moves were so urgent that making them preceded developing our strategy.

Our creditors had every right to be concerned. The collapse of the industry was on the front page of every newspaper in the country, so they were certainly aware of it, even if they didn't understand the full implications for The Entourage. It was imperative that we reached out to them quickly. Once again, we developed a plan based on our highest priorities. For the sake of expediency, we divided our creditors up into categories, according to how much we owed them. Those whom we owed less than $5,000, we would pay; those whom we owed between $5,000 and $10,000 would get an email from Jack, and those whom we owed more than $10,000 would get a phone call from Jack.

Whether we communicated via email or phone call, the message was the same: we outlined the situation clearly, acknowledged honestly that the regulatory change *did* present a financial challenge for The Entourage, and affirmed our intent to return to profitability and collaborate with them along the way. We notified each creditor that we needed fourteen days to develop a plan, and that once we had done so, we would get back in touch to outline our path forward, and propose a payment plan.

The bank, to whom we owed millions of dollars, were what's called our first ranking creditor. The Australian Tax Office, by virtue of *being the Australian Tax Office*, ranked even above the bank. These two creditors were in a league of their own, and required ongoing meetings with Jack and detailed financial reporting. They wanted to be kept abreast of how our strategy was taking shape, and how we were performing against it. Maintaining the support of these two creditors was *the biggest* risk factor of the entire exercise. If they lost confidence, they would not hesitate to pull the plug, and it would be game over.

Beyond the obvious moral obligations, we had a critical legal reason to communicate openly with our creditors. For a company to go under, one of two things must happen: either the director or an unpaid creditor makes a call to wind it up. It is illegal for a company director to trade while insolvent—in plain terms, to continue operating a business, without reasonable grounds to believe that it will be feasible to pay the bills as and when they fall due. This law is a good one because it stops businesses from running rampant, receiving goods from suppliers—other *businesses*—and racking up debts that they have no real intention of paying.

This definition of insolvency means that a business sailing close to the wind for justified reasons should always seek to reach an agreement with creditors to delay the date when bills become payable. Doing this creates a longer runway, and more precious time to trade out of the situation. This is the position we found ourselves in. Not only did we need to create a plan that could see us through our painful situation, we also needed to convince creditors that we were on the road to recovery, as opposed to spinning further out. Had we failed to do this, they might at anytime have decided to throw in the towel and shut us down.

The final aspect of our emergency financial surgery was to trim every nonessential cost out of the business, while urgently tightening our cash *collection*. Any expense that wasn't going to impact immediate performance and help us weather the storm was cut. Conversely, we focused on collecting as much outstanding cash as we could, as quickly as possible. Every additional dollar helped us to kick the can a little further down the road.

Once we had scrambled to buy ourselves a mere fourteen-day runway, it was time to get back to building our roadmap. The regulatory changes had made much of our existing **product** suite redundant, so we needed to make an immediate pivot, ensuring that we delivered to our final cohorts of accredited students while simultaneously reinvigorating the non-accredited side of our business. In addition to his existing leadership role, Tim headed up both of these essential tasks. He ensured that our accredited students received the world-class diploma they had signed up for, all while renewing and driving the development of our business coaching arm—delivering programs that catered to the real-world needs of business owners, and which were within our capacity to confidently provide.

Our next strategic imperative was to ensure that we placed adequate emphasis on sales and marketing. We had no choice but to radically redevelop our entire **sales** function—craft a new sales process, clarify our messaging, and retrain the sales team on both our new product suite and our updated OKRs. From a **marketing** perspective, the shift was even greater. We were no longer an accredited education institution for diploma students, so all marketing materials relating to that side of the business were redundant. The silver lining, however, was that our situation forced us to reassess who we truly were, and return to the heartbeat of The Entourage: a business coaching provider for real-world business owners. Every part of our marketing, from our branding to our website, from our ad sets and content messaging to our lead magnets, *all* needed to change, and fast. Further, it was essential that we stayed laser-focused on immediate lead generation. Any activity that wasn't going to translate to revenue within a thirty-day window was off the table.

When in extreme distress, the **people** side of the business is usually the most challenging. Imagine, for a second, that you're a team member of a company that has just lost 70 percent of its revenue overnight, and has just fired more than half of your co-workers and closest friends. No matter how much you love the company, or how much you believe in what they do, you *can't help* but feel unsafe, perhaps even a little bit resentful. That's the maelstrom we faced at The Entourage. The culture was teeming with every imaginable emotion: confusion, loss, fear, apathy, fatigue, and occasionally—on a good day—a glimmer of hope. Coming off the back of six years where we had known nothing but success, our management and leadership of the team suddenly required a completely different approach from previous years.

Given the circumstances, we no longer had a license to present a compelling vision for the future; to people who had just seen colleagues and friends walk out the door, such an approach would have come over as tone deaf. Instead, we concentrated on doing whatever we could to provide psychological safety. As we outlined earlier in the chapter, the way to this was not by trying to make things sound better than they were. Quite the opposite, in fact. Our challenge was demonstrating to the team that we could be honest about the situation, the risks involved, and the grounded steps we were taking every day to make things a little better. When a business is distressed, all anyone—creditors, the bank, the team— is seeking from the founders is honesty and transparency.

In the realm of **operations**, our only option was to sacrifice the pursuit of operational perfection in favor of becoming comfortable with operational imperfection. We retained the people and technology necessary to enable marketing, sales, and product delivery, but cut everything non-essential. Turning our scaleup back into a startup meant stripping the operations function down to the bare essentials, and tying its subsequent development to the growth of our new business model.

Even after building this strategy and winning the ongoing support of our creditors, we knew that we would continue to incur considerable losses for approximately nine months, while we traded our way out of the deep hole we found ourselves in. Sustaining these losses required us to raise capital from equity investors, along with any debt-financiers who were bold enough to come along for the journey. Incoming investors understood while the play we had put together was risky, it had the potential to deliver very high returns if it came off. Persuading them that we had what it took to make a success of such a bold gambit, however, required a considerable amount of Jack's time. In addition to everything we were doing to enact our operational plan, Jack spent a large amount of time meeting with potential investors, to ensure that we kept our heads above water.

Thus began the hardest fight of our lives. For the first year, The Entourage was on life support, in extreme **distress**. Even after we pulled ourselves off the canvas and started landing some punches of our own, we were still in category two: **challenged**, for an additional two years. As we mentioned in the Introduction, the hardest thing about being in distress is that every task is critical and urgent, and they all need to be completed concurrently. While those years were fraught with painful decisions and sleepless nights, the fight ultimately transformed the company into an improved version of itself and elevated it to a standard it might otherwise never have reached.

Today, we are better managers, better leaders, smarter at balancing risk, sharper money managers, and more decisive when the time comes to making the tough calls. This enables us to lead our team more effectively, and most importantly, we are better coaches and leaders for our Elevate members. From the depths of adversity, we have transformed back into a scaleup and reached a level of size and influence that dwarfs what we were capable of prior to 2016, becoming the leading movement for entrepreneurs around the globe. Our brand exists to move the world forward through entrepreneurship, and today we are doing this more powerfully than ever before.

Difficult times can either diminish or develop us. The times of our greatest challenge are the times of our greatest growth, because they force us to rise up and become our best selves. They invite us to uplevel continuously—indeed, sometimes they demand that we uplevel—constantly expanding the boundaries of what we're capable of. If we lean in, tough times make us better people, and enable us to develop stronger businesses. The three years following the loss of our accreditation business were incredibly difficult, but today we can look back and feel grateful for the lessons they taught us, knowing that we have become infinitely better *because* of those years.

NEXT UP...

Whether you are thrown into distress by a recession, a change in government policy, a new competitor entering the market, or simply from taking your hands off the wheel, the fundamental, undeniable lesson of this chapter is that, no matter how bad things get, there is always a play. The number one rule of navigating hard times is to *never waste a crisis*. Always accept the invitation and *use it* to get better. If there's one characteristic that differentiates great entrepreneurs from also-rans, it's the ability to make the right moves when there are no right moves.

Now, it's time to wrap. We've guided you through the transition from startup to scaleup, sketched out the journey from technician to entrepreneur, detailed the Six Elements present in every business, clarified the crucial distinctions between the drive-growth-focused entrepreneur and the enable-growth-focused entrepreneur, and explained how to craft your roadmap. We've dived into the Drive Growth Cycle and shared the principles you need to understand to build your marketing, sales, and product functions, and we've discussed how the Enable Growth Structure underlies this cycle, providing your business with rock-solid operations and finance, and allowing you to build a team of brilliant, inspired people.

In this part of the book, we've shown you how all these moving pieces work together in every type of business scenario, even when it seems like there's no way forward. In the next chapter, we'd like to leave you with a sendoff that we trust will help you visualize how you can turn your business into a self-managing company, and give you the push you need to take action.

CONCLUSION

Building a Self-Managing Company

We started this book by describing the entrepreneur's dream of freedom: creative freedom, financial freedom, time freedom, and lifestyle freedom. We spoke about the dynamic that affects almost every entrepreneur: while most founders set out in pursuit of freedom, their lived experience is that as their business grows, they become increasingly consumed by it. The world is full of business owners who are, sadly, yet to experience the elusive sense of freedom they've been chasing for years, sometimes decades.

We want you to be one of the few who *does* find the freedom they sought when they started, which is why we wrote this book and packed it with the tools you need to get there. As you reach the end, take a moment and imagine that two years from today, you have put in place the paradigm shifts and practical strategies that you've absorbed from these pages. What will your life be like?

Imagine that your business has transitioned from a chaotic and reactive startup to a scaleup that is growing faster than ever before, without your operational involvement. You've elevated from being the technician, with your hands constantly on the tools, working exhausting hours, to being the entrepreneur, building, leading, and shaping your company. You've successfully made the journey from business operator, buried in each of the Six Elements, to business owner, orchestrating each element like a symphony conductor. You're doing what you do best, and your company is far healthier and more successful than it ever was while you were trapped in it, trying to manage everything yourself.

Imagine that you've constructed a marketing engine that is building your brand, growing your audience and generating the perfect quantity of high-quality leads for you. You've built an attribution model that ensures every marketing activity you invest in delivers a positive return. With a profitable marketing engine, and the visibility to ensure that every dollar you spend results in greater profit, you have—in effect—an unlimited marketing budget. Your sales engine now runs without your day-to-day involvement, and you're no longer the main revenue driver in the business. Your elite sales team, highly trained on the Your Company way of selling, are helping the right people to buy more, more often, faster. As a result, conversions have increased, as has the average dollar spent per sale, while time to sale has dropped. Your revenue model is growing faster than you ever thought possible.

Your buyer's journey, through your marketing and sales functions, flows seamlessly into your customer journey as you deliver great products and delight your customers. You are highly attuned to what your customers want, meaning you have an incredibly high level of product-market fit, which makes *every* element of the business easier and more enjoyable for your team. Your growing base of happy customers is fast becoming your number one branding and marketing tool. You capture their stories, turning them into testimonials and case studies, proving to your future customers that your brand is the market leader.

This accelerated growth is supported by an operations function that ensures each element connects to the next. Your team feels supported by cohesive, comprehensive processes, and you have the right technology in place, underpinning your organization end-to-end and doing the heavy lifting. You've captured the core drivers of the business's success in your very own OKR framework, so your team members know exactly when they're succeeding and when they need to adjust. This visibility has ingrained a performance-oriented culture, with each person and each team totally clear on what they need to do to fulfill the company's highest objectives.

As your operations have strengthened, so has the financial management of the company. You've developed a good relationship with the numbers, finally making friends with finance. Knowing that you are informed about the financial performance of the business, you feel empowered. Cash management is robust, profit is higher than ever, and you know *exactly* what future scenarios will drive the most profitable growth. Each night, you rest your head on the pillow with a deep sense of confidence and comfort.

As the business has matured, your vision, mission, and values have become the heartbeat of the organization. You have a senior leadership team, equipped with everything they need to be successful: a unified company strategy, an OKR framework, financial visibility and reporting, strong leadership principles woven into the fabric of the company, and dependable management cadences. Your leaders are taking full responsibility for the commercial performance of each function, structurally developing each of the Six Elements. Your business is growing, and your organizational culture is thriving, even *without* you. You've done it; you've built a self-managing company, freeing you up to spend your time doing the things you're best at, and the things you enjoy.

You choose how and where you invest your time, energy, and money. You spend your time doing what you love, with the people you love, at work and at home. Knowing that your business is functioning smoothly, you're finally able to be fully present. You contribute in meaningful ways to the lives of those around you, self-actualizing and living a life that you find deeply meaningful. As you reflect on your journey, you're able to speak the two words that everyone longs to say: "it mattered."

To turn that image from dream to reality, you'll need to be really honest with yourself. You'll need to ask yourself one crucial question: "What could stop me from getting there?"

When it comes to making progress—in life and in business—we've all been sold the lie that "knowledge is power." Knowledge is not power. Knowledge is *potential* power. Unless it translates into action, it's worth nothing. Knowledge unapplied is worthless. Have you ever been to a seminar, or read a great book, that taught you a bunch of really great things, and then gone away and done nothing with your new insights? Of course you have; we all have. But here's the thing: all the fun and richness of life happens in the experiencing—in the doing. Not in the *knowing* of things, but in the *living* of things.

YOUR BEST NEXT STEP

This is the reason why it's critical to always have what we call a best next step. It's the reason why you always need to know exactly what you're going to *do*, not just in theory but in practice, to create the life and business that you want. Knowing your perfect best next step is not about trying to take on everything at once—that type of approach is often counterproductive. No, the ideal best next step helps you translate information into implementation, making implementation easy and fun.

By now, you've understood that simply working harder isn't the answer. The case studies in these pages share one fundamental realization: in every case, working harder was actually *preventing* our members from breaking through to the next level. They were so focused on the tasks immediately in front of them that they couldn't find the space to survey the overall workings of their business, and work smarter. Please consider this book your field guide to working smarter.

You've probably heard of the butterfly effect. This is the idea that when a butterfly flaps its wings on one side of the world, creating a tiny gust of wind, that gust of wind travels further and further out into the atmosphere, building speed and gathering momentum. That small, seemingly insignificant action can multiply exponentially, causing a tsunami on the other side of the world. In other words, changes that originally seem minor may generate large-scale shifts days, weeks, and months later. Our question for you is where does the butterfly need to flap its wings to create the greatest transformation in your life? What seemingly small actions can you commit to *right now* that will have exponential effects in years to come? What small steps can you take straight away that will create a big future?

This is why we've created the Elevate Business Growth Session, to help you take the strategies that have resonated with you from this book and begin applying them in your life and business. In your Elevate Business Growth Session, we audit your business through the lens of the Six Elements, to get a clear picture of exactly where you are today. We examine the core challenges that are keeping you stuck, and assess the key opportunities that will immediately propel the growth of your business. We also seek out the north stars that reveal what's possible for the business in the long term.

Once we've done all of the above, we work together to develop a step-by-step plan to get you there. If we then determine that we're a fit, we will work together to tailor the resources of our Elevate program to you and your business, helping you *implement* your plan and achieve your most meaningful objectives. This is a session where we take the key strategies you have learned from this book and proactively integrate them into your business. You will work with a senior entrepreneur development manager, who will take your roadblocks and help you transform them into a tailored roadmap, putting you back in the driver's seat, where you belong.

To book your complimentary, one-on-one Elevate Business Growth Session, head to www.the-entourage.com/elevate-session.

GREAT ENTREPRENEURS ARE MADE, NOT BORN

It's easy to look at the most successful entrepreneurs on the planet and imagine that they have always had everything figured out. That couldn't be further from the truth. Entrepreneurs aren't born great. Anyone who has achieved the highest level of success, in any field, has *learned* how to become great. Building a business, like anything else, is a skill. You're not born a natural entrepreneur, you *develop into one*. At its heart, business is simply a personal development program with an earnings plan attached. And that makes it the best personal development program on the planet, because as you grow, your business grows with you, serving more people, supporting more people, and reflecting that success back to you. It invites you to become more: to be constantly assessing where you can improve the things around you, and of course where you can develop yourself.

The journey of an entrepreneur is a long one. When you start out, you work exhausting hours, trading time for money. Then, as you build a team, you trade money for time; employing people in a way that exponentially expands what the business is able to achieve. And then, as your business becomes profitable and you start making smart investments, you end up trading money for more money. This is the ascension that breaks the startup cycle, lifting you out of needing to work for money. This is how you create leverage in your business and financial freedom in your life.

Sometimes, business can be so challenging, for so long, that we forget we have choice. We get so consumed by the day-to-day routine that we forget that *we're* the ones creating our lives and our world. We forget that *we're* the ones driving the bus. If there's one thing we want you to take away from this book, it's the realization that you are at choice, in your business, in your life, and in the impact you have on those around you. Everything we do here at The Entourage is to give you, the entrepreneur, choice: choice about what you work on, how you spend your time, and ultimately how you live your life. As entrepreneurs, we are explorers who yearn for the vast and endless sea of possibility and freedom. To explore that sea, we need to remember that we have infinite choice available to us, and then act on that remembering.

When an explorer has completed a long voyage through treacherous waters and unchartered territories, and finally reaches their destination, they have two choices: they can either throw away their map, or they can pass it back to the next adventurer so *they* can better navigate their own voyage, reach their destination faster, and maybe, one day, explore new horizons, traveling further than the pioneer who handed them the map. This book is our master plan for how you can build an eight- or a nine-figure company, while doing the things you love, and living a meaningful life. We discovered the blueprint by doing it ourselves, and we've chosen to hand the map over to you. Now it's time for you to grab hold of it, use the wisdom you've gleaned from these pages, and *elevate*.

ACKNOWLEDGMENTS

First and foremost, we would like to thank the team at The Entourage for your unwavering commitment to moving the world forward through entrepreneurship.

To our Elevate program members, thank you for being shining examples of precisely what the business world needs: heartfelt humans building great companies.

To all those who helped us navigate the stormy waters of 2016, in particular Said Jahani—your guidance was pivotal at the most critical of moments.

To Rob Wolf Petersen, this project is infinitely better for having you involved. We had a blast. Thank you for continuously going the extra mile —your commitment is deeply appreciated.

And to our amazing life partners, Clare and Amanda, we absolutely and unequivocally could not do what we do if it wasn't for your endless love and support.